GENDER BLENDING

GENDER BLENDING

Confronting the Limits
of Duality

HOLLY DEVOR

Indiana University Press

Bloomington and Indianapolis

Photographs by the author.

Library of Congress Cataloging-in-Publication Data

Devor, Holly.
  Gender blending.

  Bibliography: p.
  Includes index.
  1. Sex role.   I. Title.
HQ1075.D48   1989   305.4'2   88-46041
ISBN 0-253-31637-5
ISBN 0-253-20533-6 (pbk.)

4   5   6   7   8   02   01   00   99   98

CONTENTS

Acknowledgments   *vi*
Introduction   *vii*

ONE   Where It All Begins:
                 The Biological Bases of Gender   1
TWO   Learning to Be Gendered:
                 The Psychological Bases of Gender   25
THREE   Becoming Members of Society:
                 Learning the Social Meanings of Gender   43
FOUR   Growing Up Gender Blending   65
FIVE   Sexuality and Gender   89
SIX   Living with Gender Blending   107
SEVEN   Gender in Context   145

Notes   155
Bibliography   167
Index   177

Acknowledgments

It pleases me to be able to take this opportunity to say thank you to a few of the many friends and colleagues who contributed to the completion of this book through their support, encouragement, commentary, and criticism. I would especially like to thank Liora Salter, Meredith Kimball, and Anita Fellman for their support and encouragement when the way was not always entirely clear to me. Warmest thanks go to my partner in life, Jesse Gossen, whom I could always count on to challenge me to move beyond the easy answers. Lou Mitchell, Ellen Randall, and Frances Wasserlein all gave generously of their time to help me with proofreading and editing and to provide their own perceptive comments. Without the generous financial and material assistance of Simon Fraser University, the difficulty of completing this work would have been greatly increased. My thanks go in particular to Simon Fraser University's Women's Studies and Communications departments.

My most profound thanks go to the women who spoke to me so candidly about their lives. Their support of this research, shown in their willingness to trust me and participate in it, and in their openness to my questioning, made this work an enriching and rewarding experience for me. I also take this opportunity to thank those women who bravely volunteered to allow themselves to become the faces in the photographs. I hope that the women whose lives and pictures appear in this book, and other women who share their experience as gender blending females, find the result of our time together as enlightening and empowering for them as it has been for me.

Introduction

Boys will be boys, and girls will not. These two phrases together form the basis for the everyday understanding of the meaning of gender. They are understood in the language and minds of members of North American society as both a description of what is and as a prescription of how it must be. "Boys will be boys, and girls will not" describes how sex and gender are understood: males are defined by what they are, while females are defined by what they lack by comparison to males. The male sex is seen by most people as a baseline against which the female sex is seen as an incomplete version of the male. The basis for this understanding can be found in many cultural sources, ranging from the Judeo-Christian Bible, in which Eve was created as a companion for Adam out of his spare parts, to psychoanalysis, which described the healthy female psyche as founded on a reaction to "defective" female genitals.

These two phrases can also be seen as a prescription which reads: boys *will* be boys, and girls *will not*. This reading reflects the belief shared by most members of society, that there are two and only two sexes (female and male); that every person, most animals, and many things must be either one or the other; and that one cannot be both male and female, cannot be neither male nor female, and cannot change sex without the aid of surgery. Concomitant with this is the belief that there are two and only two genders (girls/women and boys/men), and that whatever a woman does will somehow have the stamp of femininity on it, while whatever a man does will likewise bear the imprint of masculinity.

It would be useful to begin with definitions of some key terms. When I use the word "sex," I refer to one's biological status as having one or the other set of primary sexual characteristics, i.e. male or female. When I say "sex identity," I mean a person's acceptance of their membership in a particular sex category as either a male or a female, as when people say of themselves, "I am a female," or "I am male." When I use the term "gender," I refer to a person's social status as either a man (boy) or a woman (girl). Gender may be either "attributed" to a person by others, as in "it's a girl," or by oneself, as in "I am a man," in which case it is called "gender identity." Sex is generally believed to so strongly determine gender that the two classifications of sex and gender are commonly conflated to the extent that many people use the terms interchangeably and fail to see any conceptual difference between the two. Finally, when I use the term "gender role," I am referring to those actions, thoughts, behaviors, and beliefs which distinguish one as a member of a gender category, i.e. masculinity and femininity.

Not all individuals in society fit within the normal patterns that presume that females will become girls and then women, and that males will become boys and then men. A small but significant number of people fall outside of the standard formula. Not all males are masculine enough to entirely satisfy the gender role demands of social stereotypes, nor are all females feminine enough to do so. Hermaphrodites cannot be clearly classified as belonging to one sex or another. Transsexuals clearly are born to one sex but have a gender identity and follow a gender role which is supposed to belong exclusively to another sex. Transvestites clearly belong to one sex and identify themselves as belonging to the corresponding gender but for short periods of time choose to live according to the demands of the gender role of another gender. Still other people indisputably belong to one sex and identify themselves as belonging to the corresponding gender while exhibiting a complex mixture of characteristics from each of the two standard gender roles. I call these people "gender blenders."

Gender blending people can be distinguished on the basis of several characteristics. They have a normal sexual status of either female or male. They have a normal gender identity which corresponds to their sexual status (females identify themselves as women, males identify themselves as men). Their gender role patterns incorporate elements which come from both the standard masculine gender role and the standard feminine gender role. They mix these characteristics in such a way that people who do not know them personally often, but not always, mistakenly attribute them with membership in a gender with which the gender blenders themselves do not identify i.e., females who think of themselves as women are mistaken for men. Gender blending people report that they do not consciously attempt to project confusing or misleading gender impressions, although they may, under certain circumstances, allow mistakes to stand uncorrected.

This work studied a small group of gender blending females with an aim to (1) identify them as a gender classification, (2) discover commonalities in their experiences of gender, (3) learn about how they came to be gender blending females, (4) come to a better understanding of what it is like to live the life of a gender blending female, and (5) consider some of the theoretical, personal, social, and political meanings and implications of a blended gender status.

Fifteen gender blending females were interviewed for this study. I used six avenues to reach potential subjects. First, I approached a tradeswomen's organization and requested that they describe my project to their members and ask for volunteers to come forward. I approached them because I assumed that women who worked in jobs which were usually reserved for men might find themselves mistaken for men simply on the basis of the clothing required on the job and people's stereotypical assumptions about, for example, welders or heavy-duty mechanics always being men. Next, I placed advertisements in a feminist newspaper asking women who were sometimes mistaken for men to phone me if they were willing to be interviewed for a research project. I approached feminists on the assumption that women who were engaged in a critique of femininity might also be engaged in a rejection of femininity. I had, in fact, found much of my inspiration for this study from my observation of more than one feminist caught in the dilemma of "becoming a man" in the eyes of others as the result of actions which she saw as a pro-woman rejection of femininity. I also posted notices at gay bars, health clubs, and gyms asking women who were sometimes mistaken for men to contact me. I went to gay bars on the assumption that there would be a sizable number of masculine women who frequented such places. I thought that some of them may have taken on the "butch" role sufficiently to qualify them as gender blenders. I advertised at health clubs and gyms on the assumption that athletic women would tend to be more muscular and physically assertive. I thought that a strong physical presence might be a factor in attributions of masculinity. At the same time, I told everyone I knew (many of whom were feminists) about my project and asked them if they knew anyone who might be willing to talk to me.

Word-of-mouth contacts proved to be the most successful method of reaching gender blending females. My credibility and integrity as a researcher and interviewer seemed to be a deciding factor for many of them when considering whether or not to "go public" about being mistaken for a boy or a man. As a result, most of the women in this study came to the work as either friends of my friends or friends of people who had already been through the interview process.

The women interviewed ranged in age from twenty-two to forty-one years, their average age being twenty-nine years. Fourteen of them were white and one was black. Six were from rural areas or small towns and nine were from cities. Fourteen grew up either in Canada or the U.S. and one lived in England until she was in her mid twenties. Fourteen were Anglophones and one was a Francophone. Fourteen were living in large cities at the time of their interviews, one in the country. All but one completed high school and at least some university. Two had postgraduate education. Two women grew up in families supported by welfare. Seven women came from working-class homes where the single working parent was either a low-ranking member of the armed forces, a technician, a tradesperson, a waitress, or a factory worker. Four women were from middle-class families that derived their incomes from small businesses or the civil service. Two women's families were upper-class ones in which both mothers were full-time housewives, one father was a highly skilled medical specialist and the other was with the diplomatic corps.

The jobs that the interviewees had worked at were mostly in fields either dominated by men or shared by men and women. Their employment histories included jobs in construction, technical and skilled trades, and unskilled labor. One woman had worked as a security guard, another as a police officer, a third worked in forestry, and a fourth woman was a rock musician. Only four of the twenty-two jobs reported were in areas dominated by women: one woman was a child-care worker, another was a nurse, a third was a parking-meter checker, and the fourth was a house cleaner. All but one identified themselves as feminists or feminist sympathizers. Four women were heterosexual, eleven were lesbian.

All but three of the women were mistakenly thought to be men or boys as often as several times a week. One woman reported that she was mistaken for a man approximately once each week, a second woman said she was mistaken about once a month, while a third woman was mistaken only once every "couple of months." For the rest of them the mistakes had been an everyday occurrence, to the point where they no longer automatically expected to be correctly identified as females by strangers. Eleven of these people had been regularly addressed as males for at least ten years and all but one of them had experienced this situation for more than five years; for five of them, such mistakes had been a lifelong experience.

Most of the women, at the time of their interviews, did not make a very feminine impression on me. Four of the women's appearances struck me as decidedly masculine, while only one woman's appearance and manner left me wondering at other people's inability to immediately recognize her femaleness. The remaining ten women seemed to me to present themselves in a manner which I could understand as confusing to members of the public who were neither interested in, nor concerned with, the details of the gender attribution process. Fourteen of the fifteen women I interviewed described their normal mode of dress as jeans or other casual slacks, plain man-tailored shirts, T-shirts or sweatshirts, and running shoes, work boots, or other flat-heeled "practical" shoes. All but one of the women wore their hair in short, very plain styles. Only two women wore any makeup at all in the course of their everyday lives, few wore any jewelry, and of those who did only one said she ever wore anything which was clearly feminine. Only four women said that they would ever wear dresses or skirts, but all fifteen women told me that they preferred or were more comfortable in their usual jeans, T-shirts, and running shoes. Seven of the fifteen women interviewed told me that they would actually feel foolish if they were to dress in typically feminine attire.

My overall impression of these women was that there were reasonable, even compelling, grounds, in most cases for their mistaken gender attributions. As several of them were quick to point out to me, many other women regularly dress as they did without suffering the same fate. My sense of them as a group was that their unfeminine mode of dress was only a small part of what made them appear more masculine than feminine. Their mannerisms, language, facial expressions, dress, and lack of feminine adornment all combined to convey a masculinity largely uncontradicted by any obvious femininity. Their experiences of mistaken gender attribution were always with persons who had never met them before, usually during very brief encounters. In such circumstances, it is common for individuals to rely heavily on stereotypes as devices for selectively directing their attention to, or away from, certain features of persons as a way of simplifying complex judgments.[1] The impression that these women made on me was predominantly, but not entirely, a masculine one. The easiest and simplest judgment, in most of their cases, would be to make an attribution of the presence of masculinity and an absence of femininity.

Each woman was interviewed in-depth for one and one-half to four hours. A few women were interviewed only once, but most talked with me twice, with no single interview lasting longer than two hours. Whenever possible I conducted interviews at the homes of the respondents so that I could glean something more about their lifestyles and self-images, and as a way to help put them at their ease. All interviews were tape recorded using a small unobtrusive tape recorder and were later transcribed. All names and identifying information were treated with complete confidentiality throughout.

The interviews covered six main areas of interest. (1) I asked for demographic information: Where was she born? How old was she? Where did she grow up? What kind of work did her parents do? What kind of work did she do? How much education had she and her parents had? How many brothers and sisters did she have? Had she ever been married or had children of her own? (2) I asked about each woman's current and previous relationships with her family and friends: What were each of her parents like? Who had she spent the most time with while she was growing up? Which parental figures or siblings had she spent the most time with and what kinds of things had they done together? Was she more like her mother or father? How? What did she like best or worst about her family members? What were her relationships with her brothers and sisters like? Who were her friends? What were they like and what kinds of things did they do together? What were her school years like? Did she fit in with her peers? Who were her current friends and what were their relationships like? What were her present family relationships like? (3) I explored memories she might have about important gender socialization experiences she had in her youth, teen years, or adulthood: Who were her earliest role models? Did she have memories of being told that she must or could not do things because she was a girl? Had she been encouraged or discouraged by friends or family to find the company of males or females? Had she been rewarded or punished by friends or family for stereotypically masculine or feminine activities? Had puberty been a difficult transition? What were her experiences of sexuality and love? (4) I asked about both representative and personally meaningful experiences related to her gender blended status: When did the mistakes first start happening? What were her initial reactions to them? Did she correct people? How long have they been going on? How often does it happen? Did the mistakes affect her sense of herself either positively or negatively? What were some memorable experiences of being mistaken for a man or boy? How have other people reacted to situations in which the mistakes occurred? (5) I asked each woman what the advantages and disadvantages were of her gender status:

Were there things that she could or could not do because she was a gender blending female? Did she feel that she had gained or lost as a result of her situation? (6) Finally, I asked whether she had an interest in altering her gender status or had attempted to do so already: Had she ever made any efforts to prevent the mistakes from happening? Why or why not? What had she done, if anything? Why did she think she was mistaken for a man or boy? What did she think she might be able to do to cause the mistakes to stop?

All of the information gathered through these in-depth interviews has necessarily been filtered through the joint mechanisms of subjective recall (sometimes going back twenty to thirty years) and the inevitable leading bias in any interviewer's questioning. In this case, the interviews were conducted from a feminist bias which led to, among others, an unintentional assumption in the interviews that being mistaken for a man would be an unpleasant experience which one would want to curtail to the greatest degree possible. Such difficulties, however, do not preclude valuable insights being gained from this work, and while it is not possible to reliably make wide-ranging generalizations on the basis of a small number of case histories, certain intriguing possibilities and patterns begin to emerge from the study of this small group of individuals.

I sifted through their answers to these questions searching for clues that would lead me to an understanding of the nature of their experiences. I searched for the reasons for their predicament both in them as individuals and as members of a larger society. It rapidly became clear to me that it was neither entirely their problem nor simply a case of inattention on the part of those who mistook their gender. It seemed to me that the answers to my larger questions were to be found in the interplay between biological impetus, individual psychology, social structure and constructs, and the dramaturgy of everyday life.

Every discussion of gender either begins or ends with the question of biological determinism. How much of what we call gender is "hard-wired" into us? Just how far can socialization take us before our physical selves draw us back on to some course preordained by evolutionary demands? This book therefore begins in chapter 1, "Where It All Begins: The Biological Bases of Gender," by examining how chromosomes and hormones affect gender development. It looks at evidence gained from both human and animal studies, tracing development from conception to birth, and from birth through adulthood. Chapter 2, "Learning to Be Gendered: The Psychological Bases of Gender," investigates the major psychological theories of gender acquisition and the evidence raised in support of them. It reviews studies and theories concerned with relationships between parental figures and their children and offers some critiques and suggestions for further study. Chapter 3, "Becoming Members of Society: Learning the Social Meanings of Gender," reviews major sociological theories of self and gender. It looks at how gender is acquired and maintained as part of the self and how gender is given meaning by a society through the agency of its institutions and its individual members. Chapter 4, "Growing Up Gender Blending," looks at the experiences of gender blending females as children and youths and explores how their relationships with family members and peers helped to shape their self-images, gender identities, gender role behaviors, and aspirations. Chapter 5, "Sexuality and Gender," explores the effects of sexuality on the gender identities and gender roles of gender blending females. It looks at the ways in which sexuality both grows out of gender identity and contributes to the solidification of gender identity. Chapter 6, "Living with Gender

Blending," examines the dilemmas that gender blending females found themselves in as adults. It explores the coping strategies and mechanisms they used to make their ways through many confusing, and often distressing, situations. Chapter 7, "Gender in Context," presents an analysis of the implications of the findings of this study of gender blending females and suggests possibilities for an improved understanding of gender.

GENDER
BLENDING

PAM

ONE

Where It All Begins

The Biological Bases of Gender

Biological Questions

Whenever people stop to think about what makes men men, women women, and some people neither, their thoughts inevitably lead to questions of genetics, hormones, and our inheritance from lower animals. Few people today would maintain that we are entirely the product of either a set of biological instructions, or of our socialization. Still, arguments rage about just how much of human behavior is controlled by genetic coding and hormonal functioning, or to what degree social factors influence the daily actions, thoughts, and desires of women and men, girls and boys. Scientific investigations of the interactions between genetics, anatomy, and physiology, on the one hand, and the social-psychological influences of gender attribution, gender identity, and gender role, on the other, help to clarify the relationship between biological sex and social gender. But no matter how detailed an investigation science has thus far made, it is still not possible to draw a clear dividing line even between male and female. The biological sciences, at best, provide only strong suggestions about why human females and males act the way they do. Human sex differences can only be described in terms of averages, tendencies, and percentages rather than clear-cut absolutes. As a result, there remains a tension between the desire for clear sex/gender distinctions in everyday life and the evidence being uncovered by the biological sciences.

In an effort to begin to understand our biological heritage, it is instructive to first look at what science has been able to determine concerning the development of human beings from conception to maturity. By examining the information available on this subject, it is possible to come to some understanding of the degree of human malleability from the time of conception and on through the maturation process. Some information presented here is fairly well accepted and documented by extensive research; some is controversial.

When reviewing reports of this research, it is important to keep in mind that researchers unintentionally carry the biases of their everyday attitudes into their work. Even the most scrupulous researcher is unable to entirely avoid this pitfall, because all humans, by virtue of being social entities, hold certain "incorrigible beliefs" which they carry with them, unchallengeable, throughout all of their actions.[1] These incorrigible beliefs remain invisible to the researcher and so fall outside of the strict discipline of the scientific method.

Incorrigible beliefs show up in research about both human and animal behavior in various ways. A common example is the assumption underlying almost all work on sex and gender that all subjects must be either male or female. This shows up in the routine practice of dividing subjects into these two groups before studying them. The very act of dividing a group of subjects in this fashion prejudices the results of any further investigation, because researchers who make this their first criterion are implicitly stating that they have already determined that there are certain sex-typed differences and that they are recognizable to them without the aid of empiricism. If one is seeking to determine the differences between the sexes, then this method does not allow for proper controls and a double blind situation.

There is also a great deal of interpretation in sex/gender research which is presented as impartial observation. Aggressive behavior, for example, is one topic which has received a great deal of attention. In the everyday world we have a commonsense understanding of what aggressive behavior is and a dictionary for further clarification. But in scientific research, terms are usually given very specific technical meanings for the purposes of exactness and repeatability. In behavioral research, it is common to see the term *aggression* used as a synonym for *fighting*. More specifically, aggression in the research reports generally means male-to-male fighting, usually for a position in a dominance hierarchy. Other forms of fighting are just as often not recognized as aggressive behavior. What this means in practice is that subjects are first divided into male groups and female groups and then fighting behavior is noted; male/male dominance fighting is noted as aggressive behavior while female/male fighting is noted as sexual in nature and female/female fighting may or may not be noted at all, or may be classified as related to the care of young, or as play, or as another nonaggressive type of behavior.[2] In ways such as these, research too often becomes self-fulfilling prophecy in support of, and based on, invisible incorrigible beliefs.

In most of the literature on the subject of gender, it is possible to find information based on actual human evidence, but it is also common to find conclusions concerning human development that are based almost entirely on evidence from animal studies. When reviewing this body of research, one must always question the applicability of animal studies to human situations. There is a great deal of research profitably undertaken on animals which could not morally or ethically be considered using human subjects. The conclusions of this kind of work are generalized to humans on the basis that we are simply highly developed animals; our instincts and biological mechanisms are assumed to be very closely related to those of our less developed cousins. No doubt there is a great deal of truth to this claim although, in this case, cautionary concerns seem compelling: it has been repeatedly and clearly demonstrated that social conditioning and human will can overshadow biological tendencies relating to sex and gender.[3] While animal studies may be, in some instances, quite firm in their findings, the transferability of animal results to human situations is, at best, highly tentative. Nonetheless, research conducted on rats and monkeys is routinely used as the basis for hypotheses attempting to explain human behavior ranging from makeup to the missionary position. It is not at all uncommon to see an analogy made between rat mounting behavior or lordosis* and human "tomboyism" and homosexuality.[4]

The fact that a body of research has faults and problems within it or that it has occasionally been used in spurious ways does not invalidate it. No research is without its flaws, nor is any evidence totally beyond question. There will always be unanswered questions and alternative interpretations of data. An overview of the present state of knowledge concerning the interplay of biological sex and social gender is necessary for an understanding of the process of the creation of gender.

The Usual Route

The process of creating human life begins when a sperm cell joins an egg cell. Under normal circumstances, when a sperm cell and an egg cell meet there are two possibilities: if both carry X chromosomes, the resulting baby will be born bearing ovaries, uterus, and vulva; if the egg cell carries an X chromosome and the sperm cell carries a Y chromosome, the resulting baby will be born equipped with penis and testes. During the development of the fetus from two cells to human baby, hormones (produced by the fetus itself, produced by its mother, or introduced into the fetal environment from external sources) influence the developing structures of parts of the brain, central nervous system, and reproductive organs.** These structures develop along different lines according to whether the fetus has XX or XY chromosomes, and as a result of the fetal hormonal environment. Many researchers maintain that once these sex differences are established in the fetus, they are irreversible. They propose that these physical differences cause male and female humans to have different sensitivities and propensities throughout life, somewhat analogous to instincts in the lower animals. Their position is that patterns established before birth account for later differences found at puberty and throughout maturity. Others believe the human animal to be far more plastic.

All human embryos start out with the potential to develop either female or male internal reproductive organs, external genitals, and behavior patterns. By the third to fourth month of fetal life fetuses start to differentiate in either the female or male direction. Fetuses with two X chromosomes normally develop into female babies whether or not functioning fetal ovaries are present, because

---

*The pattern of behavior of the female rat in sexual encounter with the male rat.

**Sex hormones are grouped into three general categories: estrogens, progestins, and androgens. Females secrete all three types, although they secrete more estrogens and progestins than androgens. Males also secrete all three kinds of sex hormones, although they secrete more androgens than progestins or estrogens.

the fetal hormonal environment provided by the mother alone is sufficient to produce a female baby in the absence of contravening masculinizing influences. The presence of a Y chromosome is normally sufficient to turn development away from the female path, to create a male baby. Shortly after an XY fetus develops properly functioning testes, they begin to secrete testosterone and a chemical called Mullerian Inhibiting Substance (MIS). If the body of the fetus responds to testosterone in a normal male fashion, the testosterone prompts the fetal external reproductive organs to grow into penis and scrotum, and MIS causes rudimentary female structures to wither.

In the first few months after birth, both male and female infants experience production spurts of some hormones. In particular they both generate higher quantities of two pituitary hormones (LH and FSH)* which in turn stimulate the secretion of the major sex hormones. Males also produce almost as much testosterone in their first few postnatal months as some men do as adults. Beyond these first few months, both female and male children grow up under the influence of roughly the same consistently low levels of all sex hormones.[5] As there is very little sex hormone production in either males or females past the first few months of life, it must be concluded that childhood gender development is the result of the effects of largely prenatal hormonal influences, overlaid with many years of postnatal socialization experiences.

At puberty, the bodies of young men and women again begin to produce significant quantities of sex hormones. Males begin to produce vastly greater amounts of testosterone than they had produced during childhood. At puberty, female androgen production also rises, but only slightly. Male testosterone levels jump by roughly ten to thirty times their childhood levels, whereas female levels only increase by, at most, a factor of two.[6] In both sexes, increased androgen production leads to an increased sex drive, a deepening of the voice, and an increase in body hair. The large amounts secreted by young males also account for the maturation of their genitals and the development of masculine bony structures and musculature.

Estrogen production also increases at puberty in both males and females. Male estrogen secretions increase to, at most, twice their childhood levels, whereas female estrogen secretions begin to follow a cyclical pattern whose peaks are approximately ten times childhood levels. Any effects which the slight increase in estrogen production in males might have at this time are entirely drowned in the sea of testosterone being produced by pubescent boys' bodies, while estrogens produced by young women's ovaries have marked effects on their physical appearances. Estrogens are responsible for the growth of hips and breasts and a general increase in subcutaneous body fat. The combined effects of hormone production stimulation from the hypothalamus-pituitary system and ovarian estrogens and progestins prompt the changes which turn young girls into women capable of conceiving and bearing children.

*LH and FSH stimulate ovulation in females. In males, LH stimulates secretion of testosterones and FSH stimulates the production of sperm.

During puberty, as children physically mature into young women and men, the changes that their bodies undergo are accompanied by changes in their social relations. Their physical changes act as catalysts for emotional upheavals and as signals to those around them that they must no longer be treated as children. Under normal circumstances, puberty is a time of marked growth and change precipitated largely by hormonal changes but enhanced and given meaning by corresponding alterations in social roles, experiences, and expectations.

Sex hormone levels in adults normally differ in that females produce estrogens and progestins in a cyclical menstrual cycle, which allows them to conceive and bear children, while males produce these hormones in smaller and more consistent quantities. Males and females both produce testosterone at vastly different, but relatively steady, levels. But even those hormone secretions usually thought of as being tonic, or acyclical, actually do regularly vary through daily cycles in both women and men.[7]

In addition, sex hormone secretion levels can affect, and be affected by, people's emotional experiences in their environments. Elevations of progestins and estrogens associated with the menstrul cycle, pregnancy, and childbirth have been linked to mood changes, while elevated androgen levels have been tied to increases in the sex drive, aggression, and dominance in both men and women. Although it is commonly believed that the actions of sex hormones on the bodies of men and women cause the emotional changes that have been correlated with changing hormone levels, this has yet to be proven; and in certain circumstances, discussed later in this chapter, the evidence is strongly in the favor of the reverse causation.

Old age brings with it changes in sex hormone secretion patterns. Females undergo menopause, during which the ovaries gradually decrease in size and ability to produce ova and hormones. These changes are accompanied by a cessation of menstrual cycles and a loss of fertility. As female production of estrogens and progestins decreases, the effects of adrenal androgens become stronger. The combined effects of these two processes can often be seen in physical changes which accompany menopause, such as loss of fullness in the breasts and increased facial hair. Males also undergo a menopausal-like climacteric in which they too experience a decrease in the productive activity of the gonads. In a similar fashion as experienced by females, the effects of male estrogens and progestins become stronger as androgen levels drop. These changes in hormone levels result in such physical changes as a gradual loss of potency and muscle tone, and increases in subcutaneous body fat. These physical changes in men and women as they age are also accompanied by changes in social statuses, roles, and expectations.

Thus it would seem that, throughout the life cycle, physical structure and function, behavior, and emotional state are affected to varying degrees by the actions of sex hormones on the body. In the prenatal period, sex chromosomes give direction to the cells of the fetal tissue, telling them what structures to form. The secretions of those structures and the fetal hormonal environment play a major role in determining whether a normal male or female child develops. In the years between birth and puberty, the production of sex hormones, and therefore their effects, are slight and roughly equivalent in both males and females. During that stage, most gender development takes place under the influence of factors other than sex hormones.

At puberty, the effects of sex hormones are dramatically dimorphic. They account for the transformation of children into adult women and men. The physical transformations which take place at this stage of development are accompanied by very strong social changes. It is therefore difficult to say with certainty exactly how much of the emotional and behavioral changes of adolescence are the result of biological changes and what part are the results of intense social pressures felt by that age group.

Adulthood brings with it a relative hormonal consistency. Females settle into monthly cycles, usually punctuated by childbirth and its associated hormonal changes. Both males and females also undergo individual daily hormonal rhythms. During this stage of life, emotional states and behavioral activities vary with hormonal vacillations. In some cases, hormonal changes are probably instigated by human perceptions of their experiences in the world; in some cases the reverse is no doubt true.

Old age brings with it a final adjustment in hormonal patterns. As men and women move into seniority, their hormonal levels shift so that the relationship between the dominant and less influential sex hormones becomes more equal. In men, androgen levels decrease and the effects of estrogens normally become more pronounced, while in women the effects of estrogens and progestins are diminished and those of androgens are advanced. As in other life transitions, old age carries with it new and different social demands and expectations. Here too it seems clear that while physical changes affect behavior and emotion, so too do social changes.

Normal human development thus can be seen as a number of steps beginning at conception and proceeding through to old age and death. Sex chromosomes set a developmental process in motion which is then carried through its various stages under the encouragement of the differing amounts of the sex hormones produced by the bodies of boys and girls, men and women, at each of those stages. Throughout the life cycle, hormonal messages are accompanied by social and environmental experiences. The messages of those social experiences work with, or against, the developmental programs set out by chromosomes and hormones to create the totality of a human life experience.

Exceptions to the Rules

Not all people follow the usual route. The study of persons whose development is in some way abnormal can uncover information concerning some of the questions which remain unclear in the study of normal developmental processes. By examining the exceptions to the rules, it sometimes becomes possible to better understand causes and effects in more usual cases.

When discussing human development it is important to bear in mind the distinction between sex and gender. Sex is usually decided by scientists on the basis of chromosomal sex. XX individuals are classified as female, XY individuals as male. In cases where this test of sex is not conclusive, a variety of methods are employed to enable a person to be classified as either male or female. In general the presence of at least one Y chromosome is sufficient to merit a male classification.

Gender is usually divided into the two categories of men (boys) and women (girls). Gender is recognized on the basis of social behavior and commonly believed to be congruent with sex. The actual characteristics used to define gender are infinitely variable over time and place. Those characteristics which might be defined as feminine in one location or time period are not the same ones as may be defined as such in another. Gender functions as the intra- and interpersonal understanding of what it means to be a female or a male. In most chromosomally normal people, gender identity and sex match. Gender role is not always in complete alignment, but usually gender role, gender identity, and sex all more or less agree.

In individuals with chromosomal or hormonal abnormalities, this easy constellation can fall apart. It is tempting to look at the normal course of human development and assume that because things usually unfold in a particular order, they do so because they must. Many people simplistically draw the conclusion that because most people with XX chromosomes become mothers, there must be something in their XX chromosomes driving them to do so; or that because there is a strong correlation between testosterone and aggression, testosterone causes aggression. Although there can be no argument that these correlations are indeed strong, the evidence of research into chromosomal and hormonal abnormalities, brain development and functioning, and gender dysphorias shows that the question of causation is far from resolved.

Chromosomes and Gender

While under normal circumstances, humans have either XX or XY sex chromosomes, a look at the cases of people who do not fit this pattern shows that, although chromosomes appear to be causative of a wide variety of sex and gender characteristics, neither sex nor gender follow slavishly from chromosomal instructions.

When a fetus develops with only one sex chromosome present in all or most of its cells, it has a condition known as Turner's Syndrome. This configuration is referred to as 45XO, or simply as XO. All Turner's Syndrome individuals are born with a female body type and are often thought to be unremarkable females at birth, but they lack normal female internal sexual organs. What can usually be found upon internal examination is a streaklike mass of tissue, which has never developed into gonads, and an underdeveloped uterus. As a result, Turner's Syndrome females develop fetally only under the influence of maternal hormones and do not grow up under the influence of any gonadal hormones of their own.

At puberty, Turner's Syndrome females find themselves shorter than most other girls and lacking in pubertal development. This syndrome, which is usually discovered at this point if it has not already been identified, is treated by the administration of estrogens. This may result in the onset of menses if the reproductive organs are sufficiently developed, and will promote the development of breasts, body hair, and the distribution of subcutaneous fat usually associated with female puberty.[8] The administration of estrogens at puberty enables XO females to live feminine lives from birth through adulthood. They develop feminine identities and gender roles, and in some cases XO females have even been described as hyperfeminine.[9] They differentiate a clearly feminine gender identity in spite of the fact that they have only one sex chromosome rather than the normal two.

There is no analogous situation where a fetus develops only a Y chromosome. The YO condition will not sustain life. There is, however, a condition in which an XY individual is unable to use androgens and thus, although producing normally sufficient quantities of androgens, does not develop under their influence. This condition is known as Androgen Insensitivity Syndrome (AIS), or Testicular Feminization. In such cases, an XY baby is born with normal-looking female external genitalia, male internal reproductive organs, and a short vagina that does not lead to a cervix or uterus. Testes may be present inside the abdomen or may be palpable within the labia. Such children appear as normal female infants at birth. Parents and medical personnel see only a female baby, and children born this way are raised as such. They grow up as apparently normal females whose condition usually only becomes recognizable at puberty.

Even their puberty is in most respects normal for a female; they develop breasts and hips and a normal female distribution of body fat. The difference is that they have no menses, as there is no uterus, and body hair is slight to nonexistent. The hormonal source of this feminine puberty in XY individuals is the small amount of estrogen secreted by the testes and adrenal glands.[10] The testes do secrete testosterone in quantities normal for a male, but the bodies of AIS individuals are unable to use it and thus are not affected by it.[11]

These chromosomally male individuals grow up with gender identities similar to the XO females in that they show themselves to be good examples of traditional femininity. Money and Ehrhardt reported on a study they conducted of ten such XY girls. They compared them with fifteen Turner's Syndrome females and with a control group of normal XX females. They compared them on the basis of identity as a tomboy, expressed satisfaction with the female role, athletic interests and skills, preference for male or female playmates, clothing perferences, and attitudes toward the maternal role. The results of their comparisons showed that both the XO and AIS XY children were as feminine as, or more feminine than, the control group in all respects.[12]

In both Turner's Syndrome and the Androgen Insensitivity Syndrome, children are unquestioningly identified by medical personnel as female at birth and reared in accordance with that assignment. In Turner's Syndrome there is only one sex chromosome, and there are no endogenous gonadal hormones to reinforce femininity, either from their prenatal effects or throughout childhood. In the Androgen Insensitivity Syndrome, a child is also assigned to the female sex at birth and reared as such. During childhood and throughout life, an AIS female has XY chromosomes, testes, and testosterone, to no apparent effect on the social or psychological functioning of an individual living wholly as a female. In both of these cases, the major restriction that their condition puts on their ability to live fully feminine lives is their infertility, a problem they share with many "normal" women. Thus, femaleness is not determined in these cases by chromosomes (or gonadal hormones) but rather by the social implications of a judgment, made at birth, on the basis of genital appearances.

These examples demonstrate that there need not be a direct link between chromosomal status and gender identity or gender role. These syndromes illustrate that it is not necessary to be an XX individual to be socially acceptable as a female, and that having XY chromosomes does not always make a person into a man. Humans may develop apparently normal female bodies in the presence of the typically male chromosomal arrangement or with a shortage of sex chromosomes. Gender identity in these cases follows from the sex assigned to a newborn baby on the basis of appearance of its genitals at the time of its birth.

Other chromosomal abnormalities include individuals with more than two sex chromosomes or with different patterns of sex chromosomes in different cells of the body.* In Klinefelter's Syndrome an individual has two or more X chromosomes combined with a single Y chromosome. Such individuals are born with normal looking male genitals. On that basis they are assigned to the male sex at birth and raised as boys. At puberty, they fail to fully develop normal male characteristics: the testes often shrink in size and breasts develop, body hair is usually light, and the voice deepens. These boys are often fertile and capable of normal male sexual activity despite their small testes and characteristically female breasts. Individuals with more than two sex chromosomes, in any combination, show increasing degrees of mental retardation with increasing number of chromosomes.[13]

The XXY chromosomes of persons with Klinefelter's Syndrome might conceivably make them females with one Y chromosome or males with an extra X chromosome. As was the case with Turner's Syndrome XO individuals and androgen insensitive XY people, the sex and gender identities of these people follow from their sex assignment at birth and from their rearing. When they reach puberty and experience difficulties, they experience them as adolescent boys, not as boys who are suddenly turning into girls.

*In normal individuals sex chromosomes are present in all cells of the body and they are the same in all cells.

Individuals found to have one X chromosome and more than one Y chromosome are born with the appearance of a normal male. As they mature they tend to grow to be unusually tall (generally well over six feet) but are otherwise physically normal.[14] As with other chromosomal abnormalities, the tendency to mental retardation increases with the number of sex chromosomes present. Their extra Y chromosome(s) do not make them into "super-males" in any sense of the word.[15]

Persons whose sex chromosomes show variety throughout the body are known as mosaics. These individuals exhibit many characteristics similar to those outlined in descriptions of other sex chromosome syndromes. Just as their sex chromosomes are a mixture, so too are their symptoms,[16] but their sex identities, gender identities, and behavior follow their sex assignment at birth and the rearing that comes with it, regardless of often apparently contradictory chromosomal complements.

Persons with chromosomal abnormalities have been estimated to account for three out of every 1,000 births. They are twice as common as Down's Syndrome individuals but generally move in society as unremarkable females and males.[17] From the fact of the unremarkableness of their fit with the gender requirements of society it must be concluded that "although the sex chromosome complement provides the initial stimulus for normal male or normal female sexual development, an abnormal sex chromosome complement seldom influences sexual development in such a way that the individual's social sex is in doubt."[18] Sex chromosomes may or may not lead to a particular body type, hormonal set, or behavior pattern. Chromosomes exert an influence on sex but they do not prove to be the single determining factor governing future developmental patterns and gender behavior.

Hormones and Gender

Sex hormones play a major role in the development of physical and behavioral patterns. Experiments using animal subjects have manipulated hormonal levels in fetuses and adults in an attempt to isolate the effects of individual hormones at specific periods of maturation. In particular, a great deal of work has focused on the effects of excessive doses of androgens on fetuses and older animals. To a lesser degree, attention has been turned to the effects of estrogens and progestins on both XX and XY fetuses and adult humans.

When examining the literature on the effects of hormones, it is important to keep in mind certain cautions. Although experiments are conducted using known quantities of drugs, it is not fully understood how they are used by the body. Chemical pathways in the body often convert one sex hormone to another before the hormone is actually used by the body. As well, all of the sex hormones are quite similar in chemical structure and can cause similar effects. The situation is further complicated by the fact that the action of sex hormones in combination can either be inhibitory or enhancing.[19] So although an experiment may be a controlled one, the results may not directly reflect the action of the hormone which has been manipulated, but rather the action of some hormone further along in a chain of reactions.

Part of the complexity of the question lies in the fact that androgens may be converted by the brains of primates into estrogens.[20] As a result, at this point in our knowledge of sex hormones we cannot say with certainty whether it is estrogens or androgens which are functionally operative in the brain. It is also believed that sensitivity to estrogen, at least in lower animals, is related to both the amounts of estrogen already retained by the body and to the amounts of progestins and androgens circulating in the organism.[21] We cannot therefore reliably determine the effects of hormones by means of simple quantitative measurement of circulating hormones without having available more detailed information concerning hormonal balance, sensitivity, and hormonal history.

The situation is still further complicated by the fact that sex hormones circulate in the body in two main states, bound or unbound. When a sex hormone is in its bound state, it is circulating in the blood stream attached to another chemical substance. A sex hormone must be in its free, or unbound state, in order for the body to be able to process it at a receptor site. Receptor sites can most easily be pictured as keyholes. A sex hormone in a bound state will not fit the keyhole and therefore cannot unlock the series of responses of an organ. Unbound hormones will release a chemical response when they bind to a receptor site, which in turn will set off other reactions which may eventually result in physical changes or behavioral responses. Males and females have different concentrations of receptor sites in various parts of their bodies which may result in dimorphic sensitivities to stimuli.

Often quoted statistics comparing hormones and hormone levels in males and females can, as a result, be misleading. John Money, a prominent, prolific, and highly respected authority on sex differences, whose work stands among the major references in the field, explains the differences in hormonal levels between female and male humans by quoting figures which "do not discriminate between bound and free circulating blood levels of the hormone but," he adds, "they do indicate the relativity of the amount secreted."[22] So although we know that women have on the average between 6 percent and 20 percent of the circulating androgens that men do, or that men have the same progesterone levels as premenstrual women and approximately 30 percent of the estrogen level of postmenstrual women, we do not yet know exactly what impact these hormones have on the development, maintenance, or sensitivity of human receptor sites.[23]

Animal studies expose important questions for research into human conditions. Animal sex-typed behavior studied in hormone research is usually divided along the lines of mounting behavior and presenting behavior. Masculinity is defined in terms of mounts and femininity is defined in terms of sexual presentations. Other behaviors which are less clearly related to actual sexuality are also divided along sex lines: activity levels, exploratory behavior, and fighting, to name a few. Human behavior patterns commonly used in hormone studies as indicators of biologically based femininity include: interest in weddings and marriage, preference for marriage over career, interest in infants and children, and an enjoyment of childhood play with dolls.[24] Evidence of biologically based masculinity is defined in terms of childhood enjoyment of toys and games requiring high levels of activity, in self-assurance, and in holding career aspirations as more important than parenting.[25] Clearly the criteria used for investigations involving humans are even more highly socially determined than those used for animals.

Many studies have been done of animals whose fetal development has been surgically manipulated. Gonads have been removed from both male and female animals, pregnant mothers have been injected with androgens or estrogens, or submitted to situations of high physical stress. It has been well established that when XX fetuses in lower animals are exposed to unusually high doses of androgens (most often testosterone), they develop into hermaphrodites who have male genitals and female internal reproductive organs. Female monkeys exposed to androgens in utero become "predisposed to the acquisition and expression of patterns of behavior that are normally characteristic of the genetic male."[26]

While not questioning the validity of these findings, it is important to recognize that monkeys are social creatures with personalities and rules governing group behavior. While admittedly their behavior is governed more by biological imperatives than is that of humans, it is still correct to say that much of their behavior is socially learned. Harry Harlow, an authority on the behavior patterns of the rhesus monkey, reports that though the rhesus monkey appears to be born with a repertoire of mating gestures available to it, it must have "good emotional bonds with its mother and peers" or else it will not "learn from them how to use these inborn gestures appropriately."[27] Thus, although research results linking prenatal androgens to masculinized female monkeys may be reliable, the interpretation of those results may overemphasize biological factors. Monkey mothers have been observed to carefully inspect the genitals of their newborn infants, presumably to determine the infants' sex.[28] Androgens may well cause masculinized external reproductive organs, but the social response of adults to those genitals may play the major role in the determination of gendered behavior pattern formation even among monkeys.

The results gained from the study of animals are usually used as a jumping off point for studies of humans. Of course, it is not possible to administer androgens to pregnant women for experimental purposes. Instead scientists study incidents in nature which they believe to most closely resemble situations that they would like to experimentally induce.

Two groups of XX individuals have been studied to this end. One group are XX individuals whose mothers took the anti-miscarriage drug diethylstilbestrol (DES) while they were in utero, and who were born with some degree of masculinization of the genitals. Some were born with what was considered at birth to be an enlarged clitoris and were assigned as females at birth, some were born with what was considered to be an undersized penis and were assigned as males at birth, and some were born with what were considered to be normal male genitals and were thus unquestioningly assigned as males at birth.[29]

In the years between 1945 and 1971 a large number of fetuses were exposed to this drug, which is often considered an androgenizing agent despite the fact that it is a progestin.[30] Progestins do move through a stage of being androgens but are used by the body in their final state as estrogens.[31] The cells of the body, including brain cells, convert both androgens and progestins into estrogens, which may be the final and useful form of all sex hormones.[32] The inclusion of DES studies with androgenizing syndromes perhaps seems more understandable in light of the fact that androgens are masculinizing hormones, and in a small number of cases, XX babies born to mothers treated with DES were born with some degree of virilization of the genitals.[33] It is important to note, however, that these children represent only a minute percentage out of the estimated 980,000 to 4.5 million children exposed to this drug in the U.S. alone.[34]

The gender identity and gender role of DES exposed and masculinized chromosomal females has been the subject of much study in an attempt to determine if their behavior was masculinized along with their genitals. There are a number of problems with this course of research: (1) As has been pointed out, DES is *not* an androgen.[35] (2) Conclusions drawn from studies regarding the effects of DES on the fetus are representative of only a tiny fraction of the individuals actually affected by this drug. If the effects in question were resultant from this drug, why have so few come to the attention of the medical establishment? (3) In all of the cases under study there was at least partial masculinization of the genitals. It is therefore impossible to say with certainty whether any masculine behavior was resultant from chemical effects on the central nervous system and other physical mechanisms or from a masculine gender identity based on the physical evidence of male-looking genitals.

Excessive prenatal exposure to progestins does not always masculinize the external sexual organs of an XX fetus. Reinisch and Karow studied girls who were exposed to excessive progestins prenatally but were not physically virilized. They compared these girls to a group of girls known to have been prenatally exposed to excess estrogens. The progestin group was found to be more independent, more self-assured, more self-sufficient, more individualistic, and more sensitive, as well as being more inner directed in their thoughts and having a tendency to feel their way through things rather than think in a dry, objective, and cognitive way.[36] The description that Reinisch and Karow gave of girls fetally exposed to high doses of progestins is one which could easily be interpreted as the personality type of a masculinized girl, yet progestins are not normally considered to be "masculine" hormones. The action of DES and other progestins are lumped together with those of androgens because of the incorrigible beliefs of researchers that some of the behavior they observe is "men's" behavior despite the fact that it is common among women and appears to be caused by what is usually referred to as a type of pregnancy hormone. This suggests that although hormones may affect behavior, the interpretation of those behavioral effects can be skewed by social definitions and constructs.

A second human group studied in an attempt to shed light on the action of hormones on humans, is XX individuals with Congenital Adrenal Hyperplasia (CAH), also called the Adrenogenital Syndrome (AGS). In this syndrome the adrenal glands of the fetus, and later the child and adult, do not function properly. The adrenal cortex fails to make cortisol in sufficient amounts. This signals the pituitary to secrete adrenocorticotrophic hormone (ACTH) in larger amounts. ACTH causes the adrenals to increase in size and the enlarged adrenals secrete more of all of their hormones including adrenal androgens.

In this syndrome the fetus becomes partially masculinized, and if uncorrected, the child and adult will continue to live under the influence of excessive amounts of adrenal androgens. This syndrome does offer a good facsimile to the studies conducted on lower animals, but the correspondence is not perfect. In the animal experiments the androgen used is some form of testosterone; in the human "experiments" the androgen is adrenal in origin.

AGS XX individuals, when born with normal-looking male genitals, live their lives with a male gender identity and behave in accordance with the masculine gender role despite their XX chromosomes and normal estrogen secretions. AGS XX individuals born with subsized genitals of a male appearance who are assigned at birth as males also live their lives with a male gender identity and behave in accordance with the masculine gender role. They may have anxieties about their abilities to perform sexually, but they show no doubts concerning their actual status as males and no lack of interest in the masculine role, again demonstrating that sex assignment at birth, and rearing, are more important in producing gender than are chromosomes.

AGS XX individuals assigned at birth as females require extensive surgery at several stages in their lives and are sustained throughout life on cortisol hormone therapy.[37] It is impossible to accurately assess the effect of this process on a girl's self-image. It is also as yet unknown what effect a lifetime of cortisol treatment might have on physiology or personality. Thus, in the study of AGS females it is difficult to separate the precise effects of adrenal androgens from other results of their abnormal hormonal condition.

Ehrhardt and Baker, and Money and Ehrhardt studied groups of AGS girls and concluded that they were more often long-term "tomboys" than the females in their control groups. The parameters that they used as positive indicators of tomboyism were: rough-and-tumble play or intense energy expenditure; preference for stereotypical boys' toys and male playmates; lack of interest in clothing and adornment; lack of interest in infants, motherhood, and marriage; and an interest in career for later life.[38] But these researchers used the label "tomboy" to support a finding of increased masculinity in girls exposed to either progestins or androgens in utero, while at the same time noting that the behavior pattern that they identified as tomboyism is in no way abnormal for the female gender role.[39]

Childhood tomboyism is so much a part of the normal female gender role pattern that it is present to a comparable degree in many females with no history of prenatal or postnatal hormonal abnormalities. In one sample of heterosexual women, 50 percent reported that they had been tomboys in their youth, while 75 percent of the lesbians studied reported childhood tomboyism. Another study similarly found 75 percent of the lesbian respondents reporting childhood tomboyism.[40] When these figures are compared with those reported by Ehrhardt and Baker in their major study of AGS girls, the implications of the phenomenon of tomboyism among AGS girls are weak. Ehrhardt and Baker reported that 59 percent of the girls that they studied were persistent tomboys.[41] This figure represents only a slightly higher rate than has been found among heterosexual females, and a considerably lower rate than has been found among lesbians. Yet these and similar results are used to support a hypothesis that both the Adrenogenital Syndrome and prenatal progestin exposure result in masculinization of the behavior of females. A more logical conclusion would take into account the fact that tomboyism is a normal feature of the feminine gender role.[42] More rationally, the female gender role could be redefined to include what are common and unremarkable facts of childhood: self-centeredness and the desire of children to play active and physical games. Thus, rather than masculinizing girl children, the effects of progestins and the AGS Syndrome might be interpreted as supporting behaviors inherent within the normal female range.

"Normal femininity," of the psychological-test variety, may actually be a rare commodity. In one study of college aged females, only 15 percent of the heterosexual sample tested as feminine on a widely accepted sex role inventory. The remaining 85 percent of heterosexual females scored as either masculine or as some combination of masculine and feminine. In the same study, only 7 percent of the lesbians scored as feminine, while the other 93 percent were rated as exhibiting some gender role which was not predominantly feminine.[43] A similar study found a less dramatic distribution among both heterosexual women and lesbian women. In a total heterosexual sample of 790 women, 41 percent were rated as feminine while 59 percent were rated as not predominantly feminine. In a smaller lesbian sample, 14 percent were found to score in the feminine range, while more than 85 percent of the lesbian sample scored as not feminine.[44] Thus it can be seen that few females of any hormonal history are particularly feminine by these standards, and the claim of hormonally induced masculinity is not well supported.

The question of the influence of prenatal hormones on human behavior is obscured by social definitions of masculinity and femininity. There are many characteristics which both males and females share, yet they are often designated by researchers as appropriate, or even natural, for only one sex and not the other. When a behavior pattern is exhibited by members of the sex deemed inappropriate to that behavior, researchers set off in search of a biological basis for that "abnormal" behavior. But prenatal influences on postnatal behavior are very difficult to isolate among the totality of human experience.

Social definition of infants starts from the moment they are identified as members of one sex and not the other. Even in the absence of a designation of sex, most adults will presume one sex or the other and proceed to interact with an infant according to their own understanding of sex and gender.[45] The effects of this social response to assigned sex are so strong that hermaphrodites whose physical bodies are similarly equipped, but who have been assigned to different sexes, have gender identities which follow their assigned sex, and gender roles which follow their gender identities. Although two hermaphrodites, in such cases, may have genitals, gonads, and hormones of the same type, they will grow up to be accepted and function in society as the different sexes they were assigned to at birth.[46] Thus it can be seen that although prenatal hormones have some influence on gender behavior patterns, the ability of researchers to isolate those influences is confused by the ambiguity of the social definitions and the meanings of gender roles. Clearly, research into the effects of excessive exposure to prenatal progestins and androgens is infused with incorrigible gender stereotypes which color what questions are asked and how results are interpreted.

Hormone levels in adult animals and humans have also been linked to behavior patterns and sensitivities. It has long been known that hormone levels in humans and other primates are responsive to events perceived by individuals in their environment. The "fight or flight" response of the adrenals is learned by every schoolchild. But the relationship between the sex hormones and environmental events is less clear. One area of investigation has centered on sex differences in hormonal responses to stress. This work has shown that in both humans and monkeys, males respond to stress both differently from females and to a greater degree than females. Contrary to popular misconceptions, male androgen levels are more excitable in stressful situations than are female hormone levels.[47]

Rose et al. studied the behavior and androgen levels of rhesus monkeys in changing dominance situations. They found that testosterone levels of male monkeys respond markedly to environmental variables. Testosterone levels in their experimental groups were highest when male monkeys were in situations where they were able to be most dominant. In the experiment, the testosterone levels of a group of male animals became elevated when they were exposed to sexually receptive females who granted them sexual access, thus allowing them to reach the top of the dominance hierarchy in that situation. When the same males were exposed to a new group of males where they were not able to establish dominance and were in fact physically overpowered, their testosterone levels fell below the baseline or pre-test level. The hormonal effects of defeat and failure were reversed entirely when the same group of males was returned to the presence of the receptive females.[48]

Similar results have been noted in observations of female monkeys and human males and females. Primate female testosterone levels rise with an elevation of their dominance rank. Human male testosterone levels have been found to rise in response to situations perceived by subjects as demonstrating their personal achievement.[49] Similarly, human females who view themselves as self-directed, action-oriented, resourceful people have also been found to have higher testosterone levels than more conventional and less self-confident women.[50]

In related work, both emotional stress and surgical stress have been shown to depress testosterone levels in humans.[51] Emotional stress in the form of depression, though, has a different effect on human males than it does on females. Depressed females decrease their secretion of adrenal androgens, while male estrogen secretion is increased by depression. This would seem to imply that when a human is in a situation which is experienced as one of high dominance or achievement, androgen levels respond by rising, and that when a human is in a situation which is perceived as one of low dominance or failure, the endocrine system responds to this external stimulus by lowering the secretion rate of androgens and raising the secretion rate of estrogens.[52]

It would not seem unreasonable then to hypothesize that situations that either encourage or allow a perception of dominance or achievement in humans actually promote the secretion of androgens. Although the link between androgens and aggressive dominance-seeking behavior has not been unequivocally established, there is a great deal of research devoted to clarifying this issue, most of which points toward a positive connection.[53]

Hormones and the Brain

The hormones circulating through the bodies of normal male and female fetuses are also thought, by many researchers, to have a strong influence on the development of the central nervous system. In particular a great deal of attention has centered on the hypothalamus of the brain. The hypothalamus is the control center for the endocrine system in general and the sex hormones in particular. Much of hypothalamic research has been done with a variety of animals, but examinations of human subjects have also been made within the bounds of ethical constraints.[54]

The hypothalamus is a very small body consisting of a number of nuclei. It is located in the brain stem directly above the pituitary gland and between the two branches of the optic nerve. Some endocrinologists see its functioning as so intricately tied with that of the pituitary gland that the two are studied as a unit, but this is not the majority approach. The hypothalamus is normally different in males and females. It is generally believed that differences in the structures of the hypothalami of males and females are the result of fetal hormonal baths during gestation and account for the later cyclical release of sex hormones in adult females and the acyclical, or tonic, release of sex hormones in males.

The hypothalamus acts as a regulator of hormone levels through feedback mechanisms. The hypothalamus stimulates or inhibits the secretion of endocrine hormones by other organs on the basis of a constant monitoring of the levels of various substances which circulate in the blood and pass through hypothalamic centers. Human secondary sex characteristics and reproductive behaviors are regulated by the action and sensitivity of the hypothalamus. Many argue that the "maleness" or "femaleness" of the hypothalamus and the hormonal systems it controls are permanently set by well-timed hormonal baths during fetal life.

It has been shown that in lower animals the hypothalamus is capable of learning responses to repeated environmental stimuli,[55] resulting in measurable physical changes in the structure of the hypothalamus. Such changes in the hypothalamus can then result in different response patterns than those initially fostered in the fetal environment. Panksepp speculated that these changes can be subtle enough that they occur before actual behavioral changes are perceptible to investigators. He suggested that behavioral changes are affected through a cycle of sensory input, hypothalamic response, hormonal response and/or motor response, and back to hypothalamic response. Panksepp argued that "the presence of cells in the hypothalamus which rapidly learn environmental contingencies suggests that the hypothalamus may extract the value of environmental events and analyze reward contingencies so that rudimentary motor output can be changed to increase the recurrence of rewards."[56]

Siegel and Edinger proposed that the hypothalamus serves a gatekeeping function between sensory inputs which have elicited behavioral responses in the past and neural messages which prompt motor centers to respond in a similar fashion again. Siegel and Edinger suggested that sex hormones sensitize the hypothalamus to such input: "The scheme presented here suggests that [sex] hormones act to increase or decrease hypothalamic excitability levels and thereby alter the bias exerted on the cortical mechanisms from which the motor patterns associated with aggressive behavior are elaborated."[57] The pattern suggested by this research is that the learning of certain behaviors is strongly mediated by the hypothalamus and that the hypothalamus itself is both mediated by, and the mediator of, the flow of sex hormones.

Gupta et al. pointed out that the sensitivity of the hypothalamic-pituitary system decreases with age.[58] But evidence presented by Arnold and Breedlove strongly suggests that the actions of sex hormones on the adult brain can still cause both permanent morphological changes to the brain and long-term reversible behavioral changes. Sex hormone effects on the brain can include alterations in the size, form, and speed of neuron growth and changes in sex hormone secretion and usage. Arnold and Breedlove further suggested that there may be critical periods, past the neonatal stages, during which the organism is most receptive to these effects.[59] Thus the evidence suggests that environmental factors can affect sensitivity and response patterns of the hormonal system and that these changes in hormonal functioning can have far-reaching effects throughout the lifetime of an organism.

It would seem then that the differing structures of the hypothalami of male and female animals, resultant from fetal endocrine baths, may be either a starting point for sex-related behaviors or a step on a twisting path. The research presented here suggests that although the intrauterine hormonal environment may predispose the endocrine-hypothalamic system to certain sensitivities, those sensitivity levels and the behaviors that they direct are subject to environmental influences throughout life. Both behavior patterns *and* their neuroendocrine correlates may be significantly shaped by the experiences of an animal in its environment both before and after birth.

This evidence suggests a pattern. Fetal hormonal secretions and environments establish a first level of hypothalamic sensitivity to environmental and hormonal stimuli, partially on the basis of genetic programming. External environmental factors then begin their direct influences at birth, and are most potent closest to the time of birth.[60] They act to reinforce or block hypothalamic activity patterns, receptor site sensitivities, and hormonal secretion patterns. Changing environmental demands may increase or obstruct secretions of hormones. The resulting changes in circulating hormones may then increase or inhibit receptor site sensitivity. Receptor site sensitivities may in turn increase or diminish hypothalamic sensitivity to environmental stimuli.[61] Thus, over time, lesser or greater environmental demands may produce lesser, equal, or greater behavioral results depending on the direction of the effects at each stage of the process.[62]

Thus it may be concluded that human experiences, and the meanings given to those experiences, play a role in the development of hormonal production and sensitivity patterns. It seems possible that forms of human social organization not only can constrain the social experiences of individuals in their worlds, but may even shape some part of our abilities to physically perceive and respond to the people and events of our world. In the final analysis, it may well turn out that much as our social selves are limited by our flesh and blood, so too are our corporal selves molded by our social experiences and the meanings that we attach to them. Chronic defeat and failure, or success and dominance, may leave far more than psychic marks—our bodies may themselves be shaped by the roles that we play every day of our lives.

Transsexualism

Transsexuals offer an interesting window on gender because they constitute a striking example of discordance between sex and gender. It is not uncommon, among the general public, to find examples of individuals who do not conform well with their socially expected gender role, but in physiologically normal females and males (other than transsexuals), sex and gender identity match: females are either girls or women, and males are either boys or men. Normally, people unquestioningly accept that they are, and should be, the sex assigned to them at birth. In the case of transsexuals this is not so. Transsexuals believe that they are persons of one gender mistakenly born into the body of the wrong sex, e.g., real men in female bodies by mistake.[63]

Transsexuals are not transvestites. For transvestites, sex and gender identity match; nonetheless, transvestites periodically dress and behave according to another gender role, i.e., males who think of themselves as men but who, for brief periods of time, dress and act like women. Transsexuals differ from transvestites in that gender identity and gender role conform to one another but are discordant with sex, e.g., female-to-male transsexuals identify and act as men but were born to the female sex. Transsexuals dress and act as they do because that is the appropriate role for persons of their gender identity; transvestites dress and act as they do to assume another role. Transsexuals are persons whose morphological sex and chromosomal sex are in agreement but whose gender identity and social gender differ from their sex. As such, they present a formidable challenge to the assumption that sex-based biological factors determine gender. Transsexual people appear to be biologically normal members of their birth sex, yet in all social respects they belong to the opposite gender and take whatever steps they can to alter their sexual status to conform to their gender.

In retrospective reports of their childhoods given by transsexuals and their family members, transsexuals are reported to have exhibited gender character-istics discordant with their assigned sex from very early childhood. Their accounts report that they expressed desires to change sex from as young as three years of age. As children they persist strongly in the belief that they can change sex and exhibit a marked preference for a gender role discordant with their assigned sex as well as an aversion to the gender role considered appro-priate to their assigned sex. Around the time of puberty they usually develop sexual and romantic interests in persons who are of the same sex as themselves but of a different gender. If they do engage in sex, they see themselves as entirely heterosexual and attempt to choose partners who also see themselves as engaging in heterosexual activities. Generally they have a great dislike for their own genitals and any of their own physical characteristics which remind them of their birth sex. Transsexuals avoid reminders of their sex status and attempt to override sex status with gender status. Eventually, many transsex-uals present themselves to doctors with the request that their bodies be made to conform to their gender.[64]

By definition, a transsexual is a person whose physical sex is unambiguous, and whose gender identity is unambiguous, but whose sex and gender do not concur. The existence of such people challenges the belief that gender is necessarily linked to chromosomes or anatomical features, and that males are masculine and females are feminine.[65] Scientists have turned to investigations of the hormonal status of transsexuals in an attempt to locate a biological source of their abnormality.

These studies have taken two approaches. The more common approach is to simply assay the hormonal levels of transsexuals. Testosterone levels are usually investigated in search of depressed testosterone levels in male-to-female transsexuals and elevated testosterone levels in female-to-male transsexuals.[66] The major authors on the subject of transsexualism report that hormonal assays have found normal levels of all sex hormones in both male-to-female and female-to-male transsexuals,[67] although there have been isolated reports of elevated testosterone levels in transsexuals, which have not been widely replicated.[68] These results strongly suggest that if there is a hormonal reason for this condition, it is not so simple or direct a cause as mismatched testosterone levels.

An alternate, and less common, approach is to investigate the ways that transsexuals process the hormones in their bodies.[69] Seyler et al. took this second approach and studied hormone processing in female-to-male transsexuals. They found that female-to-male transsexuals responded differently to experimentally administered progestins than did either average females or average males. Heterosexual women responded to ingested DES with increased blood concentrations of both luteinizing hormone (LH) and follicle stimulating hormone (FSH). Heterosexual men responded with decreased blood concentrations of both of these hormones. The female-to-male transsexuals in this study exhibited a response which was intermediate in both pattern and intensity between the average male and female responses.[70]

Midgeon et al. found similar results in their study of male-to-female transsexuals. In that study, male-to-female transsexuals, average males, and average females were administered estrogens and their responses monitored. Estrogen normally acts as an anti-testosterone agent in the sense that it increases the binding of testosterone to other molecules, thus rendering it unusable at receptor sites. Estrogen administered to either males or females will, under normal conditions, lower the blood concentration of free testosterone and increase the concentration of bound testosterone in the blood. Male-to-female transsexuals were found to react dramatically to the administered estrogens. Their blood levels of unbound testosterone were found to decrease to the point that their concentrations were even lower than those of the normal females studied.[71]

These studies indicate that transsexuals process the hormones in their bodies in an abnormal way. Seyler et al. suggested two possible explanations for the results of their investigation: first, "that the changes observed in estrogen responses are acquired due either to psychological or other disturbance. Psychological state is known to influence gonadotropic function;"[72] and second, "that the anomalous pituitary sensitization responses of transsexual women suggest that there may have been an abnormality in hormonal milieu during fetal life."[73] Other studies have demonstrated the ability of hypothalami to learn responses to external stimuli. The pituitary is controlled by the hypothalamus and the functioning of the entire endocrine system is controlled by the hypothalamic-pituitary system. These facts, combined with the widely accepted understanding that hormonal cycling in the female can be disrupted by psychological factors, strongly suggest the first hypothesis. If the second explanation offered by Seyler et al. were to be valid it would be logical to expect to find an increased incidence of transsexualism among females known to have been masculinized in utero. All studies of AGS and DES girls have found that gender identity follows sex of assignment. There have been no reports of increased incidence of transsexualism among these populations.[74] Thus, these studies add weight to the contention that human gender role behavior and environmental experience may have some causative influence on hormonal production and response mechanisms.

A model which might be used to explain the transsexual phenomenon, and possibly the gender phenomena of the everyday world, would have to account for the interactions of physiology and environment. It has been shown that among humans,[75] and perhaps among animals as well,[76] social interaction begins to shape personality from the moment of birth. Neonates enter this world with the heritage of their chromosomal influences and prenatal hormonal environment. At birth they are assigned to a sex; in every way this assignment colors the events of the remainder of their lives.

External environmental experiences set into motion a momentum which may be in continuation of prenatal influences, or in contradiction to them. In either case, social factors may be capable of overriding most, if not all, prenatal influences.[77] Social influences may actually reset the direction which future development of a hormonal system will take. They may act to suppress or enhance biological predispositions. If social forces continue to exert pressure over long periods of time, a chronic situation can develop which may crystallize into relatively stable physical configurations that reflect the direction of social pressures. In this way, hormonal abnormalities might be seen to be the result of chronic social abnormalities.

In the same way, one might interpret the gross hormonal differences between socially normal men and women as being a result, rather than a cause, of the chronic social pressures which males and females undergo in the process of becoming socially normal men and women. Thus the interaction between the hormonal systems and the environment can be seen to function as a feedback loop. If the loop is a positive one, the hormonal system and the environment reinforce one another and thus enhance the predispositions suggested by the prenatal experience. If it is a negative feedback loop, the effects of environmental experience may be capable of overriding prenatal influences to such an extent that the original impetus may become overshadowed by the demands of social environment.

The ongoing requirements of everyday social interaction may be powerful enough, in their long-term effects, to be of greater importance than hormones in shaping the behavioral sex differences found among humans. The constant feedback and reinforcement of behavior might have some determining effect on the hormonal levels in humans. The net result could well be that not only are human minds capable of learning behavioral patterns but so too are human brains and the endocrine systems which they control. Thus, although the endocrine glands and their secretions may have a controlling influence on gendered human behavior patterns, they are in a dynamic relationship with the experience of the social organism through the mediation of the brain. Not only is the human mind in dynamic interaction with its environment, constantly learning and changing, so too is the human body changing, learning, and growing through its experience within its environment.

SHEILA

___

Learning to Be Gendered

The Psychological Bases of Gender

How are little boys made?
Take one new baby,
Poke it and toss it, force it and push it,
Leave it alone a lot, and never speak softly to it.

How are little girls made?
Take one new baby,
Cuddle it and coo at it, soothe it and calm it,
And never let it stray.

What are little boys made of?
Scrapes and pains, fears not shown,
Lessons learned the hard way,
Loneliness ingrown.

What are little girls made of?
Questions and dreams, secrets never told,
Trusts nurtured and betrayed,
Life waiting to unfold.

                                        (The author)

Setting the Scene

Human babies are greeted into the world as little men and women. The people who come into contact with them throughout the years of their infancies and childhoods are always, on some level, concerned with relating "gender appropriately" to them as they mature first into girls and boys, and later into young women and men. Many people are keenly aware of their roles in the process of teaching youngsters to be gendered individuals, others give their actions little thought, while some people believe that they make no effort in this regard. Nonetheless, the evidence is strong, clear, and regularly replicated that all of us contribute, purposefully or not, to the process of giving consistent social meaning to the biological facts of sex.

The adults who welcome newborns into the world have well-established genders, personalities, and belief systems by the time they find themselves in attendance at a birth. They invariably, and often unintentionally, communicate their gender beliefs to newborns through the medium of their own personalities and actions. One way that this is manifested is in adults' strong social need to attribute membership in a sex status, and sex differences, to newborn infants. This tendency is so strong that they will often do it even when they have little or no concrete information on which to base their actions. Adults seem almost unable to relate to an "ungendered" child. When adults are presented with a baby whose sex is not specified, they will generally want to know the sex of the child before commencing social interactions with it. If that information is not forthcoming, they will usually proceed to decide for themselves what the sex and gender of the child are. These sex/gender attributions then form a basis for their subsequent understandings of, and interactions with, the child.[1]

Adults, in interaction with infants, generally believe that they are being impartial observers when they see infant behaviors which coincidentally match their own beliefs as to how females and males are "supposed" to be. People have a strong tendency to observe behaviors which correspond to the sex that we believe an infant to be, regardless of the actual sex of the infant.[2] For example, when a group of adults, in one study, was shown a videotape of a crying nine-month-old infant, they interpreted the crying as a sign of "fear" when the infant had been identified to them as female, and as a sign of "anger" when the same infant had been identified to them as male. When those adults believed an infant to be female (male) they observed feminine (masculine) behavior regardless of the actual actions, or sex, of the child.[3]

The attributions of adults in interaction with babies are neither in-consequential nor benign. Adults who hold such beliefs align their own behavior with their beliefs and in the process transmit some portion of their beliefs and behaviors to the infants in their care. Infants who are perceived by their caretakers to be tough and angry receive different care than ones who are perceived to be delicate and fearful. Furthermore, adults who perceive themselves to be tough, or delicate, will administer different styles of care to the infants involved. The net results of such situations are that many adult beliefs become translated into infant experience. When this happens consistently, over extended periods of time, to large numbers of infants and children, their experiences ultimately crystallize into physiological, emotional, and behavioral attributes which we recognize as gender.

Theoretical Models of Gender Acquisition

Babies learn many things about themselves and their environment while in the hands of their caregivers. As they continue to grow and physically complete many of the steps begun before birth, they simultaneously proceed through the first stages in the lifelong process of personality development. One of the major tasks of young children during these first years of life is the acquisition of gender identity and gender roles.[4] Very young children tend to understand the requirements of gender differently than adults, although not always in less distinct ways. Very young children do not usually see gender as immutable and often define it by terms of reference different from those used by adults.[5] Youngsters thus go through a process of developing and honing their sense of what gender is and how they, and those around them, fit within its parameters.

Psychologists are divided in opinion as to how gender identity and gender roles are acquired. The three most prominent theoretical approaches at present are the psychoanalytic identification theories such as those first presented by Freud,[6] social learning theories as put forward by Bandura[7] and his followers, and the cognitive developmental school as exemplified by Kohlberg and Gilligan.[8] More recently, Sandra Bem has proposed a gender schema theory which incorporates elements of both cognitive developmental theory and social learning theory.[9]

Psychoanalytic theorists place a major emphasis on intrapsychic patterns learned by infants in the first years of life. Psychoanalysts theorize that the experiences of these years are the bedrock on which all other experiences stand and the weave through which all other experience must be filtered in order to be understood. They hypothesize that the major psychological events of the first two to three years of life are etched into our psyches and that although the effects of those experiences can be modified, they can never be entirely erased. Psychoanalytical identification theorists suggest that young children come to identify with the gender role behaviors and attitudes of their same-sex parents due to the powerful influences that they exert on their children.

According to Freudians and neo-Freudians, children pass through a number of developmental stages in the process of growing into mature gender behaviors. As they move through these stages, their gender becomes more firmly entrenched in their psyches and comes to be more directly in line with the expectations of the society in which they live. Little girls are thought to identify with their mothers' roles at first as a result of the salience of their mothers' nurturant qualities, and later as a means of achieving feminine attractiveness to men. Little boys are believed to identify with their fathers as a result of the attractiveness of their fathers' dominant positions within their families.

Psychoanalysts usually claim that children have an innate predisposition to identify with and to emulate the behaviors and attitudes of their same-sex parents. Identification theorists propose that over a period of time this imitation process leads to an identity and a personality easily understood by any member of society as either clearly masculine or clearly feminine. They believe that this process of gender identity and gender role acquisition is a naturally occurring one and that it need not be coerced or prompted by societal pressures. They further claim that many aspects of the personalities of young children, including gender, evolve and grow as the result of forces which are universal and independent of varying social systems or customs.

Social learning theorists approach the question of gender identity and gender role development from a different perspective. They begin from the assumption that children are born completely malleable and open to the demands and expectations of the social entity into which they are born. They directly dispute the contention that humans have innate predispositions to behave in particular gendered ways. Rather, they maintain that our social behaviors may take any form that can be created and communicated through social organization.

The cornerstone of their theory of gender acquisition is the recognition that societies exert pressures on their members to conform to established social patterns. Certain behavior patterns are socially rewarded and others are selectively discouraged. They argue that children respond to systematic schedules of rewards and punishments by developing patterns of behavior which conform to the social expectations of the group of people applying the rewards and punishments. Social learning theory does not propose that this systematic reinforcement is necessarily a conscious process on the part of the persons shaping the personalities of young children, but rather a series of subtle processes whereby cultural values are transmitted to children who, over a period of time, absorb them as their own. Social learning theory thus proposes that gender is a cultural artifact learned along with other socially appropriate behaviors in the process of growing up. According to this theory, persons are entirely capable of learning whole other, and possibly wildly different, cultural meanings for gender if they are given the opportunity to reexperience the social learning process in a new social setting.

Cognitive developmental theorists believe that children take a more active role in the learning of gender. They begin with the assumption that humans are born with a need to make sense of the world they live in. They argue that it is problematic that we are presented with a tremendous amount of sensory input at all times. They assert that in order to absorb and cognitively process what we experience every day, we must somehow engage in mental processes which organize, and therefore simplify, our experiences.

Cognitive developmental theorists suggest that children proceed through a series of stages wherein their ability to understand concepts and absorb information becomes more complex as they mature. At very young ages, children begin to seek understanding of how the world around them is organized; they have a desire and a need to make sense of their experiences in life. One of the ways in which children learn to understand the world around them is by recognizing that the people of the world can be divided into two large groups on the basis of gender. Once children learn to make this distinction, they use it as a filtering device to help them classify the behaviors of others into the more easily recognizable and understandable units of gender.

Cognitive developmental theory also proposes that children desire to behave in accordance with the expectations of their social group. Therefore, once children understand what gender they are, they actively attempt to learn how others perform their gender roles and imitate them to the best of their understanding and abilities. As children grow older their conceptual abilities become more sophisticated, and their gender roles acquire more subtle nuances and phrasing.

Thus, cognitive developmental theories differ from Freudian theories in that they claim that gender is a socially variable product with no biologically based tendencies toward any particular forms. Cognitive developmental theories share with Freudian theories the idea that we are born with certain psychological needs, but for the cognitive developmentalists the need is for cognitive order in general rather than for any specific form of gendered thought or behavior.

Cognitive developmental theories share with social learning theories the concept that gender behaviors are learned by children through their experiences in social interactions. But these two theories differ in their perception of the nature of that learning process. For the cognitive developmental theorists, children initiate and actively compel that process, while social learning theorists believe that people are passive recipients of the effects of powerful social forces.

Gender schema theory accepts and incorporates the cognitive developmental ideas that children desire to understand their world and that they have a propensity to categorize their experiences. Gender schema theory also borrows from social learning theory the concept that children learn through their social experience that the categories of male and female are important social classifications. The net result then, according to this theory, is that children learn to classify themselves and others according to a sex-typed gender schema. They learn to do this because they have a cognitive desire to classify, and a social impetus to classify according to sex or gender, rather than according to any number of other possible classification schemata.[10]

Gender schema theory further suggests that people who have learned to be most conforming to social expectations of gender are most likely to use gender as a cognitive schema for understanding their interchanges with other people. What this can mean in practice is that sex-typed people, who use gender as a rationale for their own behaviors, are more likely to see gender as the reason for the behaviors they expect and observe in others, even when there may be many other valid or plausible explanations.[11]

Thus gender schema theory takes cognitive developmental theories and social learning theories one step further in the explanation of how gender is learned in society. This theory argues that an innate desire for cognitive order is satisfied by a socially learned cognitive gender schema. According to this theory, we have little freedom to reject the gender schema which dominates in a society, and once we have learned it, we perferentially use it to explain social phenomena which might easily be explained using other terms of reference. This theory, then, asserts that while the need for schematic information processing may be innate, gender schemata are socially imposed and highly pervasive in their effects.

Each of these theoretical models has its strengths and weaknesses. Psychoanalytic theories recognize and acknowledge largely unconscious motivations and needs which spring from the child, but they fail to take adequate account of the external social demands which impinge on children or of the conscious and active needs of children to understand their world. Social learning theories explain the influences of people and external social forces in the creation of gender, but they tend to develop a picture of children as passive recipients of these forces. Cognitive developmental theories describe children as active participants in the shaping of their own personalities but inadequately attend to questions of either internal unconscious forces or external social pressures. Gender schema theory describes the interaction between the cognitive development of children and their social milieu, but it largely ignores the role of unconscious dynamics and their effects on young minds. Each of these theoretical perspectives seen individually is lacking in some essential area; the four taken together provide a more complete picture.

It would also seem necessary that a theoretical perspective which attempts to explain the deep and enduring nature of the lessons learned during childhood must take into account the physiological effects of these learning processes. The periods of most intense early childhood gender learning and personality formation, the first years after birth, correspond to the period during which the brain is undergoing its most intense postnatal period of growth.[12]

At the time of birth, human brains have the capacity to respond to a very broad range of stimuli with a seemingly limitless variety of responses.[13] As infants experience their environments, their brains begin to build a repertoire of response patterns that reflect their experiences. These learning processes, which occur within rapidly maturing brains, are reflected in neural growth patterns that become physically encoded in the brain in the form of synaptic traces. Such neural growth formations facilitate the occurrence of later responses of a similar nature. As response patterns become established in the brain through repeated use, they become more efficient and rapidly occurring responses. In this way, experience becomes facility. Patterns of thought and behavior learned by infants and young children under the age of six can become translated into neural growth which then acts as a template around which the young brain forms itself during this most plastic of periods in the life of the brain. Thus the experiences of the first two years of life can become the original source of many of the patterns which the brain, and the human organism, will follow throughout life. In a neurological sense, many of the foundations on which an entire life might be built are laid during the first two years of life.[14]

The hypothalamic centers in the brain, which control the excitability and sensitivity levels of sensations such as pleasure and pain, hunger and satiation, rage and fear, sexual arousal, and the corresponding hormonal levels associated with each of these states, are also immature at birth and develop concurrently with personality and gender.[15] It would therefore seem possible that personality and gender patterns that become habitual during these first years of major brain growth may become encoded in synaptic patterns as lifelong sensitivities or propensities of a physiological nature. Thus sex differences which are discernible in the brains and behavior of children as young as six months of age[16] may well be a result of an overlay of their social experiences of gender on the effects of prenatal chromosomal and hormonal influences.[17]

Defining Gender Roles

Since the 1930s, psychologists have been developing a body of work which has attempted to systematically describe popular concepts of masculinity and femininity. Their attempts have been hindered by the shifting nature of popular opinion and by their own inevitable positions as members of the very societies they have been attempting to study. Their positions influence the questions which they ask, the ways that they are asked, and the interpretations which they apply to the data they collect. The subjects whom researchers investigate also carry with them values and beliefs gained from earlier investigations into the nature of masculinity and femininity as they reach the public in their more popularized forms, and the beliefs and behaviors generated from the realities of their experience of gender, race, class, culture, sexual orientation, age, or ethnicity. Thus, the scales and instruments used in psychological research, and the results obtained from them, are often little more than historical artifacts of the times and places in which they were designed.[18] Standards of femininity and masculinity differ across class, age, race, ethnicity, and time, as well as with changing political and sexual persuasions. The gender role standards of a female, inner city, native youth of today will differ from those of a middle-aged rural white male during the 1950s. Such factors have rarely been adequately taken into account in investigations of gender roles.

The earliest models of gender roles were based on an assumption of a continuum ranging from masculinity to femininity. Such models required a subject to be classified as masculine or feminine and allowed for no overlap or middle ground. Later models included a concept of layers or levels of personality wherein one might be outwardly masculine but inwardly feminine.[19] More recently, Sandra Bem introduced the idea that gender roles need not be seen as an either/or sort of arrangement; that one individual might be both highly feminine *and* highly masculine, or neither, thus introducing the concepts of androgynous and undifferentiated personalities. In using Bem's Sex Role Inventory, individuals may be classified as masculine, feminine, androgynous (both masculine and feminine), and undifferentiated (neither masculine nor feminine), thus allowing for two new gender measurement concepts to be added to the discourse.[20]

Unfortunately, some of the early and influential work done in this field was based on highly unrepresentative samples. For example, the for many years widely used Minnesota Multiphasic Personality Inventory (MMPI) male-female (m-f) scale was based on an original sample consisting of "fifty-four male soldiers, sixty-seven female airline employees and thirteen male homosexuals in the early 1940's." The median educational level of the sample as a whole was only eight years.[21] Although such a collection of people might arguably represent a variety of individuals, the sum of those 134 persons could not represent the full range of social attitudes either in the 1940s or today.

The Gough Femininity (Fe) scale was created in 1952 based on the opinions of a group of high school students in Wisconsin and a group of university students in California. By 1966, more than half of the items on the scale were shown to no longer differentiate between males and females in a group of U.S. college students.[22] The Gough (Fe) scale was still widely used in 1974 when Bem proposed the Bem Sex-Role Inventory (BSRI) as an alternative. Bem's Inventory was based on the opinions of 100 Stanford University undergraduates in 1972, half of whom were female and half of whom were male. Bem's sampling might account for some of the changes brought by time, but her sample did not take into account, in any systematic way, other variables such as class, race, age, ethnicity, sexual orientation, or regionality.

Gender role standards as described by psychological testing and as subscribed to by members of the public are far from neutral in their impact. Members of the general public and practicing psychologists, psychiatrists, social workers, and therapists attach differing degrees of value to various gender role characteristics. In 1970, Broverman et al. found that clinicians held a different standard of mental health for females than they held for males. The standards for psychologically healthy males used by the clinicians in the study corresponded closely with their standards for healthy individuals in general, whereas their standards for psychologically healthy females did not.[23]

Clearly, the impact of judgments of mental health made by clinicians can be very far reaching indeed. Female clients of therapists who hold such views can find themselves caught in situations where the price of being deemed as healthy adults is flawed femininity. Not surprisingly, a survey taken in the 1960s found that women were twelve times more likely than males to have preferred to have been born as the other sex,[24] while another, more recent study found that both feminine males and feminine females wished to become more masculine.[25] These studies indicate that a wide range of people place greater value on masculinity than they do on femininity.

A perusal of the qualities used by the Broverman study, and later by Bem, to characterize masculinity and femininity reveals some of the bases for the more positive valuation of masculine qualities.[26] Masculine qualities are instrumental ones which are more likely to lead to behaviors that qualify one for success in a patriarchal and capitalist society. A comparison of masculine qualities with those of femininity clarifies why femininity is not highly valued and rewarded in patriarchal societies. Some of the terms used in the Broverman study to characterize masculinity were: "very aggressive," "very logical," "very self-confident," "very ambitious," "can make decisions easily," "knows the ways of the world," "easily able to separate feelings from ideas," and "likes math and science." Feminine characteristics in the same study included: "very talkative," "very gentle," "very aware of the feelings of others," "very interested in own appearance," and a "very strong need for security."[27] Bem later characterized masculine persons as: "aggressive," "ambitious," "assertive," "analytical," "forceful," "self-reliant," and "willing to take a stand." Bem's feminine scale included: "cheerful," "childlike," "flatterable," "gentle," "gullible," "shy," "sympathetic," "warm," and "yielding."[28] Clearly, feminine attributes qualify one for secondary expressive and cooperative social roles, while masculine characteristics train one for primary instrumental and dominant social roles in a patriarchal and capitalistic social structure.

Furthermore, several studies have found that masculinity and social adaptability, dominance, or high self-esteem tend to be found together in individuals regardless of their sex or gender identity: masculine males tend to have the greatest self-confidence, self-esteem, and flexibility; feminine females tend to exhibit these qualities the least; while all others fall between the two extremes.[29] Femininity, then, can be a social behavior pattern which can be maladaptive to emotional well-being and material success in a patriarchal society. Masculinity, by contrast, can be seen to function as a minimum basic requirement for social success in mainstream society regardless of one's sex or gender identity.

Femininity and masculinity can best be understood as ideological constructions whose human manifestations (women and men, girls and boys) are recreated in each generation according to the intermeshing requirements of social, cultural, economic, and biological necessities. The apparent naturalness of femininity and masculinity does not stem from an inevitable and overwhelming biological imperative, but rather from the pervasiveness of a patriarchal social structure founded on the division of humanity by sex; a division which a patriarchal society demands must be at all times, and under all circumstances, unequivocal and obvious.

The imbeddedness of members of society within this belief system leads them to experience themselves and those around them as verifying the "intrinsicness" of femininity and masculinity. They then transfer not only their beliefs but also psychological and physiological reproductions of those beliefs to the infants in their care. In this way, the "universality" of gender as the primary organizing principle of all human endeavor is continuously reinforced and reconstituted within, and between, each succeeding generation.

Parental Influences on Infant Gender Development

The bulk of children's experiences during the first few years of their lives occur in interactions with family members. In most North American families the major caregivers during those years are mothers. Fathers, for the most part, play supplemental roles in child rearing, especially during the earliest years of upbringing. Although they spend fewer hours with their children, the role of fathers in the gender development of their children is far from inconsequential.

Parental attitudes and beliefs about their children's genders come into play even before their babies are born. Most parents in both North America and England prefer the births of sons. Fathers show a stronger preference in this direction, especially if there are no other sons in their families, while mothers most often desire to have sons in order to please their husbands or other family members. Mothers only slightly prefer the birth of sons over daughters, while fathers' preference for the birth of sons is three times greater than their preference for daughters.[30] Such projective partiality and bias in parents' attitudes toward their unborn babies must differentially affect the behaviors and attitudes of parents toward their newborn sons and daughters. It seems inevitable that disappointed parents will convey different messages to their infants than will happy and satisfied parents.

Parental gender stereotypes come into active play immediately upon the birth of a child. Studies of parents of newborns only a few days old have found that parents' observations of their days old infants reflect the common stereotypes that females are "soft, fine-featured, little, inattentive, weak, and delicate," and that boys are not.[31] Parents, fathers more so than mothers, tend to perceive their infants as acting in these ways despite the fact that female infants at birth are generally more mature, active, and alert than male infants.[32] This once again illustrates that people perceive babies on the basis of their own beliefs about what they are "supposed" to be like, rather than on the basis of what babies actually do.

It is not surprising then to find that fathers and mothers interact differently with daughters and sons. Fathers, visiting their newborn children in hospital on the day of their birth, tend to spend more time with their sons than with their daughters, holding their sons more than their daughters and speaking more to their sons. Mothers, on the other hand, have been found to be more equal in their attentions to their sons and daughters, perhaps reflecting their initially more equal interest in the birth of either sons or daughters.[33] Moreover, this pattern has been shown to continue throughout children's upbringings, with fathers showing greater interest in their boy children than their girls, and with mothers tending to instruct their growing children in less stereotyped ways than fathers do.[34]

This theme is further played out in the differences in how parents spend time with their young children. Mothers of infants pass more time with their children than do fathers and engage in activities of a different nature.[35] Fathers tend to spend most of their time playing with infants, while mothers spend the majority of their time with infants being involved in caretaking activities.[36] As a result, infants experience their two parents through different patterns of activities. Fathers come to be experienced by babies as infrequent, but fun, visitors to their worlds while mothers personify the regularity and structure of their daily lives.

Babies involved in play activities with their parents find that their two parents have significantly different styles of play. Mothers and fathers play with their babies in ways which reflect their own sex roles and their attitudes about male and female babies. Fathers tend to play more physically active games, while mothers are more verbal and play less vigorous games. Fathers, who play more physically active and less verbal games with both sons and daughters, are most physically active and least verbal with their sons.[37] Both parents, but especially fathers, tend to handle boy children in ways which conform to the dominant cultural attitudes that males are tougher, more aggressive, more independent, stronger, and more intellectually competent than females. By contrast, female infants are treated in a more protected manner reflecting socially held beliefs that they are more delicate and fragile than boys, despite sound medical evidence to the contrary. Thus their play behaviors further reinforce babies' experiences of male and female adults as significantly different creatures who do different things, or at least do the same things differently.

Both parents, but especially fathers, tend to encourage independence in their sons and dependence in their daughters. Sons are rewarded for exploring and taking risks, while daughters are encouraged to stay close to their parents and are praised for adult-oriented, help-seeking behaviors. Mothers tend to exhibit fewer sex-biased differences in their handling of their youngsters, but the overall effect of their child-rearing practices is to foster more dependency in their daughters than in their sons.[38]

These differing play and care patterns which infants experience at the hands of their mothers and fathers must be considered not only in light of the fact that sons receive more of their fathers' attentions, but also in light of the fact that fathers tend to be more strict with their sons in terms of gender role behavior, and less lenient than mothers are with either their sons or daughters.[39] Fathers have been consistently found to be more intensely concerned with their children's conformity to socially acceptable gender roles than have mothers. Fathers, although they spend less time with their offspring, devote more of their child-care energy to gender role training than do mothers, and are most intent that their boy children behave as proper little men.[40]

This combination of circumstances results in infants assigned to different sexes having considerably different experiences of the world starting in hospital at birth and extending throughout their first, most impressionable, months and years of life. These differences in interaction with caretakers affect the ways infants act in response to masculine and feminine adults. Infants at least as young as nine months of age have been found to be able to differentiate adults on the basis of the gender of the adults, and to show a greater preference for interaction with adults of one gender over the other.[41] For example, Lichtenberg reported that a young baby when "talked to from behind by the mother will show a smooth, controlled response. When the father's voice is heard the baby will respond with jerky excitement,"[42] thus displaying what would seem to be conditioned responses to the different patterns of interaction characteristic of mothers and fathers.

Lamb, Owen, and Chase-Lansdale have proposed that the major gender role lesson of the first year of life is the learning of such response patterns. They argue: "Learning to recognize masculine and feminine interaction styles has more important implications for sex-role development than any explicit attempts on the part of parents to differentially shape the behaviour of their sons and daughters."[43] Long before a child is old enough to have an intellectual concept of gender, it begins to learn to distinguish between masculine and feminine on the basis of nonverbal behavioral cues such as styles of physical movement, tones of voice, facial expressions, and the types of activities that adults engage in with children. Thus the sex-typed behaviors of parents all but demand of infants that they make gender one of their first lessons in social propriety.

At the same time as infants are learning to distinguish between different types of adults, they are also learning other basic lessons about how to survive and thrive in the world of humans. Through their interactions with the adults around them, infants come to learn many things about what is expected of them and what is safe for them to do. The different interaction styles of women and men communicate different messages to young children. Children whose interactions with the world of adults are characterized by warmth, caring, and protection will develop markedly different personalities from those whose experiences of the world of adults have been characterized by rough handling and a cool or distant caring. The question has been raised by Doering, and others, as to whether such differences in the handling of an infant might also have lifelong physiological effects.[44]

It would seem logical to infer that infants who experience life as consistently, or often, dangerous or hostile might more often use those portions of the brain devoted to sensing and responding to such experiences. With repeated stimulation and use, these portions of the brain might become strengthened, more highly sensitized, and more adept at response. Other areas of the brain which were called into use less often might become sluggish, or even atrophy, from disuse.[45] In a brain that is experiencing its greatest postnatal period of growth, such effects might be dramatic indeed, resulting in sensitivity and response patterns which, if continually reinforced throughout the growth period, might become entrenched for life.[46] Once so entrenched, such patterns might also be passed on to later generations by way of similar behavioral conditioning of their young.[47]

Thus it might be inferred that the early experiences of young children play a major role in shaping not only their personalities but also their physical propensities. If the brain and its mechanisms are plastic and impressionable, then the experiences of the young organism, especially if forcefully and consistently repeated, might play a role in determining the form into which the developing brain, and the mechanisms which it controls, will ultimately stabilize. Such patterns could then become the resource basis for more mature learning processes. Triggering mechanisms, intensities of response levels, and physical response patterns might all be set into motion, tempered, or enhanced, by the early experiences of a young and sensitive organism.

Separating the Boys from the Girls

One of children's most important lessons during the first months and years of their lives is to develop individual identities. Margaret Mahler proposed that children's development during this time occurs in several stages. The first stage, lasting approximately through the first three months of life, she called the symbiotic stage. During this phase, infants have very little definition of themselves as separate and distinct from their primary caregivers (who Mahler assumed to be their mothers) and only gradually become aware of themselves as separate from their mothers in body and in person. This process of learning one's physical and psychological boundaries in relation to one's primary caregiver was termed by Mahler the separation-individuation process. Mahler saw this process as consisting of "two complementary developments": separation being the process of learning one's physical and psychological boundaries, or who, or what, one is not, and individuation being the process of learning who, or what, one is. The separation-individuation phase is characterized by the mother and infant sharing in an exploratory process wherein the infant takes ever more adventurous steps away from the security of the mother while always returning between explorations to the safety of the symbiotic state. In this way infants slowly learn their own boundaries and those of their mothers, and they also learn to define themselves against the changing background of an ever expanding territory. This separation-individuation process, according to Mahler, occupies young children through roughly the first three years of their lives.[48]

Although Mahler suggested that all young children go through these processes, not all children experience their symbiosis or separation-individuation in the same way. Caregivers may have differing levels of attachment to their children, or different styles of expressing their affections, or may be prevented by other obligations, or by physical or mental illness from caring for their children in the way that they may optimally wish to. Their children may have physical or psychological characteristics which cause their caregivers to experience anxiety or alienation or otherwise affect the type of care that an infant receives. Caregivers also hold beliefs about what constitutes ideal infant and child care, beliefs which likewise influence the kind of care that youngsters receive.

One of the largest contributing factors to the style of care an infant receives is the sex of the child. A second major variable in the equation is the sex of major caregivers who, in most societies around the world, are children's biological mothers.[49] Mothers relate differently to their sons and daughters; by the very fact of their mutual femaleness, mothers tend to identify more strongly with their daughters than they do with their sons. This suggests that the symbiotic attachments between mother and daughter can often be more potent than between mother and son.

Yet mothers are not without conflict in their identification with their infant daughters. They may be aware of the difficulties of being female in a patriarchal world, and so wish that their daughters might be spared the difficulties of being born female into such a world. Mothers' closeness with their daughters might also be tainted by unconscious fears of lesbian attachments and tendencies within themselves. Or, they may harbor a wish that their daughters grow to be more successfully feminine than they themselves have been. Any of these maternal feelings can affect the degree of intimacy between mothers and daughters during the early formative years of children.

A symbiotic period which is disrupted by such ambivalences on the part of a mother can lay an unstable foundation for the later phase of separation-individuation in which a girl child discovers who she is and who she is not.[50] Yet, it is difficult to imagine any mother in a patriarchal world who would not be beset by such conflicting desires and emotions. Further, if the father or other family members have been disappointed at the birth of a female child, these feelings may well become magnified. If, in addition, a female child is physically ill-matched to the prevailing stereotypical vision of how a female child should look or act, the situation may become more difficult still. In situations where a female child is unusually large, uncuddly, or coarse looking, or when a parent, or parents, strongly preferred a male child, a female child may find herself being unconsciously reared by her parents as a surrogate son.[51] Thus it would seem likely that the "normal" attachment and separation processes between mothers and daughters may go awry on a great number of accounts.

Mothers likewise often have conflicting feelings and attitudes toward their young sons. All women are aware of the greater power which society affords to males solely on the basis of their maleness. This, in itself, is sufficient to engender a different sort of attachment between mothers and sons. Mothers know that their infant sons are slated to grow to be more privileged in the world than they themselves have been. As well, most women have in their lives experienced some level of fear of male violence and know that their male infants will grow to become members of an often violent and dangerous fraternity. It would seem inevitable then that mothers would relate to their infant sons as more "other" than they would to their daughters.

Sons must also learn to identify themselves through such a sense of "otherness." Male children learn to define themselves as boys after a symbiotic phase in which they have identified themselves with their female mothers. Male children must therefore build their masculine identities through stronger denial of their earlier identification and attachments to their mothers than is required of girl children. Boys, unlike their sisters, must repudiate not just their identification with one woman, but with all women. Thus male identity, in a society where early child care is almost exclusively the province of females, must be established in opposition to female indentity.[52] Male children must learn to take their identity from the fact of their being "not female." They must be more distinct in their definitions of themselves than must their sisters and must do so at an earlier age. They are obliged to see themselves as profoundly different from the most powerful persons in their lives: their mothers. This establishes in male children a self-identity, a gender-identity, based on a defensive sense of separateness, and on a denial of relationship and connection.[53]

The degree to which parents actively participate in these processes varies not only with their parenting skills but also as a result of their beliefs and attitudes. Parents who hold aspirations for their children that may in some ways contravene the usual socially prescribed procedures, or outcomes, may vary their behavior accordingly. Parents who subscribe to alternative cultural or political traditions, or who simply want more for their children than the social limitations which are imposed by the happenstance of their social status, often consciously break from traditional child-rearing practices. Such parents may specifically encourage unconventional personality development in their children.

Adult caregivers may also be oddly influenced by their own attitudes about the essential natures of males and females. Henry Biller has found that "parents and others seem to expect more masculine behavior from tall, broad, and/or mesomorphic boys."[54] Others have suggested that parents of girl babies who find that their infants are large, active, or "not pretty" may likewise see masculinity in their children and unintentionally relate to them in ways which evoke masculinity.[55] Thus parents who are seemingly orthodox in their gender beliefs and attitudes may produce unexpected gender anomalies in their offspring.

As children grow older and begin to have a separate and individual sense of themselves, they begin to absorb social lessons from a larger sphere than the mother-child bond. Both female and male children become increasingly aware of their fathers, elder siblings, and other adults with whom they have regular contact. Both boys and girls reach out to these other people to help them in their quest for separation and individuation during the first years of their personality development. These people make themselves available to children in different ways according to their own sex and the sex of the children, the specifics of their actions being mediated by social and cultural beliefs concerning gender roles.

Fathers play an increasingly important role in the development of gender as their offspring grow from babies into young children. Early in the second year of their sons' lives, fathers tend to increase the amount of attention they pay to them.[56] Around that time they may begin to spend as much as twice the time with their sons that they spend with their daughters.[57] This higher level of interaction between fathers and sons can have several effects on the developing gender of both male and female children. The greater saliency of fathers to their sons serves to increase the likelihood that sons will identify with their fathers as major role models and imitate their gender behavior. The increased amount of time that fathers spend with their sons also increases the opportunities that fathers have for actively participating in the shaping of their sons' social learning and cognitive development. These factors, in combination with the high degree of gender rigidity demanded by fathers of their sons, ensure a continuation of a pattern of greater masculine subscription to gender role stereotypes.

Fathers simultaneously make themselves less available to their daughters as models for their gender development. This relative inaccessibility of fathers may foster in girl children a greater motivation to receive fatherly attentions and an intensified desire to please their fathers.[58] The fact that fathers show less interest and concern for the gender development of their female children may mean that when they do become involved with the lives of their young daughters, the influence of their demands and responses may become further pronounced through the enhancement effects of intermittent reinforcement.[59] In the majority of situations, pleasing fathers requires daughters to exhibit conformity to feminine gender role stereotypes. Fathers are therefore able to function as major gender educators despite their relatively slight time involvement with their children.

Fathers tend to be more stereotyped in their gender attitudes than mothers.[60] As they act out their gender attitudes in the contacts they have with children, they communicate as gender role models. While parents of both sexes contribute to gender role training in this way, they do not do so equally. The social pressures on boys to be masculine are greater than those on girls to be feminine. Maccoby reported relevant data from a Langlois and Downs study of parental responses to children's play with "sex-inappropriate" toys. The fathers in that study reacted negatively to inappropriate toy use in boys almost four and a half times more often than they did to such play in girls. Mothers, in the same study, also showed more negative reactions to unconventional toy use among boys, but only by a margin of approximately 20 percent.[61] Thus, boys are strongly trained by both parents, and most strongly by their fathers, to abandon their interests in all things feminine and to learn the ways of masculinity.

Fathers' style of interaction with youngsters also contributes to children's understandings of the power relations between the sexes. Fathers demonstrate through their behavior with their sons that men and boys are allowed more room for the expression of aggression and are held more responsible for problem solving. Daughters learn from their time with their male parents that males hold the power to control situations, that males provide solutions to problems, and that aggression, anger, and vigorous physical activities are inappropriate to femininity.[62] Thus, infants or children who are consistently related to as if they are in need of help and protection grow to think of themselves in those terms, and their more assertive tendencies may become extinguished, while young children who are treated as responsible and active persons grow into those qualities. In this way, children often become what their parents expect them to be.

At the same time as fathers are taking more prominent positions in the gender role training of their young sons, the power of mothers in the lives of their growing children gradually declines. As children expand their awareness to include social relations outside of the mother-child symbiotic bond, and outside of the family structure, their vision of their mothers as all-powerful persons necessarily decreases. This occurs partly because in patriarchal societies, it is very common for children to see men dominate both within and outside of families, at the same time as mothers are teaching their youngsters to respect male authority. In this way the credibility and desirability of mothers as role models is often diminished for both girls and boys as they mature.[63]

The lessons of these first years of human relationship set the basis for a child's "stance towards itself and its world—its emotions, its quality of self-love . . . or self-hate."[64] When the needs of a child are not adequately met, for whatever reason, the ramifications may be very far reaching. Chodorow, in a discussion of the preverbal period of infancy, speculated that:

> When there is some major discrepancy in the early phases between needs and material and psychological care, including attention and affection, the person develops a "basic fault," an all pervasive sense, sustained by enormous anxiety, that something is not right, is lacking in her or him. This sense, which may be covered over by later developments and defenses, informs the person's fundamental nature, and may be partly irreversible.[65]

It would seem possible then, that similar effects might result from similar conflicts at a slightly later developmental stage. If Mahler and others were correct in their assertions of a universal symbiotic phase through which all infants pass, and if separation were a painful, albiet natural process, then all adults might harbor within them such a "basic fault." When the process has been felt as deeply painful or abrupt, it can become amplified and result in "a tendency to make excessive demands on others and to be anxious and angry when they are not met" and in a blockage in the ability of children, and the adults they become, to form meaningful intimate relationships.[66]

The separation process is not experienced identically by male and female children. Male children are encouraged to separate from their mothers more quickly and radically than are female children, thus fostering in them an early sense of themselves as "not female," or male. Female children are allowed and encouraged to maintain their attachment to their mothers longer and to let go of their mothers in a slower and more gradual release, thus protecting them from some of the inevitable anxiety associated with the path toward masculinity. A feminine identity is therefore bound up more profoundly with a sense of connection and continuity, while a masculine one is in essence one of separation and denial.[67] Masculinity then might be seen as a double duty shield defending people from contamination by femininity or femaleness, and partially compensating them for a pervasive anxiety, aggression, and difficulty with intimacy born of a premature and severe separation phase. In a sense, masculinity might be a socially sanctioned and encouraged example of the sort of "basic fault" which Chodorow has described.

The development of femininity, although seemingly grounded in a more secure sense of positive identity, can also create fundamental anxieties. Children are characteristically curious and exploratory. Social definitions of femininity foster a curtailment in female children of such natural tendencies to self-education. Mothers, having themselves been raised to be feminine, tend to have a less clear sense of their own boundaries in relation to their daughters than in relation to their sons. Such a situation might serve to further intensify the mother-daughter bond and thereby increase the difficulty in the mother-daughter separation process.[68] One result of this could be a degree of frustration of the needs of female children for separation and individuation. Thus people trained to femininity might also suffer from a "basic fault" as a result of inopportune timing, or a delay, in their separation process.

In a society which classifies infants on the basis of a simple binary system, thereby denying the infinite diversity of nature, many children, both male and female, do not easily fit within the stereotypical notions of femininity and masculinity. Nonetheless, society demands that parents and other adults attempt to teach children to conform to their society's norms of masculinity and femininity. Parents are not always entirely adept at their tasks, and infants and young children are individuals who have their own agendas. Although it is possible to make generalizations about the development of masculinity and femininity, few, if any, real-life children are entirely feminine or masculine either physically or psychologically.

RUTH

THREE

Becoming Members of Society

Learning the Social Meanings of Gender

The Gendered Self

The task of learning to be properly gendered members of society only begins with the establishment of gender identity. Gender identities act as cognitive filtering devices guiding people to attend to and learn gender role behaviors appropriate to their statuses. Learning to behave in accordance with one's gender identity is a lifelong process. As we move through our lives, society demands different gender performances from us and rewards, tolerates, or punishes us differently for conformity to, or digression from, social norms. As children, and later adults, learn the rules of membership in society, they come to see themselves in terms they have learned from the people around them.

Children begin to settle into a gender identity between the age of eighteen months and two years.[1] By the age of two, children usually understand that they are members of a gender grouping and can correctly identify other members of their gender.[2] By age three they have a fairly firm and consistent concept of gender. Generally, it is not until children are five to seven years old that they become convinced that they are permanent members of their gender grouping.[3]

Researchers test the establishment, depth, and tenacity of gender identity through the use of language and the concepts mediated by language. The language systems used in populations studied by most researchers in this field conceptualize gender as binary and permanent. All persons are either male or female. All males are first boys and then men; all females are first girls and then women. People are believed to be unable to change genders without sex change surgery, and those who do change sex are considered to be both disturbed and exceedingly rare.

This is by no means the only way that gender is conceived in all cultures. Many aboriginal cultures have more than two gender cateogories and accept the idea that, under certain circumstances, gender may be changed without changes being made to biological sex characteristics. Many North and South American native peoples had a legitimate social category for persons who wished to live according to the gender role of another sex. Such people were sometimes revered, sometimes ignored, and occasionally scorned. Each culture had its own word to describe such persons, most commonly translated into

English as "berdache." Similar institutions and linguistic concepts have also been recorded in early Siberian, Madagascan, and Polynesian societies, as well as in medieval Europe.[4]

Very young children learn their culture's social definitions of gender and gender identity at the same time that they learn what gender behaviors are appropriate for them. But they only gradually come to understand the meaning of gender in the same way as the adults of their society do. Very young children may learn the words which describe their gender and be able to apply them to themselves appropriately, but their comprehension of their meaning is often different from that used by adults. Five year olds, for example, may be able to accurately recognize their own gender and the genders of the people around them, but they will often make such ascriptions on the basis of role information, such as hair style, rather than physical attributes, such as genitals, even when physical cues are clearly known to them. One result of this level of understanding of gender is that children in this age group often believe that people may change their gender with a change in clothing, hair style, or activity.[5]

The characteristics most salient to young minds are the more culturally specific qualities which grow out of gender role prescriptions. In one study, young school age children, who were given dolls and asked to identify their gender, overwhelmingly identified the gender of the dolls on the basis of attributes such as hair length or clothing style, in spite of the fact that the dolls were anatomically correct. Only 17 percent of the children identified the dolls on the basis of their primary or secondary sex characteristics.[6] Children, five to seven years old, understand gender as a function of role rather than as a function of anatomy. Their understanding is that gender (role) is supposed to be stable but that it is possible to alter it at will. This demonstrates that although the standard social definition of gender is based on genitalia, this is not the way that young children first learn to distinguish gender. The process of learning to think about gender in an adult fashion is one prerequisite to becoming a full member of society. Thus, as children grow older, they learn to think of themselves and others in terms more like those used by adults.

Children's developing concepts of themselves as individuals are necessarily bound up in their need to understand the expectations of the society of which they are a part. As they develop concepts of themselves as individuals, they do so while observing themselves as reflected in the eyes of others. Children start to understand themselves as individuals separate from others during the years that they first acquire gender identities and gender roles. As they do so, they begin to understand that others see them and respond to them as particular people. In this way they develop concepts of themselves as individuals, as an "I" (a proactive subject) simultaneously with self-images of themselves as individuals, as a "me" (a member of society, a subjective object). Children learn that they are both as they see themselves and as others see them.[7]

To some extent, children initially acquire the values of the society around them almost indiscriminately. To the degree that children absorb the generalized standards of society into their personal concept of what is correct behavior, they can be said to hold within themselves the attitude of the "generalized other."[8] This "generalized other" functions as a sort of monitoring or measuring device with which individuals may judge their own actions against those of their generalized conceptions of how members of society are expected to act. In this way members of society have available to them a guide, or an internalized observer, to turn the more private "I" into the object of public scrutiny, the "me." In this way, people can monitor their own behavioral impulses and censor actions which might earn them social disapproval or scorn. The tension created by the constant interplay of the personal "I" and the social "me" is the creature known as the "self."

But not all others are of equal significance in our lives, and therefore not all others are of equal impact on the development of the self. Any person is available to become part of one's "generalized other," but certain individuals, by virtue of the sheer volume of time spent in interaction with someone, or by virtue of the nature of particular interactions, become more significant in the shaping of people's values. These "significant others" become prominent in the formation of one's self-image and one's ideals and goals. As such they carry disproportionate weight in one's personal "generalized other."[9] Thus, children's individualistic impulses are shaped into a socially acceptable form both by particular individuals and by a more generalized pressure to conformity exerted by innumerable faceless members of society. Gender identity is one of the most central portions of that developing sense of self.

Gender as a Cognitive Schema

The first important molders of children's concepts of social standards reside within the immediate family group, but very early in life children become exposed to the standards of others in a larger social context. Often the various people in children's lives give them conflicting or confusing messages as to the nature of social standards. Children are only able to make sense of such variety according to their cognitive abilities and within the context of the experiences they have already had and the lessons they have already learned.

Certain ways of understanding social exchanges become more firmly established through repeated experience with them. These cognitive frameworks become more useful to children as they learn that they are the ways that many other people around them share. Different societies, or social groupings within societies, teach children and adults their own ways of recognizing and organizing knowledge. When members of societies share common ways of understanding the people, objects, and events of their lives, they use similar conceptual structures to organize their experience into cognitive bits which make sense to them, and which may be effectively communicated to others. Any conceptual structure that organizes social experience so that this sort of understanding and shared meaning can exist is called a cognitive schema.

Cognitive schemata are therefore basic to social organization and communication. They make it possible for persons to come to common understandings of shared experiences. Without socially accepted cognitive schemata, individuals who experienced the same events could place such diverse interpretations on their simultaneous experiences that it would be difficult to believe that they had all been at the same place at the same time.[10]

Most societies use sex and gender as a major cognitive schema for understanding the world around them.[11] People, objects, and abstract ideas are commonly classified as inherently female or male. The attributes, qualities, or objects actually associated with each class vary widely from society to society, but most do use gender as a most basic groundwork. Gender, then, becomes a nearly universally accepted early cognitive tool used by most children to help them understand the world. This means that children learn that gender is a legitimate way to classify the contents of the world and that others will readily understand them if they communicate through such a framework. Children also learn from those around them what to allocate to the categories of male and female, what elements of all things are considered to fall under the influence of the feminine principle, and which are classified as within the masculine sphere.

In North American society, the gender schema most widely in use is biologically deterministic. While there is some widespread belief and understanding that social factors have an influence on questions of gender, the dominant view remains that biological demands set the limits on the possible effects of social factors. In the script of the dominant gender schema, and in the parlance of the everyday world, the relationship between the main concepts is roughly as follows:[12] It is presumed that there are normally two, and only two, sexes, that all persons are either one sex or the other, and that no person may change sexes without extensive surgical intervention. Sex is believed to so strongly determine gender that these two classifications are commonly conflated to the extent that the terms are used interchangeably, and many people fail to see any conceptual difference between the two. Thus it is also believed that there are two, and only two, genders, and that individuals can effectively change genders only by also changing their sex. Gender roles are that part of the sex/gender bundle that may culturally vary within the constraints of biological imperatives. Gender roles, usually seen to be somewhat determined by social factors, are therefore thought to be less precisely tied to sex and gender than sex and gender are to each other.

Thus, sex is seen as wholly determining gender and largely determining gender role. The practices of gender roles are thought to be biologically constrained by the demands of one's biological sex/gender and socially defined by one's particular rearing within their gender (see Figure 1).

FIGURE 1. DOMINANT GENDER SCHEMA

SEX → GENDER
            ↓
       GENDER ROLE

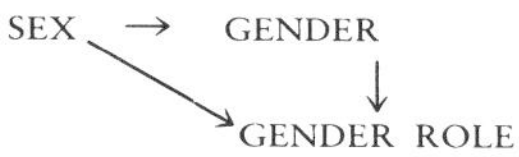

The specifics of the definitions of appropriate gender roles for members of each sex/gender class in North American societies vary mainly by age, race, regionality, socio-economic class, ethnicity, and by membership in sexually defined minority groups. Nonetheless, each sub-group generally subscribes to the main premises of the dominant gender schema and forms its particular definitions of appropriate gender roles from within those limitations.

In strongly sex-typed societies, or individuals, a gender schema tends to be a predominant mode of thought. In any given situation, there are always a number of cognitive frameworks one might use to understand the dynamics of that situation. Other major frameworks which might be used to understand situations involving human beings might revolve around race, social class, age, or physical size, but sex-typed individuals, and societies, tend to regard gender as one of the most significant factors in understanding themselves and the situations they find themselves in.

During the period in children's lives when they are first learning their gender identity and gender role, they also learn the definitions and usages of a gender schema. Children learn that they are girls or boys and that everyone else is either a girl or a boy. They learn that girls and boys are different by virtue of the different ways that they act and look, and that certain objects and ideas are associated with maleness and femaleness. As children assimilate the concepts and classifications of the gender schema of their social group, they learn to define themselves and those around them by its terms of reference. A process begins in young minds whereby it becomes not only legitimate but also expedient to sift all experience through the mesh of a gender schema.[13]

Children who are raised within a society which revolves around a gender schema learn to embrace those aspects of the schema which apply to the gender group that they have been assigned to. Because an element of our gender schema is that there are two distinct, non-overlapping gender groups, children also learn to reject those elements of their schema which do not apply to themselves. But it is important that members of society do not so thoroughly reject the gender lessons of the other gender that they become unable to recognize its members and respond appropriately to their cues. As gender schemata are highly complex and can be used to understand almost any experience, children are engaged in this process with increasing sophistication as their cognitive abilities improve with age.

The Male Standard

In North America, the dominant gender schema is patriarchal, and its assumptions underlie psychological, social, economic, and political definitions of gender. Psychological examinations of personality, for instance, routinely start by dividing subjects into classifications of male and female. The results obtained from such research thus have built into them the parameters of gender. In ways such as this, the division of persons by gender is both legitimized and reinforced. The same kind of emphasis carries through into social, political, and economic research as well as into research involving animals. Gender is thus forced to become a relevant variable in almost every situation studied.

Research has been undertaken to investigate what people do when they are denied information which readily allows them to use their gender schema as an organizer of information. In one study, adults were exposed to infants whose sex was not disclosed to them. It was found that when adults assumed a sex for a child in the study they most often assumed the child to be male.[14] The attribution of a gender, and the more frequent assumption of maleness, suggest schematic information processing according to a patriarchal gender schema which claims that (1) all persons must be either male or female, and that (2) maleness is primary and generally inclusive of lesser categories.

Adults themselves are so thoroughly imbued with the dominant gender schema that it is virtually impossible to gather any group of them who would be so totally devoid of gender cues as to make suitable confederates for similar studies. Kessler and McKenna, in the mid 1970s, however, did devise a study using line drawings of adults exhibiting mixtures of common gender cues in order to examine how adults recognize and ascribe gender in other adults. By combining nine sex or gender cues (long hair, short hair, wide hips, narrow hips, breasts, flat chest, body hair, penis, and vulva) with two non-gender cues ("unisex" pants and shirt), they were able to produce ninety-six different combinations of characteristics which they overlaid on simple drawings having the same arms, hands, legs, feet, shoulders, waistlines, and faces. The ninety-six different drawings were each shown to equal numbers of male and female adults who were asked to identify the figure they were shown as male or female, to rate the confidence that they had in their appraisal, and to suggest how the figure might be changed to render it a member of the other sex or gender. The results of this study strongly suggested that people see maleness almost whenever there is *any* indication of it. A single strong visual indicator of maleness tended to take precedence in the attribution process over almost any number of indications of femaleness.[15]

Common wisdom and, to a large degree, medical opinion tell us that gender is determined on the basis of genitalia. Thirty-two of the figures used in the Kessler and McKenna study had their genitalia covered by a non–gender specific pair of pants while displaying various combinations of the other possible characteristics. Male and female cues were evenly distributed among the thirty-two drawings of figures wearing pants, but more than two-thirds (69 percent) of the 320 people who viewed these figures saw them as male. Surprisingly, a majority of the figures (57 percent) wearing pants and showing bare breasts were among those seen as male.[16] Thus, more than half of the people who viewed the figures displaying bare breasts were able to ignore, or rationalize away, a major female secondary sex characteristic and somehow still label the figure in the drawing as male.

The tendency to see maleness was even more pronounced among the remaining 640 persons who viewed drawings of figures with exposed genitals.

Kessler and McKenna found that although in theory genitalia determine the sex of an individual, in fact, only male genitals serve this function. In this study, it was overwhelmingly the presence or absence of the male genital cue which determined the sex attributed to the drawings. (No figure had both male and female genitals portrayed.) The drawings which exhibited a penis were almost unanimously (96 percent) identified as male regardless of the presence of any number of female cues such as breast or wide hips.[17] The female genital cue did not have this same power.

The presence of a vulva in a drawing was, by contrast, sufficient to elicit a female identification in only a little less than two-thirds (64 percent) of the representations. In the remaining more than one-third (36 percent) of the drawings where a vulva was in evidence, the people who viewed the drawings were able to disregard that information in favor of male cues which were also present. There were only two combinations of cues that produced a rate of female identification equal to the rate of male identification achieved with the presence of the penis in combination with *any* other cues (male or female). These were the drawings which showed a figure with vulva and wide hips, wearing a "unisex" shirt and long hair; or a figure with vulva, no body hair, breasts, and long hair. In other words, for a figure to be seen virtually every single time as male required only the presence of a penis; for a figure to be identified as female equally as often required the presence of a vulva *plus* one of two specific combinations of three additional cues.[18] Thus, the power of the presence of a penis to elicit a male identification was a full 50 percent stronger than the ability of the presence of a vulva to cue a female identification.

This study demonstrates that even in situations of conflicting, confusing, or absent gender cues, people were willing, able, and likely to attribute gender. It also shows that when there is a doubt as to the gender of an individual, people have a pronounced tendency to see maleness. This study also suggests that maleness is readily seen whenever there are indicators of it, whereas femaleness is seen only when there are compelling female cues and an absence of male cues. This way of seeing corresponds closely to patriarchal gender schema notions of maleness as a positive force and femaleness as a negative force; of maleness as a presence and femaleness as an absence; of maleness as primary and femaleness as derivative. Thus, in North American society, the dominant gender schema rests on and supports patriarchy. It assumes that maleness and its attributes are the definitive standard against which all gender questions shall be judged. This means that femaleness, as well as all that becomes associated with it, is defined by the dominant patriarchal gender schema as inherently flawed and lacking.

Gender Role Behaviors and Attitudes

The clusters of social definitions used to identify persons by gender are collectively known as femininity and masculinity. Masculine characteristics are used to identify persons as males, while feminine ones are used as signifiers for femaleness. People use femininity or masculinity to claim and communicate their membership in their assigned, or chosen, sex or gender. Others recognize our sex or gender more on the basis of these characteristics than on the basis of sex characteristics, which are usually largely covered by clothing in daily life.

These two clusters of attributes are most commonly seen as mirror images of one another with masculinity usually characterized by dominance and aggression, and femininity by passivity and submission. A more even-handed description of the social qualities subsumed by femininity and masculinity might be to label masculinity as generally concerned with egoistic dominance and femininity as striving for cooperation or communion.[19] Characterizing femininity and masculinity in such a way does not portray the two clusters of characteristics as being in a hierarchical relationship to one another but rather as being two different approaches to the same question, that question being centrally concerned with the goals, means, and use of power. Such an alternative conception of gender roles captures the hierarchical and competitive masculine thirst for power, which can, but need not, lead to aggression, and the feminine quest for harmony and communal well-being, which can, but need not, result in passivity and dependence.

Many activities and modes of expression are recognized by most members of society as feminine. Any of these can be, and often are, displayed by persons of either gender. In some cases, cross gender behaviors are ignored by observers, and therefore do not compromise the integrity of a person's gender display. In other cases, they are labeled as inappropriate gender role behaviors. Although these behaviors are closely linked to sexual status in the minds and experiences of most people, research shows that dominant persons of either gender tend to use influence tactics and verbal styles usually associated with men and masculinity, while subordinate persons, of either gender, tend to use those considered to be the province of women.[20] Thus it seems likely that many aspects of masculinity and femininity are the result, rather than the cause, of status inequalities.

Popular conceptions of femininity and masculinity instead revolve around hierarchical appraisals of the "natural" roles of males and females. Members of both genders are believed to share many of the same human characteristics, although in different relative proportions; both males and females are popularly thought to be able to do many of the same things, but most activities are divided into suitable and unsuitable categories for each gender class. Persons who perform the activities considered appropriate for another gender will be expected to perform them poorly; if they succeed adequately, or even well, at their endeavors, they may be rewarded with ridicule or scorn for blurring the gender dividing line.

The patriarchal gender schema currently in use in mainstream North American society reserves highly valued attributes for males and actively supports the high evaluation of any characteristics which might inadvertently become associated with maleness. The ideology which the schema grows out of postulates that the cultural superiority of males is a natural outgrowth of the innate predisposition of males toward aggression and dominance, which is assumed to flow inevitably from evolutionary and biological sources. Female attributes are likewise postulated to find their source in innate predispositions acquired in the evolution of the species. Feminine characteristics are thought to be intrinsic to the female facility for childbirth and breastfeeding. Hence, it is popularly believed that the social position of females is biologically mandated to be intertwined with the care of children and a "natural" dependency on men for the maintenance of mother-child units. Thus the goals of femininity and, by implication, of all biological females are presumed to revolve around hetero-sexuality and maternity.[21]

Femininity, according to this traditional formulation, "would result in warm and continued relationships with men, a sense of maternity, interest in caring for children, and the capacity to work productively and continuously in female occupations."[22] This recipe translates into a vast number of pro-scriptions and prescriptions. Warm and continued relations with men and an interest in maternity require that females be heterosexually oriented. A hetero-sexual orientation requires women to dress, move, speak, and act in ways that men will find attractive. As patriarchy has reserved active expressions of power as a masculine attribute, femininity must be expressed through modes of dress, movement, speech, and action which communicate weakness, dependency, ineffectualness, availability for sexual or emotional service, and sensitivity to the needs of others.

Some, but not all, of these modes of interrelation also serve the demands of maternity and many female job ghettos. In many cases, though, femininity is not particularly useful in maternity or employment. Both mothers and workers often need to be strong, independent, and effectual in order to do their jobs well. Thus femininity, as a role, is best suited to satisfying a masculine vision of heterosexual attractiveness.

Body postures and demeanors which communicate subordinate status and vulnerability to trespass through a message of "no threat" make people appear to be feminine. They demonstrate subordination through a minimizing of spatial use: people appear feminine when they keep their arms closer to their bodies, their legs closer together, and their torsos and heads less vertical then do masculine-looking individuals. People also look feminine when they point their toes inward and use their hands in small or childlike gestures. Other people also tend to stand closer to people they see as feminine, often invading their personal space, while people who make frequent appeasement gestures, such as smiling, also give the appearance of femininity. Perhaps as an out-growth of a subordinate status and the need to avoid conflict with more socially powerful people, women tend to excel over men at the ability to correctly interpret, and effectively display, nonverbal communication cues.[23]

Speech characterized by inflections, intonations, and phrases that convey nonaggression and subordinate status also make a speaker appear more femi-nine. Subordinate speakers who use more polite expressions and ask more questions in conversation seem more feminine. Speech characterized by sounds of higher frequencies are often interpreted by listeners as feminine, childlike, and ineffectual.[24] Feminine styles of dress likewise display subordinate status through greater restriction of the free movement of the body, greater exposure of the bare skin, and an emphasis on sexual characteristics. The more gender distinct the dress, the more this is the case.

Masculinity, like femininity, can be demonstrated through a wide variety of cues. Pleck has argued that it is commonly expressed in North American society through the attainment of some level of proficiency at some, or all, of the following four main attitudes of masculinity. Persons who display success and high status in their social group, who exhibit "a manly air of toughness, confidence, and self-reliance" and "the aura of aggression, violence, and daring," and who conscientiously avoid anything associated with femininity are seen as exuding masculinity.[25] These requirements reflect the patriarchal ideology that masculinity results from an excess of testosterone, the assumption being that androgens supply a natural impetus toward aggression, which in turn impels males toward achievement and success. This vision of masculinity also reflects the ideological stance that ideal maleness (masculinity) must remain untainted by female (feminine) pollutants.

Masculinity, then, requires of its actors that they organize themselves and their society in a hierarchical manner so as to be able to explicitly quantify the achievement of success. The achievement of high status in one's social group requires competitive and aggressive behavior from those who wish to obtain it. Competition which is motivated by a goal of individual achievement, or egoistic dominance, also requires of its participants a degree of emotional insensitivity to feelings of hurt and loss in defeated others, and a measure of emotional insularity to protect oneself from becoming vulnerable to manipulation by others. Such values lead those who subscribe to them to view feminine persons as "born losers" and to strive to eliminate any similarities to feminine people from their own personalities. In patriarchally organized societies, masculine values become the ideological structure of the society as a whole. Masculinity thus becomes "innately" valuable and femininity serves a countrapuntal function to delineate and magnify the hierarchical dominance of masculinity.

Body postures, speech patterns, and styles of dress which demonstrate and support the assumption of dominance and authority convey an impression of masculinity. Typical masculine body postures tend to be expansive and aggressive. People who hold their arms and hands in positions away from their bodies, and who stand, sit, or lie with their legs apart—thus maximizing the amount of space that they physically occupy—appear most physically masculine. Persons who communicate an air of authority or a readiness for aggression by standing erect and moving forcefully also tend to appear more masculine. Movements that are abrupt and stiff, communicating force and threat rather than flexiblity and cooperation, make an actor look masculine. Masculinity can also be conveyed by stern or serious facial expressions that suggest minimal receptivity to the influence of others, a characteristic which is an important element in the attainment and maintenance of egoistic dominance.[26]

Speech and dress which likewise demonstrate or claim superior status are also seen as characteristically masculine behavior patterns. Masculine speech patterns display a tendency toward expansiveness similar to that found in masculine body postures. People who attempt to control the direction of conversations seem more masculine.[27] Those who tend to speak more loudly, use less polite and more assertive forms, and tend to interrupt the conversations of others more often also communicate masculinity to others. Styles of dress which emphasize the size of upper body musculature, allow freedom of movement, and encourage an illusion of physical power and a look of easy physicality all suggest masculinity. Such appearances of strength and readiness to action serve to create or enhance an aura of aggressiveness and intimidation central to an appearance of masculinity. Expansive postures and gestures combine with these qualities to insinuate that a position of secure dominance is a masculine one.

Gender role characteristics reflect the ideological contentions underlying the dominant gender schema in North American society. That schema leads us to believe that female and male behaviors are the result of socially directed hormonal instructions which specify that females will want to have children and will therefore find themselves relatively helpless and dependent on males for support and protection. The schema claims that males are innately aggressive and competitive and therefore will dominate over females. The social hegemony of this ideology ensures that we are all raised to practice gender roles which will confirm this vision of the nature of the sexes. Fortunately, our training to gender roles is neither complete nor uniform. As a result, it is possible to point to multitudinous exceptions to, and variations on, these themes. Biological evidence is equivocal about the source of gender roles,[28] psychological androgyny is a widely accepted concept.[29] It seems most likely that gender roles are the result of systematic power imbalances based on gender discrimination.[30]

Gendered Values

Feminine people experience, and therefore understand, the world from a very different status position than do masculine persons. Their differing access to power and privilege engender in them different value systems, priorities, and goals. Many theorists have suggested that the early childhood experiences of boys and girls begin the process of shaping them into their assigned gender roles by creating deep psychological needs in individuals which predispose them toward the social roles into which they will be encouraged to grow.

Nancy Chodorow hypothesized that the primary emotional bonds of all children are the ones they first had with their mothers. She suggested that the closeness of these first bonds acts as a largely unconscious model for people in the relationships they form in later life. She maintained that the desire to recreate mother-child bonds is a motive force behind attitudes of both masculinity and femininity. Chodorow argued that femininity revolves around the need to replicate the primary symbiotic bonds experienced by young girl children with their mothers. She also suggested that masculinity stems, in part, from the need to reproduce the one-on-one emotional closeness lost to young male children as they are forced to reject their bonds to their mothers and cleave to social definitions of masculinity. Chodorow's argument essentially states that our emotional lives are driven by needs to feel symbiotically attached to other persons in the way that we all once felt, however briefly, with our mothers. But because of the different gender role training that males and females receive from the moment of birth onward, both the symbiotic stage and the separation-individuation processes are experienced differently by the two sexes. Therefore our attempts to recreate our infantile states, and our adult relational needs, reflect these differences.

The men that boys become strive, on one level, to duplicate the emotional closeness and security of their earlier mother-child bonds within the privacy of their emotionally intimate relationships. On another level, masculine people suffer from a need to assert their masculinity through independence from women, and freedom from dependency in any guise.[31] The role of masculinity, therefore, requires of those who wish to enjoy its privileges, that they regard vulnerability to other people as a dangerous weakness at the same time as they crave emotional intimacy. These conflicting needs make emotionally intimate relationships very problematic. It is difficult, if not impossible, for people to conduct satisfying intimate relationships when they are suspicious of emotional intimacy. The recreation of the closeness of a mother-child bond is therefore stymied by the successful practice of masculinity, because masculinity is, in essence, about separation and emotionally distant relationships.

Feminine persons, who tend to grow out of more secure and enduring attachments to their mothers, also wish to simulate the experience of union in their intimate relationships. Heterosexual women, however, are often frustrated in their attempts to find intimacy with the men in their lives, because of the conflicting masculine needs to receive unconditional love and to assert independence from the source of that love. Women therefore tend to turn to other women and, more commonly, to their own children for a reconstruction of the love they received as children. But the recreation of a mother-child bond through motherhood is not an entirely satisfactory solution. Those women who become mothers do not have the opportunity to feel themselves playing the desired role of child in the mother-child dyad. For this feeling, they must have the cooperation of another adult. Hence women's often frustrated desire for intimacy with men can be supplemented, but not fully replaced, by emotional intimacy with children.

Chodorow argues that in societies where women do virtually all early child care, and in which there exists a dichotomized, male-dominated, and hierarchical gender schema, femininity has two major components: maternal and heterosexual. The heterosexual component of femininity serves as a means for women to achieve both maternity and some satisfaction of their needs for emotional intimacy. Femininity, as characterized by Chodorow, is motivated by a need for union with others, a need which is socially channeled toward childbearing and heterosexuality.

The socially dominant needs of masculinity also require that femininity be defined heterosexually so that the masculine psychological goal of surrogate mothering for grown males may be accomplished.[32] Child rearing is an integral part of femininity which, although it may serve other important masculine goals of egoistic dominance,[33] is often only a tolerated impediment to the emotional goals of masculinity. Masculinity then might be characterized as a cluster of psychological needs which vibrate with the conflict between a largely unconscious need for emotional submersion and a continuously socially reinforced gender role need for independence.

Not all females equally accept the feminine role. Some females reject the heterosexual component of the female role without abandoning an interest in the recreation of the mother-child bond. Many women turn directly to other women, rather than to children, for an approximation of the sort of love that they recall from their childhoods. Many women desire, and do have, children without forming heterosexual bonds to men. Many women form loving bonds with other women and children in non-heterosexual family groups. Concerning these other ways of satisfying the need for intimacy and union, Adrienne Rich has asked:

> If women are the earliest sources of emotional caring and nurture for both female and male children, it would seem logical from a feminist perspective at least, to pose the following questions: whether the search for love and tenderness in both sexes does not originally lead toward women; *why in fact would women ever redirect that search;* why species survival, the means of impregnation and emotional/erotic relationships should ever become so rigidly identified with each other; and why such violent strictures should be found necessary to enforce women's total emotional, erotic loyalty and subservience to men. (Emphasis in the original)[34]

The answers to these questions might be found in an analysis which focuses on the masculine needs of motherly attention and egoistic independence within a morality which allows the assertion of masculine needs to dominate over a more cooperative balancing of masculine and feminine goals.

Catharine MacKinnon analyzed heterosexuality as a defining characteristic of femininity, and hence the social meaning of femaleness. She argued that social recognition of femaleness is defined entirely within sexual terms. More specifically, she proposed that to be seen as female one must be heterosexual, and that to claim femaleness and not be heterosexually within the power of males is to be in defiance of the social meaning of femaleness.[35] Femininity, from this perspective, can be seen as a structure designed for the purpose of satisfying the egoistic needs of males for dominance, and heterosexuality can be seen as a component of femininity which ensures that females are accessible to those who need and demand patriarchal power. It is through the institution of heterosexuality that females remain in intimate and continued contact with the people who require them to function in support of masculinity. The institution of heterosexuality ensures that females never stray far from a masculine reminder of patriarchal definitions of femininity.

Masculinity is less rigidly defined in terms of heterosexuality. Although masculinity requires access to the sexuality of women, it does not pivot around that sexuality in the same way as the feminine role does. Masculinity has other dimensions which can be sufficient to independently delineate one as male. Outwardly directed states are more important to masculinity than are emotional or home-centered interests. Economic achievement, bureaucratic power, physical strength, aggression, and emotional toughness are major indicators of masculinity;[36] heterosexuality is a minor indicator. Insufficient or nonexistent heterosexuality will cast a doubt on a person's masculinity,[37] but if other more outwardly directed qualities are strongly in evidence, the negative effect of a defective heterosexuality may be diminished or erased.

Thus, although adult femininity and masculinity share common elements, the function of those elements is quite different. Both masculinity and femininity are in part defined through their heterosexual and child-caring roles, but those roles carry very different values in their applications to the lives of men and women. The feminine role, to a great degree, derives from the need of the masculine role for support functions. Masculinity requires emotional nurturing from a quasi-maternal source; femininity is dedicated to satisfying that requirement. Masculinity further requires independence from that quasi-maternal source of emotional stability, and to this end the dominant patriarchal gender schema attributes greater masculinity to outwardly reaching, emotionally cool, achievement activities; and greater femininity to the child rearing which femininity offers as an alternative source of emotional intimacy to those who find themselves emotionally abandoned by their masculine partners.

These different motivations and statuses result in different moral standards for feminine and masculine persons, different styles of interaction based on differing standards of right and wrong, differing value systems, and differing assumptions about the motivations and goals of others. More masculine people, who tend to relate to the world on the basis of an assumption of the separation of individuals and place a high moral value on the results of separation, find intimacy threatening. More feminine people, who tend to value and strive for interactive styles and situations which are based in a desire for attachment and communion, place the highest value on caring for the needs and feelings of others. As a result of these differences, women tend to approach moral questions and problems within a context of conflicting responsibilities, while men tend to approach these same situations as questions of conflicting rights.[38]

Masculinity fosters an ethic wherein separate and independent individuals assert their rights within a set of laws which provide guidelines for resolving whose competing interests will take precedence when conflicts arise. It is understood as inevitable and fair, in such a system of justice, that there will exist a hierarchy of rights and individuals. Where separation is the theme, order is the method.

Femininity demands an approach to questions of morality from another perspective. Feminine morality is predicated on the desire for the greatest communal good for the greatest number of people. Feminine justice is based in an ethic of caring for others and directs conflicts to be resolved through a minimizing of power differences. Where attachment is the theme, empathy is the method.

An aggressive assertion of power sustains a masculine ethic of domination through rights, while a contextual and supportive balancing of power through empathy and nurturance underlies the feminine ethic of cooperation. In North American patriarchal society, aggressive masculine striving for egoistic dominance backed by a patriarchal social, political, and economic reality ensures the negative social valuation of femininity, the marginal status of femaleness, and the subordination of the ethic of cooperation.

Gender Role Strain

When people come together in social exchanges, they bring with them the sum of their experiences to that point, the cognitive schemata they used to make sense of those experiences, and the results of the application of the latter to the former. Each individual in social interaction acts, and perceives the actions of others, from the perspective of their own gender role values, training, and experience. All persons in society are constantly engaged in an ad hoc process of negotiation aimed at interpreting experience and developing shared meanings. Each of these interactions is built upon an exchange of social cues which individuals use to construct their understandings of the meanings of actions, words, and events. Such dyadic and small group negotiations of meaning take place within a larger shared contextual framework made up of the cognitive schemata and norms of a society. All interpretations of interactions between members of a society are normally understood within that larger context at the same time as cognitive schemata are applied idiosyncratically and subjectively to everyday events.

Social actors simultaneously receiving information from others are also attempting to project information about themselves which both reflects their self-images and conforms to their understandings of the requirements of their social setting.[39] This process is open-ended, to some degree, as people are often willing to reformulate earlier conclusions as new information suggests a more "sensible" interpretation of prior events.[40] Nonetheless, all members of society are social actors attempting to manage the impressions that they make on others, so that they might be perceived in the most advantageous light possible.

Individuals are able to understand social experiences only within the restrictions imposed on them by their own frames of reference, or from within the boundaries of their own cognitive schemata.[41] To simplify and organize experience so as to make it more manageable, people call upon a loosely organized commonsense "stock of knowledge at hand,"[42] which they presume that "anyone like us necessarily knows."[43] Such a stock of knowledge constitutes a set of cognitive schemata that offer them guidelines around which they may structure their perceptions. Together, people involved in face-to-face interactions strive to develop a shared understanding of the meaning of their experiences through an ongoing interactive process, which is actually a subtle bargaining process about whose version of reality will become accepted as the working definition in an interaction.[44]

When two individuals meet they must establish certain facts about themselves as a basis for the smooth progress of their interaction. As all individuals in society are presumed to belong to gender groups which are governed by certain etiquettes and proprieties, adult members of society generally consider that a social failure has occurred if a person's gender is not displayed obviously, immediately, and consistently.

A subtle but powerful process of interaction revolves around the cueing and countercueing of gender display. Members of society signal to one another, through their simple everyday talk and actions, the complex message which is an unmistakable gender.[45] Social actors exchange this information through both direct and indirect means of communication. Persons put forward presentations which they would like to have accepted by their audiences as the "true" state of affairs. Observers respond in ways which indicate either acceptance or the need for further negotiations to establish a mutually acceptable definition of their situation. In the case of gender attributions, these cues and responses are largely nonverbal, but vast in number. And because, as Goffman maintained, "any scene . . . can be defined as an occasion for the depiction of gender difference, and in any scene a resource can be found for effecting this display,"[46] there may be no plausible excuse for adults to fail to properly display their gender.

Children, on the other hand, who are young enough to be conceivably still learning the proper application of their society's gender schema, are usually benignly tolerated if they fail to display gender behaviors appropriate to their assigned genders. But this tolerance is not evenly distributed between the two gender classes. Masculinity would seem to be more highly valued in children than is femininity. Boys are strongly encouraged toward masculinity, while masculine behavior in female children is tolerated as quite harmless, perhaps even salubrious. Feminine behavior in male children, on the other hand, is only poorly tolerated and often seen as a cause for alarm,[47] while femininity is valued but not required in prepubescent girls.

Girl children who exhibit masculine behaviors are colloquially known as "tomboys," boy children who display femininity are called "sissies." Both parents and peers show strong disapproval of femininity in boys, the label "sissy" carrying with it significant social stigma. On the other hand, "tomboy" is used in a tongue-in-cheek pejorative way when applied to prepubescent girls. There almost seems to be a guarded respect for girls who enjoy some of the privileges and skills which are usually reserved for the socially dominant gender. Masculine girls call forth an amused, bittersweet admiration for their striving to socially "better" themselves. By contrast, feminine boys evoke, in most people, a disdain for their seeming disregard for the superior opportunities and privileges available to them. Masculinity in children then, as in adults,[48] is more highly valued than femininity, regardless of the gender of the children exhibiting it.

Children learn the greater value of masculine behaviors and the lesser value of feminine ones by observing the actions of the adults around them. Although children do receive a great deal of social training as to the "correct" ways for boys and girls to act, they also receive the message of the dominant gender schema that maleness is the standard against which all things associated with gender are measured. Thus, children learn that to be masculine is better than to be feminine: to be male and masculine is to be best; to be female and masculine is to be second best; to be female and feminine is to be a "good girl," but second class; and to be male and feminine is to be a traitor. Masculine males take full advantage of their superior social options, and so gain the greatest social approval and rewards. Masculine females can improve their social status by acquiring some of the characteristic behavior patterns of men, thereby cueing others to grant them some of the respect and privileges usually reserved for men. Feminine females behave in accordance with their prescribed social roles. They therefore earn social approval for their conformity, but the role they perform affords them fewer rights and privileges than masculinity does. Feminine males forfeit many of the special advantages usually associated with maleness, because they not only fail to cue for them, but also compromise the appearance of innate, biologically based, male rights to socially dominant roles. They therefore elicit disrespect and distrust from most members of society, because they not only turn their backs on their own opportunities for social power, but they also threaten the credibility of other men's claims of "natural" superiority. Thus, it is not cross gender role behavior that is censured so much as it is gender behavior which lowers an individual's or a gender class's social value.

Cognitive developmental theorists have suggested that people desire to learn and conform to what is appropriate for their gender grouping. This process of identification and modeling is complicated by the diversity in gender schema definitions. There may exist severe, or subtle, disjunctions between the gender schemata projected by various "significant others," or between "significant others" and a person's "generalized other." As the actual prescriptions and proscriptions of gender schemata are constantly in flux and undergoing challenge from competing social and cultural ideological sources, individual representatives of society subscribe to different individual versions of a gender schema which in itself contains confusions and contradictions. The media, peers, schools, workplaces, and families may deliver sharply competing messages about desirable gender role behaviors. When social agents transmit their gender schemata, they are rarely clear and uncontradictory.

Further complications arise despite the best intentions and abilities of people to subscribe to a gender schema as they understand it. People also carry within themselves certain individual dispositions and talents. It is not uncommon that gender role requirements as outlined in a gender schema conflict with the personalities, talents, and dispositions of growing and changing people. Such conflicts can result in gender role strain, wherein individuals find it difficult to negotiate their assigned gender role as they understand it.[49] In such situations the disjuncture between a person's "I" and "me" can become uncomfortably large, and a sense of oneself as a coherent "self" might become endangered. Such conflict might result in an internalized power struggle between one's "I" and one's "generalized other." In other words, when people do not see themselves as they believe others see them, and as they themselves believe they ought to be, personality disintegration is possible.

Persons experiencing such conflict have several avenues open to them. They might adjust their behavior, so that others can see them more as they see themselves. They might choose to alter their definitions of themselves so that they see themselves as others see them. Or they may shift their locus of social standards to reside with a different social group whose criteria coincide more exactly with their personal self-images. This last option can allow people suffering from an I/me conflict to align the way that other people see them with the way that they see themselves by changing their "significant others" to persons whose values match their own.

The first option has certain inherent limitations. When persons perceive that their private definitions of themselves vary significantly from their public image, they may attempt to display their private selves more openly in an attempt to bring others to see them as they "really" are. But one must be cautious not to display attributes which might bring social censure; therefore individuals who perceive themselves to be experiencing a conflict between their public and private selves may be able to use this option only in limited ways if their private self-image is not in conformity with social norms.

Another way to negotiate a more perfect conjunction of "I" and "me" is to adjust one's personal self-image to match more closely the way one is seen by others. This approach has the advantage of running the least risk of offending public sensibilities. It is safer in that social expectations are being met rather than questioned, but it carries with it the greatest challenge to the self because it necessitates alteration of the "I," the most deeply rooted and intensely personal part of the self.

The method for partially relieving gender role strain which least threatens the self, and most effectively avoids conflict and social disapproval, revolves around the constituency of the "generalized other." People may choose to allow the standards of certain individuals or ideologies to take prominence within their cognitive schemata. A gender schema need not be one's preeminent cognitive schema, nor must it be constructed according to the demands of the dominant ideologies of society. Individuals or groups of individuals may choose either to give other cognitive schemata dominance within their own cognitive frameworks, or to minimize their use of gender schemata whenever possible in their own lives and social interactions. Gender role strain might therefore be relieved by a willful effort to shift one's cognitive schema priorities.

Such a shift could be reinforced and bolstered by a similar effort to shift one's "significant others" and "generalized others" to include persons of similar persuasions. Gender role strain may then be lessened to the degree that individuals are able to restrict their social contacts to persons of similar minds. Such a strategy would be limited in its effectiveness to the same degree that any social deviation might be. Major social deviations are rarely tolerated easily, and individual or group deviation from gender schema prescriptions can be perceived as extremely threatening to a social order which is, to a large degree, predicated on the use of gender as a major cognitive schema. Those who threaten the social order can be, and often are, severely punished for their transgressions.

Each option must be understood within a larger social context. Gender schemata exist in society as widely accepted ways of making sense out of everyday experience; everyone may not agree on exactly how a schema is to be defined but, in general, gender schemata are universally used cognitive techniques and, as such, are a most basic part of social sense. If individuals were to contradict, in behavior, speech, attitude, or in any other way, the basic tenets of the gender schema of their society, they would be challenging a widely accepted social definition of sense. One result of such a situation might be that such individuals would simply be misunderstood. If such misunderstanding were viewed benignly, there might be no further implications. Were this behavior aschematic enough, it might be considered dangerous, criminal, or even insane. The ramifications in such situations could be severe.

Persons who find themselves unable to conform satisfactorily to their assigned gender role may become socially stigmatized for such failure. Normally, in North American society, when people join together in social situations, they expect from one another a certain level of social collusion so that all participants in an interaction will be able to share a common meaning and understand the intentions and actions of one another. The most generally applicable way to establish a common language of communication is to agree to collectively subscribe to elements of the dominant social language. This dominant social language is composed not only of words but also of a shared understanding of the meanings of nonverbal communications and by a set of values and attitudes.[50] Persons who do not, willingly or unwillingly, share in these common creations of meaning become people who carry with them a stigma. Persons who carry a stigma come to be seen by others as "not quite human," and they can thus become partially or fully disqualified from social acceptance.[51]

People who are aware that they have a disjuncture in their gendered selves between their "I," their "me," and their "generalized other" must manage themselves in such a way so as to minimize any possible stigma which might result from others becoming aware of their situation. Such people may attempt to disguise or compensate for the offending parts of their gender behavior which they feel unable or unwilling to modify. Individuals who take such an approach carry with them at all times the awareness that they are secretly in transgression of social laws. At any time they may become exposed not only as persons with stigma but also as persons engaged in deceit.

Inappropriate gender role behaviors are treated differently depending on the ways in which they are inappropriate. Minor transgressions of prescribed gender roles normally elicit social ridicule or chastisement. More major transgression can earn one the status of mentally ill. Sufficient variation from the norm can cause one to forfeit the gender attribution which they would normally expect on the basis of their sex and gender identity. Most extremely, chronic transgressions of gender role norms can lead to insecurity in, or even loss of, one's gender/sex identity. Hence, the power of gender role norms lies in the threat of possible loss of basic identity as a result of insufficient conformity to their demands. This power is possible only because of the strength of the dominant gender schema to define the core person in terms of these behaviors.

Thus, stigmatized persons, who believe themselves to be stigmatized for reasons beyond their control, have few options open to them. They may allow their nonconforming "I's" to be fully visible to public scrutiny and become subject to the full force of social affront at social nonconformity. They may attempt to hide whatever offending behavior that they are able to and run the risk of exposure and the subsequent further discredit associated with false-hood, as well as suffer the anxiety of leading a life mired in duplicity. Or they may allow their stigma to become public while safeguarding themselves by limiting their social contact to persons who will be sympathetic to their situation. In any case, full social acceptance and peace of mind are not easily available to persons who do not conform to the requirements of the "generalized others" among whom they live.

HEATHER

FOUR

Growing Up Gender Blending

Mothers, Fathers, and Other Parental Figures

The gender blending adults who constituted the core of this research learned their first lessons about the meaning and making of gender from their parents, siblings, and peers, from the schools and the media, and from their experiences with the diverse group of people who make up the public. As they aged into adulthood, they went through a developmental process of consolidating their gender identities and establishing their own methods of presenting themselves to the world around them. The identities that they grew into, and the ways that they chose to represent themselves to those around them, were built from the social messages which had been conveyed to them by their environment. They made their choices on the basis of the options which they perceived as available to them. They chose from among the behaviors of those around them and within the restrictions and encouragements they received from the people with whom they interacted in their youths.

Most of these gender blending females' families of origin contained at least one element which may have transmitted to them a conservative framework in which to understand gender and gender roles, in other words, a traditional gender schema. Environments of these types tend to emphasize the social distinctions between males and females, allow males greater freedoms and privileges, and celebrate masculine accomplishments while disregarding or belittling feminine ones. Twelve of the fifteen families in which these women grew up were probably governed, to some considerable degree, by such traditional values. Six of the respondents were sent to Catholic schools or described themselves or their families as "religious"; four of them grew up in or around the armed forces community; three of them were raised, at least during their earliest years, by grandparents; and three women merely described their upbringings as "strict."

Religious families, schools, and communities tend to subscribe to and teach some of the most conservative versions of the dominant patriarchal gender schema. The teachings of the church, having the endorsement of god, can gain strength and enduring tenacity above and beyond the power of more mundane social pressures to conformity. The armed forces community likewise teaches conservative gender values. The social structure of the armed forces is rigidly hierarchical. As such, it teaches children that it is legitimate and desirable that people be ranked and accorded power and privilege on the basis of their hierarchical status. In the fifties, sixties, and seventies, during which time these women were growing up under the army's disciplined social environment, that hierarchical structure was controlled and populated by men. The status of women and children was entirely based on the status of the men with whom they were associated. Thus, as children whose lives were touched by the army, they were taught that women had no access to power, privilege, or status in their own right. The three whose early years were strongly influenced by their grandparents might also safely by assumed to have been exposed to traditional gender values. Their grandparents most likely conveyed to them their own version of the gender schema of a more conservative era. The remaining three women in this group felt that their parents had been stricter with them than their friends' parents had been. Thus, twelve of the fifteen women studied identified clear sources of gender conservatism in their upbringings.

Social psychological theories of gender identity and gender role acquisition stress that children learn their gender through imitation of the behavior of major figures in their lives, in response to pressures placed on them to conform to social expectations, and as a result of their own individual needs for growth and social expression.[1] The relationships that these gender blending females had with their parental figures while they were young provide some clues as to how and why they developed the gender role behaviors which they did.

The relationships that these women had with their mothers were generally not conducive to strong identification or role modeling. Their mothers, often full-time homemakers, were not perceived by these daughters as strong, competent, admirable figures whom they wished to emulate. Grandmothers or elder sisters, when they were present, did not fare much better in the eyes of these women, while in many cases, fathers, grandfathers, or elder brothers were far more exciting and attractive to them. As a result, the behaviors and attitudes of male family members tended to exert a positive influence on the girls, while female family members were often used by the girls as negative examples or role models.

Most of the women interviewed said that their mothers were in the home, working as homemakers, during most of their childhoods. The sole exception in the group was the only single parent who never remarried. As a result of her double burden of child rearing and full-time employment in support of her family, this mother put her daughter in the care of her grandmother or boarded her with friends of the family for periods of time while she was growing up. One other mother was also a single parent until her daughter reached the age of six, when the mother remarried and subsequently became a full-time homemaker.

Although the remaining thirteen mothers were ostensibly full-time homemakers, their presence in the home and in the lives of their daughters was not, in most cases, constant and stabilizing. Two mothers worked part-time outside of the home or in family businesses, and one returned to school when her daughter was seven years old. One woman's mother died when she was five years old, and the girl was subsequently raised by her grandmother.

Another was raised principally by her grandmother for her first three years while her mother devoted herself to caring for her critically ill husband. One woman's mother abused pills and another's was simply emotionally withdrawn from her daughter much of the time. While all but three of the women studied came from families where the mother was in the home on a full-time basis for all or most of their youth, several of them felt that they did not get the attention that they desired and believed that they deserved from their mothers.

Most of the women studied came from larger than average families. Twelve of them came from families having three or more children, and seven of them grew up in families which had more than six children. Their origins in larger than average families also suggest that, although these women consistently had available to them a visible female role model in their homes, they probably did not have the benefit of a great deal of her undivided attention, a fact which several women mentioned in the course of their interviews.

Some of the women made comments which indicated that they viewed their full-time homemaker mothers as having devoted their lives to a job dominated by thankless drudgery and powerlessness. One woman rationalized her mother's inattention to her childhood emotional problems by saying that her mother was "just really sick of kids, you know, by the time I was ten she had been dealing with kids for twenty-five years and she was really tired." She felt that her mother "was bitter . . . she'd had five kids, she probably didn't want any of them, she didn't particularly like my father, I don't think she liked the kids." Another woman sadly described her mother as "everybody's servant," who never contradicted her husband and who "didn't used to go out at all. She would just sit at home and wait for my father to come home all the time. And she didn't seem to have very many friends, mostly just other housewives." Still another woman, who seemed to want very badly to be able to speak well of her mother, described her as "a worrying neurotic wimp": "I think when I started seeing her as really wimpy was when I started spending more time around her and dad. And I started to get angry that around dad she seemed more wimpy, and pretended to be stupid, and yet when he wasn't there she was really strong." An additional three women specifically said that they felt "embarrassed by," "ashamed of," or "disappointed in" their mothers, and one simply said that her mother "wasn't a very strong person." The reasons they gave included their mothers' lack of employment, their mothers' appearances, and most prominently their mothers' depressed or resigned attitudes in the face of their fathers' abusive or domineering ways. In all, six of the fifteen women expressed strongly negative sentiments about their mothers.

Few of these women expressed strongly positive feelings about their female parental figures. Many of those who did so contradicted their positive statements with later more negative comments. A few made cautiously neutral or vaguely positive comments about their maternal figures. One woman, who said that she was embarrassed by her own mother, talked more favorably about a beloved but distant aunt who she used as a role model while she was growing up. She described her aunt as "exciting" and "unconventional" while her own mother was "always just there." Another woman, who described her mother as "just really busy all the time," had fonder memories of the care she received from her grandmother when she was very young, and of her high school lunch breaks alone in the kitchen with her mother when she was considerably older. Only one woman remained almost silent about her parental figures. Her mother had died when she was very young, and she was raised by her grandmother and her alcoholic father, about whom she would say very little one way or the other.

Much of what the women remembered about their time with their mothers was concerned with conflicts or resentments about the rules of gender. They seemed to remember their mothers as either downtrodden embarrassments to them, or as persons who were trying to make them conform to an unfair sexist set of expectations. Five of the women interviewed talked about their fathers either physically or verbally abusing their mothers, or taking mistresses and flirting with other woman in full view of friends and family. All of the women who reported on such circumstances also reported feeling humiliation for their mothers' passivity in the face of their fathers' philandering and disrespect. Another woman started out loving and respecting her mother but turned sharply against her when her mother failed to recognize that she was being abused by her brothers. The girl who survived physical and sexual abuse from her brothers went from being "mother's little helper" to describing her mother as a "bitch" and "mean." Another woman said that she was close to her mother when she was younger, but that as she grew older she realized she could not "just live at home like she does." She described herself instead as "very much like my father." Of the remaining mothers, two were generally absent from their daughters' lives, and one was the family disciplinarian. The strongest terms that any of the other five women used to describe their relationships with their mothers was "pretty affectionate."

A common theme in the women's reports about their relationships with their mothers and grandmothers was the issue of their parents' training them to femininity. Eleven of the fifteen women mentioned that the wearing of skirts and dresses was an issue between them and their female parents. All of the women recalled that as girls they had preferred to wear pants as often as possible. In some families this was a major issue, in others it was of little import. Seven women reported that as children their mothers were only occasionally concerned about whether they wore dresses or not. Another two women told stories about their mothers defending their right to dress boyishly when a neighbor, in one case, and the girl's grandmother, in the other, objected to the girl's unfeminine appearance. Four women related tales of major ongoing struggles with their mothers over the issue of wearing skirts and dresses. One woman described shopping for outfits for special occasions: "We'd go around shopping for the whole weekend. We'd go into the city and she would finally break down and buy me a pant suit. She would realize that dresses don't look good on me. And after a while it just wore off and she stopped bugging me about dresses." Another woman told a similar story about her feelings about makeup and dresses:

I didn't rebel against it, I was just so blatantly disinterested that I think that she just realized that she was fighting an uphill battle. I was never interested in fancy clothes either. I always hated to go shopping. My mother finally gave up and learned how to make jeans and T-shirts on her sewing machine because she would be making these fancy things and I wouldn't wear them.

A third woman recalled that when she "threw a tantrum" at age ten, her parents bought her a boy's bathing suit and let her wear it to the local public swimming pool. The same woman also remembered being allowed to go to the corner store barechested that same summer. Clearly her parents did not rigidly enforce femininity in their young daughter. Nonetheless, she believed her parents opposed her desire to dress boyishly: "It seemed like my family was always trying to make me be more girlish. I just hated that. Why couldn't they just let me be like I was? . . . Which was like a boy." Only one woman made no mention of clothing being an issue in her youth. Several women also mentioned difficulties with their mothers over what they saw as an unfair distribution of household chores.

These women reported dissatisfaction with the accomplishments of their mothers and the grandmothers who raised them, and they rebelled against becoming little ladies. Some of them had good relationships with their mothers, but more of them were either unenthusiastic or negative about the women who raised them. Many of these complaints are common among young girls growing up in a patriarchal society which requires girls to be trained to subservient, highly sexualized roles. It is not unusual for young girls to resist many of the more restrictive aspects of femininity initially, but most eventually conform. These girls grew up into women who continued to refuse to comply with many social expectations of femininity.

When their relationships with their mothers are compared to those they remembered having with their fathers and grandfathers, the contrast is stark. On the whole, these women seemed either to have quietly endured uninspiring relationships with their mothers, or to have actively disliked the women who raised them. A few had other female parental figures who were positive influences on them. Most turned to the males in their lives for inspiration. Of the fifteen women interviewed, one never had a father figure in the home while she was growing up. For her, an older brother became an important masculine role model. The other fourteen women had either a father, a grandfather, or both, in their homes while they were young. Generally, these women reported admiration or respect for their father figures. Only two women expressed clearly negative opinions about their fathers, who were alcoholics throughout the women's youths. Of the twelve remaining fathers, all received at least critical admiration from their daughters.

Ten women expressed clear admiration and respect for their fathers, and a few of them expressed exceptionally strong positive feelings toward them. One woman said of her father, who had thrown her out of the house at age seventeen for objecting to his keeping a mistress, "I always loved him. My first love was him. He was a very special guy, patriarchal but feminine. And I liked his feminine part." Another woman described her father as "confident, humanistic, honest, famous, good, brilliant, skilled, and great at home" at the same time as she called him "emotionally constipated, on most levels pompous and very in control." Nevertheless she wanted "to follow in his footsteps" and avoid "becoming like mom," whom she had described as a "neurotic wimp." A third woman, who had called her mother a "bitch," said that her father was "a nice guy" and "really decent." Another said of her alcoholic father, "the guy is tremendous." Still another woman disparaged her mother for being a "loser" around authority but admired her father because "he always did exactly what he wanted to do." Even the woman who described her father as "a goof" and "a clown" said "he's a nice guy, warm, friendly, affectionate sort of person." Overall, these women seemed to hold significantly more positive attitudes toward their fathers than they had expressed about their mothers. The only two who entirely rejected their fathers did so because they were socially nonfunctional alcoholics.

Eight women specifically portrayed their fathers as firmly holding the power in their families. Seven of these women recalled that their fathers often expressed their power and authority by being disrespectful, abusive, or humiliating toward their mothers. Several women mentioned wishing that their mothers had been more able to assert themselves with their fathers, and being disappointed by their mothers' failure to do so. This situation might have led the girls experiencing it to see the power of their fathers amplified by contrast to the apparent powerlessness of their mothers. Such a situation could have served to increase the attractiveness of their fathers as role models, while decreasing the appeal of their mothers as feminine examples.

Perhaps more importantly, many of their fathers took a special interest in their daughters. Much research has shown that fathers play a significant part in the development of gender roles in their children. One of the ways that they usually do this is by devoting more time to their sons than to their daughters. By making themselves more available as role models for their boy children, they encourage them to identify with their masculinity and discourage feminine behaviors. Fathers ordinarily encourage femininity in their daughters by making themselves relatively unavailable for role modeling and by reinforcing heterosexuality and femininity in their interchanges with their girl children.[2]

The fathers of eight of these girls interacted with them in a pattern which strongly encouraged masculinity rather than femininity. Five women stated that they had been their fathers' favorite child. As a result, they passed large amounts of time in the company of their fathers, learning to enjoy and be skilled at masculinity. All of these women, who claimed the distinction of their fathers' favoritism, had brothers with whom they were competing for their fathers' attentions, and several of them specifically mentioned this rivalry and competition. Their rivalry took the form of attempts to outdo their brothers at typically masculine activities such as team sports, fighting, heavy manual labor, fishing, and hunting. One father took his daughter along with him when he worked as a heavy-duty mechanic in the bush, riding in his dump truck or his logging truck, flying in his bush plane, or fishing in the back woods. Another woman recalled that her father "spent a lot of time with me," and several recalled going on fishing trips with their fathers. Another woman's father took her to work with him and taught her as much as he could about his work as a surgeon, encouraging her interest in becoming a doctor like himself. Others, as girls who only weakly identified with other females, found that they could get the coveted attention of their fathers by excelling at sports.

Three other women, who had only sisters, also had especially close relationships with their fathers. In these cases, one daughter chose, or was chosen, to play the role of surrogate son, following after her father while her sisters followed the lead of their mother. One woman's relationship with her father illustrates this most graphically. Her mother told her that her "father was raised with a bunch of boys and now he got married and wanted to have sons but he had two daughters and although he loved you both very much, he still needed to have a male to identify with." She was motivated by this situation to strive even harder to please her father because she thought that "me, as myself, no matter how good or bad I was, could never amount to his image of a son." Her father chose her, his first born daughter, to become his son. He called her by the masculine nickname "Bud"* and encouraged others to relate to her as a boy. She recalled:

> I can remember people coming up and my father would be talking to them and they'd say "Well, is this your son?" And my father would laugh and say "This is my son Dorothy." . . . He was really good about it. . . . He didn't think that I had to wear dresses or be feminine to be a girl. . . . I was his little boy.

Another woman, who fought against her father's attempts to make her do feminine household chores, told of how he chose her, his oldest of three daughters, to share with him those chores that a father might otherwise share with a son.

> He taught me a lot of things, outdoors, like fixing a car, everything I know about cars. And he was an electronics tech so I know a lot about wiring of houses. We built our basement in three houses that we lived in, so I helped with that and helped with the wiring and stuff. So a lot of the typical trades I learned from him . . . because he needed help and it was usually me he called on, because there was no way that my sister would have done it.

Each of these women was singled out to satisfy her father's need for a son to do masculine things with. While their families were not explicitly telling them to be boys, it seems clear that boyish behavior was encouraged and rewarded in many ways.

Six women expressly mentioned coming to conflict with their fathers during their teenage years. They were discouraged to find that, when they began to mature physically, their fathers were no longer pleased by their

---

*All names have been changed.

boyishness. Warm and supportive relationships turned painful for the girls who were suddenly feeling pressures from their fathers to become more feminine. The same men who had always been their partners in masculine pursuits no longer wanted their companionship and began to actively encourage their daughters toward an unaccustomed femininity. One woman recalled that it was at puberty that her father first began to shape her femininity in earnest. He both stopped supporting her sports activities and started urging her to lose weight and wear pretty dresses:

> I remember . . . quite a noticeable about-face . . . when I started menstruating, my parents went from driving me to the ball games, coming to my ball games . . . being real proud of the fact that I hit home runs . . . and suddenly it became an embarrassment.

She also remembered her father's attempts to correct her way of walking.

> One time I got off the bus at the corner, I was walking down the street and my father was sitting on the front verandah. I had to walk up the street. When I arrived at the porch he said, "I was just noticing you walking along the street, you have a really long and mannish stride. You should shorten your stride, the way you walk."

One result of her father's criticisms was that she came to think of herself as ungainly and ugly.

Another woman, who had described herself as a "best buddy" with her father when she was younger, told of her father turning against her when she started to physically mature into a woman. Her father, who had always been demeaning to her mother, began to make humiliating comments about his daughter's appearance in the presence of both his and her own friends. He called her ugly and insinuated that no man would ever be romantically or sexually interested in her, at the same time as he openly flirted with her girlfriends when they came to visit her at her home. A third woman was brutally condemned by the father she idolized when he discovered that she had become sexually active in her late teens. He rebuked her by writing to her on the reverse of an adoring poem she had earlier written to him. The daughter recalled: "He was basically saying 'you're not even worth it, you're a piece of shit, you're a slut, you're a whore.' I mean I got totally shattered!" The women who spoke of the new pressures they experienced around the time of their puberty were not alone. Most of the women reported their teenage years as difficult times for them when their boyishness was no longer looked upon as a harmless childishness.

Sisters and Brothers

The relationships that children have with their siblings during their younger years can be very influential in the formation of their gender beliefs and behaviors. Younger children, in particular, often look up to their elder siblings as role models for gender behaviors. Older children often, both purposefully and inadvertently, act as gender teachers in the lives of their younger siblings.

When there are a large number of children in a family, the influence of parents is often rivaled by the combined force of sibling peer pressure. In particular, when older siblings are brothers and younger siblings are sisters, the time that they spend together is more often devoted to activities preferred by the brothers. The relational styles fostered by such contacts also likewise favor masculine patterns, and the girls who grow up in close contact with their older brothers tend to be less femininely gender stereotyped in their behaviors and attitudes. Older sisters with younger sisters are more likely to reinforce and solidify stereotypical gender role training unless there are other mediating factors which may push a girl's development in another direction.[3]

None of the women interviewed were only children; most came from larger than average families. Three women had only sisters, two had only brothers. Nine of the twelve women who had brothers had older brothers, six had younger brothers, and three had both younger and older brothers. Nine of the thirteen women who had sisters had older sisters, six had younger sisters, three had both younger and older sisters, and one gave no information on the subject. The relationships that these women had with their sisters were generally weaker than those they had with their brothers. They tended more strongly to admire or like their older brothers, and to dislike or resent their older sisters.

Three women had only sisters. Two of these women were the oldest child in the family, while one was only a year and a half younger than her sister. In all three cases, the gender blending woman was not close to her sister, was moderately comfortable with her mother, but had a special surrogate-son type of relationship with her father. One of these women said that her youngest sister was too small to play with, and her next youngest sister "didn't like any of the things I played and she said I played too rough." This same woman was chosen by her father to be his apprentice in his numerous household improvements and other masculine projects. Another of these three women was the one whose father had wanted to have sons and laughingly referred to her by a masculine nickname. She said about her family dynamics, "Wherever my mother was, my sister would follow, and my father, I would follow." Clearly, she had become the "boy" in the family. The third woman recalled that her parents had wanted one boy and one girl. She said in her interview, "my sister was born first, and I was going to be the boy." She also echoed the comments of the previous woman when describing the roles in her family: "In our life styles, my mother and my sister are very much the same. I'm very much like my father." In each of the cases where there were no sons in their families, one girl was singled out to fill the role of the missing son. It would seem that the father was the prime gender role educator in each of these instances, but the girls themselves, their sisters, and their mothers all seemed to be willing to cooperate in the situation.

Two women had brothers, but no sisters. Both of these women had only older brothers. In one case the older brother was very close in age to the woman who was interviewed, and the two of them were the only children in their fatherless family. She remembered being very close to her older brother when they were younger. She said that there were not a lot of other children near to their ages in the vicinity of their home. and so neither of them had many other friends to play with. She recalled that he was "the main motivator" in their play together and that she happily followed his lead in all things. She said, "Anything my brother did, I thought was great!" She took this feeling so far that as a young child she "was real pissed off" that she could not be a boy, and felt that her desire to be a boy could have been "partly because I admired my brother." The other woman who had only brothers said very little about them except to say that they were "very alienated" from their alcoholic father, and that she had wanted to be a mechanic like her father and brothers. This woman and her father seem to have worked together to compensate for her father's emotional loss of his sons. She said that she spent a lot of time with her father and that he taught her things "the way men teach." As a youth she became "the most aggressive kid on the block," and as she became a young adult she took pride in being tougher than most of the men she could imagine. She went fishing and hunting, studied military history, rode big motorcycles, flew an airplane, and did aerobatics for fun. She seemed intent on becoming a son her father could be pleased to have love him, providing compensation to him for the loss of her distant older brothers. The first of these two women adored and emulated her older brother; the other strove to bring satisfaction to her father by being the best son he could ever want.

Among the ten remaining women, seven had older brothers. Two of the three women who had no older brothers had never been mistaken for a man or a boy before they reached puberty, by which time one woman found herself taller and heavier and with a deeper speaking voice than most other girls, and the other woman had begun to grow extensive facial hair. The first of these women remembered being "embarrassed by" her mother, although she had an aunt who provided a distant but positive role model. She remembered her father as being "mild mannered" and supportive of her "tomboyism" before puberty, but she had a negative relationship with her only older sister, whom she described as "a bitch, a total bitch." This woman grew up feeling ugly and oversized for a woman. She recalled:

> I remember my sisters being oohed and ahhed over for being pretty. I don't think I was ever oohed and ahhed over but I would get points for other things. No one ever said I was ugly but no one ever said I wasn't. . . . I knew that I was ugly from when I was a kid. Not revolting to look at but not pretty. I had two very pretty sisters, and I got points for other things.

She rebelled against the norms of femininity by rejecting family pressures to try to be prettier:

> You got dressed up to look pretty, and I knew I wasn't going to look pretty, so nobody was going to accuse me of trying and not being it. . . . I rebelled and I'm really glad I did, on whatever principle. . . . because I wasn't going to give anybody the satisfaction of thinking that I was going to try and look pretty.

Her attitude toward looking pretty combined with her size, manner, and deep voice to give an impression of masculinity.

The second woman who had no older brothers was the oldest child in her family. She recalled that her relationships with both of her parents were "strict," but she said, "I think I probably had one of the most well adjusted childhoods of anybody I ever heard of." She did not remember ever being mistaken for a man or a boy in her youth, and she traced her later problem of being mistaken for a man as being directly proportional to the amount of her copious facial hair that she allowed to show.

A third woman came from a family of ten children. She mentioned having a particularly combative relationship with her oldest sister, thinking of her mother as a loser, and generally not ever feeling like she belonged in her family. She spoke well of only two family members: a younger brother, about whom she had only mild comments, and her father, who she felt was most similar to her of all the people in her family. She remembered being her father's favorite child but did not say a great deal more about their realtionship, probably because he had moved out of the family home while she was still quite young and remained only in intermittent contact with the family throughout her childhood.

Thus, among the three women who had no older brothers to train them to masculinity, one was her father's favorite child in a large family where he was the only person she felt close to. Neither of the other two women had any strong attachments either to their parents or siblings of either sex, but did develop physical characteristics at puberty which contributed to the masculine impressions they made on others.

Three of the seven remaining women with older brothers told of being sexually assaulted or molested by male family members, and another strongly implied that she may have been sexually abused by her father. For each of these women, masculinity seemed to offer a degree of protection from further sexual violence both by disguising their femaleness on night streets and in a more intrapsychic way. One woman, who had described her father "as my first love," later married a man who raped her and beat her "many times" during their marriage. She said that when she finally became assertive, "it was like assuming that I was as good as my father." For her, becoming assertive was a way to free herself from years of abuse by her husband. She said "I was raped many times by my husband, so now I decided that I was going . . . to be the man." Masculinity provided her with a powerful position from which "to serve myself in the way of a revenge."

Another woman, who admired her father, developed strong negative feelings about her mother when her mother failed to recognize or intervene in her two older brothers' physical and sexual abuse of her. As a young child she had idolized her older brothers and had "spent all my time chasing after them." When her older brothers started beating and raping her, around the age of eight, she began to hate her mother and to want to become a boy herself. She at first became withdrawn and later began a long period of sometimes violent, and often self-destructive, behavior which landed her in hospital or jail more than once. One of her first responses to her situation was to try to become a boy. Together with another eight-year-old girl, she hatched a scheme:

> She was the world's best boy and I was the second best boy . . . we were tough, very tough. . . . We both had brothers and they had a lot of fun. And they had black rubber boots with orange around it and we weren't allowed to have them because we were girls. And they used to get to go out on Saturday mornings and we didn't because we were girls so we called each other boys.

She forced other children to comply with her fantasy by beating them up in schoolyard battles. At home, her father, but not her mother, cooperated with her plan by referring to her as a boy, thus increasing her loyalty to her father and further alienating her from her mother.

Another woman had one older brother who attempted to rape her and another who beat her badly. This woman idolized her father and, like the woman above turned against her mother around the time of the attempted rape. Her relationship with the brother who attempted to rape her had been extremely close, albeit highly competitive, up until that point, and he had pressed her for sex on several other occasions as well. This same woman, who was later raped by a man she met at a party, has been sexually promiscuous with both men and women. At the time of her interview, she expressed a strong fascination with the idea of becoming a man. She railed against sexual objectification by men and said that she would not be happy if she were always recognized as a woman when out in public because "I'd be totally vulnerable all the time." She clearly found that appearing to be a man provided her with a shield against sexual assault.

The fourth woman only implied that her father had sexually molested her. This woman seemed to both fear and adore her father, who had been brutally violent to her other brothers, sister, and mother. She tried to win his favor by "tagging along behind him most of the time" and by "doing extra things without being told." From the age of five until she was eighteen years old she had a secret fantasy life in which she was a boy who was beaten and abused by his family but who himself was "all good." At age eighteen she abandoned this fantasy to begin a three-year period in which she lived more or less full-time as a man. As she went through puberty, her father publicly derided her for the changes in her body, and she began to desire a sex change. Her desire to become a man intensified still further after her father's death when she was seventeen years old. In her early twenties she abandoned her hopes of qualifying for a sex change operation and came to an uneasy acceptance of her womanhood.

These four women suffered cruelty and violence from men they loved. None of them felt that the other women in their lives were able to protect them from this abuse, and they knew that their mothers and sisters were also subject to sexual attack from men. It seems possible that, in each of these cases, the desire to become, or be seen as, a boy or a man was motivated by the survivors' feelings of vulnerability as women and their understanding that men and boys have the power to resist, if not perpetrate, such violent intrusions.

The final three women in the group all had older brothers. In one case, the woman's older brother was close to her in age and they spent a great deal of time together as they were growing up. As a girl, she was "embarrassed" by her mother and had little to do with her alcoholic father. Her brother became her best friend and constant companion to the extent that "people thought we were twins." As might be expected of twins, they "liked doing the same things." As might be expected when the older sibling is a boy, the things that they liked doing together were typically masculine things such as fishing, football, and softball. She said, with some pride, of their time together: "He taught me how to throw a baseball and how to catch it. . . . He taught me how to fix my bicycle. He always wanted me to go places with him. Occasionally he didn't want his little sister there, but he liked having me around."

The second woman avoided talking about her family at all but attributed her gender status to the dark hair on her upper lip. The final woman of the group was the second youngest in a family of six children. She remembered having fairly comfortable relationships with both of her parents, although she did seem to favor her father slightly. She also recalled having a "wonderful" relationship with one of her grandmothers who lived with the family for her first few years. Her most difficult sibling relationship was with her older sisters who "wanted to turn me into a girl." Her closest family friend was her next oldest brother with whom she did things "like playing baseball and football, and riding around, and generally being rough." But the family seemed to have been dominated by her oldest brother, who became a professional athlete. She professed a jealousy of the disproportionate amount of attention that he received from her father. At the time of her interview she still felt resentment and jealousy, and she reported that as a motivating factor in some portion of her childhood attempts to gain her father's attention and approval through excellence in sports.

The dynamics of the families in which many of these girls grew up strongly encouraged them toward masculinity. They grew up in families largely dominated by traditional gender schemata. As would be expected in families governed by such values, their mothers held little power in their families and were often the target of physical or verbal abuse and sexualized humiliation. One result of growing up in such an environment was that these girls held their mothers generally in low esteem and thus were not strongly inclined to use them as their role models as they searched for their own identities. They turned instead to the men and boys in their families for more positive visions of how they might grow into self-respecting adults. Often, they were aided by other brothers or fathers who willingly took on the job of shaping their development after their own. In several instances, their fathers chose them to be sons to them; in one case the girl seems to have appointed herself to the role. In other cases, older brothers provided the impetus by leading them into the pleasures of masculine pursuits. In no instance was there an older sister present who compensated for the girls' lack of interest in their mothers, nor were there any older sisters who were able to mold their younger sisters' interests in the same way as their older brothers had been able to do so successfully.

Peers

Family members play crucial roles in helping young children to form their self-identities and to learn the appropriate ways to act as they move out into the world beyond their family homes. As children form play groups in their neighborhoods and enter the school system, the role of nonfamilial peers increasingly gains importance in their development, becoming especially influential during the teen years. Peers serve, in large measure, as the body of persons that children and teens use as their "generalized others" in the process of learning to conform to social expectations. The ridicule or support of peer groups carry a great deal of weight in young people's development of self-esteem and a sense of belonging.

Very young children often have little choice in their playmates; they play mostly with siblings, close neighbors, and friends of the family. When they enter school, their choices widen somewhat, but limited access to transportation still restricts their ability to reach more distant peers after school hours. Therefore, local childhood friends and sibling peers help to shape activity choices, and those activity choices in turn dictate how play groups will be formed and propagate.

All of the women interviewed described themselves as active children who enjoyed sports or other vigorous outdoor pastimes. It is impossible to say where this propensity came from: whether it was the result of some biological predisposition, whether it was a product of patterns of family dynamics, or whether it was learned by the girls from the playmates they serendipitously found themselves associating with. Whatever the source of their tendencies to "rough-and-tumble" play, all fifteen of the women in this study said that they had been "tomboys" in their youths. While none of the women reported that their preference for active outdoor play, or the wearing of trousers, was a major problem for them in their youths, eight of them did say that these interests became a problem for them when they reached puberty.

These women reported that as girls they enjoyed physical activities such as track and field, swimming, playing on northern ice floes, climbing trees, playing hockey, football, soccer, and baseball, snowball fighting, and childish daredevil games. Seven of the ten women who regularly played sports said that sports were tremendously important to them in their youths. One woman said that she played sports "constantly, whenever I could get a chance," another said "my parents got us into every sport when we were little." A third woman said that "sports was the only thing that kept me in high school," and a fourth said that she was "incredibly active" in sports, which were the most important thing in her childhood. She said, "I played hockey from two hours before school and five or six hours after school." The only woman who did not participate in sports or other vigorous outdoor exercise was physically unable to do so. Even she spent as much time outdoors as possible and enjoyed less demanding sports such as fishing. She also reported that she was a regular playground fighter who beat up other children who made fun of the orthopedic shoes she had to wear.

Several commonalities resulted from their unanimous enjoyment of sports and physical exertion. Their preference for vigorous outdoor activities influenced who they chose as their peers. These women, in their youths, spent most of their time in the company either of boys, or of other girls who also preferred sports and outdoor activities. Those few girls who could not find friends to share their preferences said that they spent periods of their youths as loners. Nine women specifically stated that they played mostly with boys during their youths. Seven women, including three who said that they played with boys, described themselves as basically loners when they were young, although two of those women did have brothers with whom they were close. Only one woman remembered her strongest peer relationship being other girls, and they were girls with whom she played team sports at her Catholic girls' school. All of them also had a strong preference for the convenience of wearing pants whenever possible. Many of them expressed a clear dislike of dresses when they were young because, they said, they made rough-and-tumble play more difficult.

Their preferences for sports and other active games meant that they spent little time in the company of more traditionally oriented girls. As a result, they felt little peer pressure training them to be feminine and much peer pressure toward masculinity. Those for whom sports and the company of boys were a major part part of their lives usually excelled at the games they played. They received trophies and awards, or merely reaped praise from friends and family members for their accomplishments. They reported that such rewards boosted their self-confidence and increased their attachments to sports and the people who commended them for their participation. In most cases, this meant that they became strongly emotionally attached to boys' and sporting communities dominated by masculine values of aggressive competition, hierarchy, team discipline, and the subjugation of individuality.

Several women commented on the unavailability of girls with whom they could enjoy their favorite activities. One woman simply said, "All my life I associated mostly with boys because the girls . . . just didn't seem to want to have the same kind of fun as I do." Another said that she did not like being around girls, "because they weren't rough like I was." Others were less even-handed in their appraisals of the other girls they knew. One woman explained: "I had never found women who were good enough to play with me, who I found challenging. And I really got bored and I didn't like playing with women because they weren't good enough, because it slowed me down." A second woman explained her dislike of other girls: "What I saw of girls in school was that they weren't very smart and they didn't do very many things, that they weren't strong in their bodies and they didn't use their minds."

Another woman would play sports only on the street with the local boys because in school "everything that we did that was women's sports was sappy." Still another woman felt that she did not really fit in very well with either the boys or the girls whom she knew, but since there were not any other tomboys for her to play with, she opted to be with the boys when she was not off alone in the woods. She said of the local girls:

> I didn't really like the games they played and also they were really, really tight with each other and mean . . . They were always playing Prince Charming and Cinderella, non-action, pretend games that I didn't have any fun with. . . . But, also, I wasn't really part of their group either. If they needed any nerdy thing done, that was what I had to do to be part of that and that wasn't really worth it.

She felt that the boys treated her in a similar second-class way, but because she preferred their games she played along. She felt that "being the goalie in hockey wasn't really that bad."

When these girls did play with other girls, they often took on male roles in their play, or otherwise transformed stereotypically feminine activities into less feminine ones. When they played alone, they often featured themselves in their fantasies as male characters engaged in masculine pursuits. Three women recalled that when they played house or doctor with their friends, they always took on male roles in the games; two of them refused to play unless they could have those roles. Two other women remembered that they occasionally played with dolls but that their play was out of the ordinary. One woman hated dolls other than the Davy Crockett explorer doll that she inherited from her older brother. The other woman said that when she was young she and a girl friend concocted this version of playing house:

> It was not the kind of dolls you usually play. . . . It was the woman would beat the man up and tell him to go to bed. And she was always the one who worked and he was the one who stayed home and did things around the house. . . . We thought we were being very bold.

Thus, they rebelled against their feminine role even as they played with stereotypically feminine toys.

These women and five of the others also featured themselves in their fantasies as boys or men. Some merely imagined that their lives would be better if they were boys; others envisioned themselves as princes rescuing princesses in distress, or soldiers in combat zones. One woman, who said, "I didn't want to be identified as a girl" and often fantasized that she was Huck Finn, recollected: "My role models were . . . biker gangs. . . . The tough image, the T-shirt and jeans, and the leather jacket. I would have loved to have been able to dress up like that. I did to a certain extent. . . . I had the jeans and the T-shirt." Another woman probably summed up the feelings of many when she talked about her resentments against the feminine role:

I was very conscious of the different ways that boys and girls were treated from an early age . . . I was a feminist when I was eight . . . boys got treated this way and girls got treated that way and they got the better deal for the most part and I didn't want to put up with that. . . . They didn't get hassled about hanging out by the river so much. People weren't so afraid of them drowning. It wasn't such a big deal for them to go off into the hills. I wasn't supposed to go unless my brother was with me when I was little but he could go by himself. I wasn't supposed to play football. I wasn't supposed to get quite as dirty.

She, like the others, felt that the feminine role did not offer her the possibilities that she craved.

All of these women, as adults, shared a preference, which dated from childhood, for wearing pants. Some recalled that as children they were strongly disturbed by the fact that they had to wear dresses or skirts to school or special occasions. Others uncomplainingly wore skirts or dresses to school but changed into pants as soon as they arrived home. The woman who did not want to be identified as a girl, and whose role models were biker gangs, explained her dislike of dresses:

I remember when I was a tiny kid, one of my earliest memories—this is in the old house so I would have been less than five years old. I was wearing a pink dress and panties with little ruffles on the bum. Like I was a little kid, three or four, and my mom had the gals over for tea, or a sewing bee, or something, and she had me come out and raise the back of my skirt so they could see my ruffly bum and I was horribly embarrassed. . . . I didn't like dresses because I didn't like people seeing my underpants or I didn't like that sort of coyness of if the wind blows or if you bend over, you can't do a head stand or hanging by your knees in the jungle gym. That whole trip, it's embarrasing and degrading and I was aware of that as a kid.

The woman whose father had called her by a masculine nickname remembered that she had already acquired a taste for pants and certain masculine mannerisms by the age of two, when her beloved grandfather died.

There was actually a girl stage in my life . . . It was amazing, like I had long hair. I don't remember this but [in a picture] . . . I looked like a little girl, and then the next picture I saw of me, which was only about five months later, I was in this little jump suit, and my hair was all cut off short and I was sitting on this horse, right? And you know there was a hell of a change between those two pictures. From then on, I guess that's when people thought I was a little boy. And it was the way I carried myself too . . . like my grandfather the huge truck driver. . . . I've always had a problem with dresses. . . . When my mother first put a dress on me I stood there going like this, looking for the pockets.

She felt that wearing a dress was "lowering" herself and wore shorts underneath any dresses that she was forced to wear "so that I would feel more like I could run and play and do somersaults and not expose my underwear and not feel vulnerable." Another woman, who always felt large and clumsy off of the playing fields, said that she never learned how to be comfortable in feminine clothing.

> I think the other part of it is that I just don't feel comfortable in those kind of stupid clothes. I just don't know how to sit right. I always feel uncomfortable and clunky. . . . I can remember times that I did dress up, and you know, had to put on the prescribed outfit. I would get all this, quote positive reinforcement. "Oh, that looks real nice!" And I never believed it so I found that really humiliating, the compliments, because I never, ever, believed it. I felt horrible and I felt really like I looked stupid.

Another woman's discomfort in dresses during her adolescence was so severe that she said, "I think that's part of the reason I dropped out of high school. I didn't want to have to wear clothes that I didn't particularly feel comfortable in."

Thus, these women all grew up with an awareness that the trappings of femininity were not highly compatible with the active lives which they enjoyed and preferred. Some of them were able to find other girls who shared their pleasure in rough-and-tumble play. They were able to both reject feminine attire and postures, and sustain a relatively strong connection, in their own minds, between femaleness and the things they enjoyed most. Others were not so fortunate as to find like-minded girl friends and thus grew up, in large part, rejecting femininity and retaining a less secure identification with other females.

In their early years these fifteen women were funneled toward masculinity by some or all of the following factors. (1) They grew up in homes in which traditional gender values were relatively strong. (2) Their mothers, and/or older sisters, and/or grandmothers either were not prominent in their lives during their early years or were seen by these girls as weak and ineffectual people. (3) They had fathers who enlisted them as surrogate sons or provided them with affection only as a reward for masculinity. (4) Their experience of incest made maleness seem invulnerable. (5) They took pleasure in vigorous physical activity and were encouraged in this direction by other family members and/or peers (usually male). (6) Their peer group was dominated by boys who supported and reinforced tendencies toward masculinity while discouraging and punishing femininity. In individuals where most of these factors were strongly present, the feminine identities of the girls were so deeply suppressed as to result in self-doubts regarding their own femaleness. Three women in this group had seriously considered sex-change operations at some time prior to their interviews.

Adolescence Means Change

The problems that many of these women experienced in adapting to their prescribed gender roles increased dramatically during their teen years. Pressures to be feminine intensified from both family members and peers and caused many of these women to experience a great deal of discomfort. Their manner of dressing, moving, and talking all became problematic as they were pushed to become ladies and abandon their boyish ways. Their society had allowed them a period of freedom from the demands of femininity, but as their bodies matured they were expected to leave their masculine pleasures behind; there was no benign category called "tom-men" into which they could mature.

As their bodies became more adult and they turned unmistakably into women, several of them suffered rejection from male family members or peers. Others spoke of the discomfort they felt as they began to receive unwanted sexualized attention from boys with whom they would have preferred to play sports. Still others complained that the girls whose company they had enjoyed in their games and sports activities deserted them to become young ladies who were now more concerned about hemlines than goal lines. All resisted the inevitable curtailment of their freedoms as long and as hard as they were able. One woman, who expressed her feelings about adolescence this way, probably summed it up well for most of the other women when she said: "I guess in a way it just really seemed like the whole idea of growing up really bothered me. When this change occurs then all of a sudden you won't be able to be a tomboy anymore, you'll have to be a girl." She said that she had had other plans for her future besides turning into a girl and getting married. She said "I wanted to grow up to bigger and better things, drive a truck."

Several women found that their significant others were no more thrilled about the changes expected of them at adolescence than they themselves were. One woman recalled that when she started to mature, her mother began to disparage her plans to join the army and "work on jeeps" or fly airplanes. At the same time, her father turned sharply against her, becoming viciously verbally abusive about her looks, strength, and size. In her mid-teens she suffered severe emotional problems which led to serious physical illness and the desire for a sex change. She recalled:

> I could do anything I wanted to when I was a kid . . . I was never scared of anything. And I remember I started shaking when I was sixteen . . . I hated my body. When I left home, I wouldn't take anything with me that reminded me of being a female. I took shirts with me, and jeans, and maybe cords. I wouldn't take any female clothing that I had, and I had lots of female clothing. I wouldn't take anything with me. I left my bras behind.

Two other women told stories about rejections they received from their male friends as they reached puberty and started to change from "one of the boys" into women. One woman told about this incident during her junior high school years:

> I sort of was a dual personality. I still wanted to be a boy and I still wanted to wear jeans and climb trees. . . . I remember once I went to my grandmother's house . . . usually I wore my jeans and I'd go through the back lots and back alleys and climb over brambles and under fences to get there. One day . . . I decided that I wanted to

be a girl that day. I thought, now what do my girlfriends wear? They wear pedal pushers and sleeveless cotton blouses and they carry purses. So I put on pedal pushers and this blouse, I'd never worn a sleeveless cotton blouse before, I wore whatever they were wearing, bobbysox and carried a purse and walked down the sidewalk. And I went by this house where there were three boys living we used to play with when we'd play sports, and they looked up at me, I remember the one kid was my age, and said, "Why don't you go home and change into some real clothes and come back and play with us? Go and get rid of that stuff and come back and play." . . . I thought they were being funny and unimaginative. But it sort of was a little surprise, you know, that finally I was dressing to be socially acceptable and I was not socially acceptable. So that was the only time I remember doing that.

Another remembered that when she got her first bra her pals appreciated its merits even less than she did.

I told the guys and they were just aghast, they didn't know what to make of it. It was like a barrier, which really sort of embarrassed me because I just sort of thought that it was something that, you know, girls have, . . . and they've got to wear one. And I thought fine. . . . Well it turned out to be physically constraining. Well I mean it is, it's a god damned harness! . . . That lasted about a year and then I ran into the women's movement who legitimized not wearing a bra. So, you know I pretended that it was political but it wasn't, it was physical comfort.

The same woman also recalled that the boys that she had played hockey with on the street forced her out of their games as she reached puberty even though she described herself as "the best hockey player in the neighborhood. No question. I was a superb hockey player." She also said of herself, "I was also a very tough girl, you know, so to refuse me was to get a hockey stick over the head." Nonetheless, by the time she was seventeen years old the boys had successfully forced her out of their games because she was "too obviously a girl." She said, "I quit hockey when I did, not because I wanted to, but because I had to." Each of these women found that although she was expected by family, peers, and social conventions to become more feminine in her teen years, her significant others and many among her generalized others were either ambivalent or antagonistic about such changes. It thus became even more difficult for these women to wholeheartedly embrace the behavioral changes which they felt were expected of them in their teens.

Others found that as they reached puberty their male playmates became less interested in their physiques and more interested in their figures. One woman remembers her puberty as a difficult time because the changes which were happening to her body were not something which she welcomed, nor were they possible to hide from others.

Grade 8 was the worst year for me. It was the transition year. It was the year that . . . there was this whole new social pressure to dress and look nice at school . . . It was just terrible . . . It bothered me because it meant that I was a girl and I had to start doing something different, that people expected me to do something different.

Everybody wanted me to get a bra which I didn't want to do. I was mortified. The whole thing embarrassed me. My mother had never talked to me about it, I didn't have a close sister I could talk to and I didn't have any close girlfriends . . . I hung out with boys . . . they talked about other things. . . . Things started changing then, there was more of this boy-girl thing. Boys wanted to go out with girls and wanted to feel them up. . . . And I had fairly large breasts for all the girls my age, and I used to hide them. . . . I would get so embarrassed by them.

This same woman began to seriously object to dresses in her teen years, partly because relations between boys and girls had become sexualized:

I hated dresses, I just hated them. It was a very big deal . . . They are impractical . . . when I was eight I guess I didn't care if somebody saw my underwear . . . when you get older you have to wear nylons and high heels and you just become this ineffectual little bo-bo staggering around. You can't go out and run, you can't go out and sit behind the bleachers and smoke dope on the grass.

She, and others like her, felt betrayed both by her own body and by the boys who used to be her friends. Several of these women spoke of feeling discomfort and alienation in their bodies as they became more obviously women. They experienced their maturation as a loss of freedom and status.

Some of the women were able to retain friendships with their girl friends during their teen years. Others mourned the loss of their friends of both sexes. The female friends that these women were able to retain through their adolescence were other girls who, like themselves, were tomboys resisting the socially expected change into femininity. One woman remembered that she had a best girl friend at the time who was exceptionally athletic along with her. Her friend shared her desire to be a boy and was also mistaken for a boy during their teen years together. She recalled that they lifted weights together all through high school and were generally concerned with strength and fitness. "They had this super-fits program. Betsy and I were the only girls, and they were all guys, and we'd do things like hand stands, do sit-ups, or have somebody laying on your back and you'd do push-ups. . . . I was the fittest in my high school." Another woman, who had a very different experience, recounted how disappointed and hurt she had been when her female friends "deserted" her to become more feminine.

I got really hurt because I started seeing all my jock friends turning into these idiots when we got older. I met a few of them and they just got into it. Being what I call fem-bots, you know, being pretty and "Oh, I'm working as a secretary now!" . . . I get really upset and I got really angry and I just kept saying I'm never going to do that.

At the time of her interview she had held true to her vow. She had so rejected traditional femininity that she considered that she might be better off having a sex change.

All of the women interviewed resisted adult femininity as long as they were able. All of them resisted obviously feminine clothing, and some made a special effort to hide the changes occurring in their bodies. One woman went through a period of wearing "a lot of long bulky shirts" that hid her newly developed shape. Another said,

> In high school, I wasn't allowed to wear pants so I wore the next best thing, tailored clothes. . . . I wore total camouflage clothes, dark green, navy blue, grey and brown. I never wore dresses. I only wore skirts and knee socks and V-neck sweaters. Nothing frilly. . . . Tailored, I dressed tailored, in dull, dark colors.

A third woman said that she avoided feminine attire and makeup because she felt it was a falsification of her true self. "I wasn't really into femmey stuff . . . I thought it was a waste of time because it was a deception. Here you go to all this trouble to make yourself be something that you weren't. How long were you going to be able to pull it off for?" She was a loner who made her own decisions to be true to herself as she felt most comfortable.

Many of the women in this study went through a brief period in their teens when they experimented with feminine fashions. Their adolescent years were the times when they first felt that their boyish ways were actually "wrong," rather than simply expressions of their individuality. They were expected to outgrow their childish toying with masculinity. Most did give femininity a try. Two of the women who did so stayed with their experiment for several years. All of the rest rapidly came to the conclusion that they were far more adept and comfortable in their old ways, and so chose to remain with them despite social expectations to the contrary.

Most of the women in this study also resisted becoming involved in heterosexual relations until their late teens or early twenties. All but one went through adolescence in the 1960s and 1970s when there was increasing pressure on teens to become heterosexually involved while still in high school. Two of the fifteen did not divulge at what age they first became sexually active, but of the remaining thirteen women, ten of them did not become sexually active until they were out of high school. The three women who engaged in sexual activity during high school did so with others girls. Thus, all of the women about whom information is available were successful at evading, until a relatively advanced age, the heterosexual component intrinsic to traditional conceptions of adult femininity. This avoidance of and general lack of interest in dating and heterosexual romance was just one more aspect of their resistance to the demands of the dominant gender schema.

Adolescence for these women, as for most women, was a time when they were expected to take their appointed places as feminine actors in society. In North America, the dominant gender schema allows young girls to play with boys and to do stereotypically masculine things. Such tomboys are usually looked upon with benign amusement as ambitious youngsters eager to get the most out of their childhoods. At adolescence, when girls become women, tomboys are expected to become feminine. The dominant gender schema demands that females who are physically capable of reproduction must learn to play the feminine role which reflects, supports, and nurtures the power of men. Girls who want to retain that power for themselves threaten the order of patriarchal society.

These gender blending females found themselves caught in an inconsistency in the dominant gender schema. Because patriarchy sees the value of females as residing almost entirely in their reproductive capacities, young girls are allowed relative freedom before they reach puberty. These women, their families and peers, took full advantage of this laxness. When they began to mature into women, everyone knew that it was time for them to grow out of their boyishness. Most of them tried to cooperate. All of them eventually found that they wanted to continue on the path they had been on all along. This reality flew in the face of society's norms and expectations. Theirs was not an easy course to negotiate.

 JAN

F I V E

Sexuality and Gender

Sexuality and Gender Identity

People's identities as males or females, men or women, are partially based on their understandings of the meanings given to sexuality in their sociocultural context. Thus, sexuality is a major component both in people's gender identities and in their sex identities. In North America, the dominant gender schema of the late twentieth century presumes that femaleness will result in feminine behavior, which is characterized by an often highly sexualized heterosexuality. In particular, feminine heterosexuality demands that those who would be women must be both sexually attracted to men and sexually attractive to men.

Masculinity likewise is partially defined by heterosexuality. Masculine heterosexuality similarly requires that those who would claim full rights to maleness must be both sexually attracted to women and sexually attractive to them. Feminine sexuality emphasizes allure and desire, while masculine sexuality is more concerned with actual genital sexual activity. Thus, although gender identity for both men and women is partly defined in terms of their sexuality, masculine sexuality is defined in more concrete performance terms, while feminine sexuality is more passively concerned with impressions and their management.[1]

Gender dictates sexuality in many direct ways. Sexuality is, in large part, a social construction. This means that although sexual drives may be biologically based, the forms and courses which sexual desires and activities take are learned behaviors. Gender identity forms one basis of sexuality. Persons who see themselves as women or men make some effort to conform to the social expectations for their gender. At the same time, social pressures to conformity normally direct individuals into sexual behavior patterns which are appropriate for members of their gender. In any event, by the time that individual emotional and behavioral sexual patterns begin to form, the gender role behaviors and beliefs which underlie them are already well established.

The propensities, skills, and tendencies which make up gender role behaviors constrain the possible forms that a person's sexuality might take. Masculine socialization produces masculine behavior patterns and aspirations in the persons who experience it; persons who have been raised to think of themselves as active and aggressive competitors are not likely to develop a sexuality based on passivity and coyness. By the same token, persons who have grown up using older males as role models are not likely to cease to model themselves after them in the formation of their sexuality. Thus, females who have been substantially socialized in accordance with masculine patterns will find masculine patterns of sexuality more readily available to them as they enter into their own patterns of sexual desire and activity.

Sexuality also doubles back to form a basis for gender identity. Members of society are aware of social expectations that adult females should possess a feminine sexuality, and that the sexuality of male persons should take a masculine form. When persons conform well with the social expectations for their gender, they, and others, see their conformity as a confirmation of their gender. Such confirmations serve to reinforce individuals' gender identities and therefore support further activity of the same variety.[2] In a similar manner, sexual behavior or desires which are non-stereotypical for persons' genders may cause confusion and insecurity in their gender identities and in the gender attributions made by others about them.

Thus adult females, who develop a sexuality which reflects the dictates of the dominant gender schema that female persons should be romantically and sexually attracted to men and that men should find them sexually attractive, find that their sexuality reinforces their identities as women. By contrast, females whose sexual desires are directed toward other women, or whose patterns of sexual activity are aggressively focused on genital sexuality, can find themselves, and others, doubting the authenticity of their identities as women and as females.

The Making of Sexual Preferences

As the gender blending females in this study passed through adolescence, they had to make choices about their sexuality and about their sexual preferences. They made their choices from within the context of the possibilities offered to them in their social environment and the personality traits they had thus far developed. They made choices which allowed them to live as comfortably as possible with themselves and with their society.

During early adolescence, all of these women felt a pointed pressure toward a femininity which demanded of them that they change their appearances and behaviors so as to become sexually attractive to men or boys. Most of them made some efforts, during their early teens, to at least "try on" the new femininity that was expected of them. Ten of the fourteen women who provided information about their sexuality reported that they were neither sexual nor romantically interested in boys during high school. Twelve women said that they had participated in heterosexual activity early in their sexual careers, but by the time of their interviews only four remained exclusively heterosexual. Of the eleven women who were exclusively lesbian at the time of their interviews, seven had previously been either heterosexually or bisexually oriented, two gave no information on the subject, and two had always been lesbian. None of the women claimed bisexuality at the time of their interviews.

The four women who were exclusively heterosexual throughout their teen and adult years, and one other woman who became lesbian after approximately fifteen years of heterosexual activity, a marriage, and the birth of three sons, were each reluctant entrants into the world of heterosexuality. One woman, who did not start dating until she was nineteen years old, said that she "liked boys as playmates not as dates." Another, who as a teen had had a serious crush on a woman at her church, and who had begun dating at age eighteen, said, "I just wasn't interested in guys at that time. . . . I was a little retarded as far as dating." Another woman, who was unusually tall for her age as a young teen and found that older men and boys were interested in dating her because they misjudged her age, complained that men were interested in sex, whereas she was only interested in their friendship. She said, "I was quite negative on men actually when I was younger because, I guess, because of being mistaken as older." She said of her relationships with boys during her teen years: "I never had a boyfriend. I had a very good friend. My best friend for a long time always had a boyfriend and it always ended up that I would be his friend and she would be his girlfriend. She'd be his girlfriend, and then they'd be fighting, and then he'd come to me. I always had a lot of guy friends." She put off serious dating until she was nineteen years old. The two other women in this group both avoided dating by resisting thinking of themselves as adult women. During their teens, one exclusively heterosexual woman wanted a sex change and went so far as to schedule surgery intended to alter her appearance to make her look more masculine. The other woman merely went through a phase during which she recalled that, "As a teenager I gave serious thought to 'Why should I be a girl? I would have been such a good boy! If I had been a boy, there wouldn't have been this problem.' . . . It would have been easier, the things that I do naturally, if I had been a boy." By tenaciously clinging to their boyishness, those gender blending teens who were to become heterosexual women avoided and postponed the heterosexual aspect of their transition to womanhood as long as they were able.

The women who continued to have mostly male friends into their late teens, well after most of their female friends had become romantically interested in boys, experienced an unusually extended period of masculine companionship. As a result, they were exposed to masculine peer group socialization longer than are most girls. Those extra years in the company of boys could only have served to reinforce and further entrench the gender role lessons they had already learned in their youths. Thus, it should not be surprising that these teens later became heterosexual women whose patterns of desire reflected their high estimation of men, masculinity, and masculine values.

Two women reported that they were sexually and romantically attracted to hypermasculine men. One woman described the type of men that she is attracted to as "real men, tall, muscular, physical," to which she added "I don't like wimps." She described her then-current and longest-lasting boyfriend as "really good looking and well built and everything, and it seems like he can do anything he bloody well pleases and nobody bothers him really." She said that when she had wanted to become a man she had wanted to be the type of man that she is attracted to, and she speculated that if she had become a man she might have been homosexual because of the strength of her preference for men. It seemed that because she had resigned herself to the fact that "I could never really be a real man, as much of a man as I'd like to be," she instead contented herself with romantic liaisons with the type of man that she would herself have preferred to become.

The other woman who preferred hypermasculine men seemed to want a partner who was at least as masculine as herself, so that she could share her favorite activities with him. She reported that when she was in her early twenties she considered herself more deserving of masculine privileges than most men. She told this story about her attitude toward "wimps" in her younger adult years:

> I remember I had taken my brother's 750 [cc motorcycle] to work one day. And it was a bigger, tougher, better bike than anybody else in the workplace had. It hit me that I could drive it right up the boss's desk, put the front wheel on his chest, and I would still get less wages than some wimp. And it really, really bothered me. It just bothered me beyond belief.

Clearly, this woman would not be satisfied with the companionship of any man who was less masculine than herself. She reported that it was only recently in her life that she began to appreciate that it was not necessarily only men who could provide her with the type of companionship that she enjoyed most. She said,

> All my closest and dearest friends are all males. . . . I feel a real affinity with men. That's changed now that I've met women that are interested in the topics I'm interested in. For instance I know about three women hunters. I now know a lot of women scientists, I now know a lot of women in trades. These women have the same sort of experiences that I have.

Nonetheless, she was heterosexually oriented and her companion at the time of her interview seemed to satisfy her requirements of highly developed masculinity.

Both of these women had made a compromise with themselves and with the society in which they lived. Both had grown up strongly preferring stereotypically masculine activities, both had intense relationships with their fathers, both had adolescent fantasies of being boys. As adults, they were not interested in abandoning masculine companionship or activities, and so their desire became directed at the men that they might have become. Their involvements with men more masculine than themselves allowed them to continue on the masculine path they had chosen. They were able to continue to enjoy masculine pursuits and companionship while availing themselves of the validation of their femininity that heterosexual relations with "real men" afforded them.

Three of the heterosexual women described themselves as having engaged in stereotypically masculine aggressive and predatory sexual behavior. One woman simply said that her friends and acquaintances think of her as sexually aggressive. A second woman displayed a somewhat dispassionate aggressive attitude toward sexuality in several of her comments. When she described her first forays into sexual activity she said that she had coolly made a decision to lose her virginity and then acted upon it.

> I decided that I was tired of being a virgin. . . . Well, I got turned on. That was the first time I wanted to, after I hit college. I think my German teacher started it, he was real cute. I remember sitting in the dorm and thinking (now this was '67–'68), "I have to be a virgin until I'm married, Why?" I knew that there's some horrible ominous thing that will happen to me if I lose my virginity, and I was trying to figure out what it was. I couldn't figure it out. I decided that I didn't want to marry a man who insisted on having a virgin. I just sat a while. I had to really think about it and realize that I wouldn't go straight to hell tomorrow if I lost it tonight. So I went out and seduced this guy and had a good time. Actually it wasn't that good a time. He wasn't a good lover, but, nonetheless, I did manage to unburden myself. . . . From there it was a series of lovers.

This woman also described becoming sexually attracted to another man whom she turned into a sexual conquest. She took a decidedly unfeminine attitude toward her love life.

> My last year of university a friend hauled me off to a karate class. And the teacher was real pretty. I wasn't that interested in karate because it looked very robotic and I knew it took years to get confidence. But it was sort of like going to ballet class and not really being interested in ballet but if Rudolf Nureyev is teaching the class, you sort of go whoa, I think I'll stay in this class for a while. So I was really impressed with the grace and strength of his movements and I wanted to have that too. And I wanted to have him too. So I managed to.

The third woman went through a period which she referred to as "my male phase" during which time she felt that she was avenging herself for all of the physical and sexual abuse that her husband had inflicted on her. She went to bars where she was "just picking up boys just to serve myself in a way of revenge." She said, "I thought I was really acting as a male chauvinist pig, and I was using men. . . . I was treating them as objects, as I was treated as an object." She continued in this phase until she had an experience that convinced her that she had gone "overboard." When one of her "pick-ups" doubted the veracity of her femaleness she decided to stop objectifying and sexually using men.

> So I come in the bar and I forgot my cigarettes in my coat. So I ask the first guy I see "Do you have any cigarettes?" and he says "No, but I have cigars." That's great, I take a cigar. And I really love cigars because I'm smoking black tobacco. So it was a great big cigar, a couple of bucks cigar. He thought it was funny but he gave it to me. He was really happy to do it, and so he gave it to me. I light it up, and then I go

around and that guy there, about thirty, very nice looking, comes up to me with a big smile and I am smoking my cigar. He says "How are you?" and starts paying scotches. He had like double scotches. So I said, "Why not? If I have to deal with a man tonight."

Then I take him back home because I never went to the guy's place. I take him back to my place. He goes to the bathroom. I go to bed. He comes back, he comes into my bed, he takes one of my breasts and he pinches it. I'm just mad and I stand up. I say "You're a complete fool! I don't want any of this and get out of here!" And he says, "How come it hurts?" I say, "How come it hurts? Christ! That's my breast!" He says, "I thought transsexual breasts didn't hurt." I say, "What do you mean? You pig! That's a womb I have there and I had three children through it and you won't be able to do that in your life, try it or not, to be a transsexual or whatever!" I was so mad that I picked up the guy's coat, I had an apartment with a huge balcony at the front and on a very busy street, went out of my balcony doors, took his clothes and threw them into the street. The guy was standing there nude in my apartment. I was so powerfully mad, I kicked him out. . . . I was so mad that it was like complete madness.

Her experience prompted her to "look into my relations with men, and what I saw is that I was just hating them." Shortly thereafter, feeling that she could not lead a life based on misandry, she came "into a new reincarnation" as a lesbian.

These three women took on a stereotypically masculine attitude toward their sexual relationships with men. They made no pretense of romanticism, they sexually objectified the men they were interested in, and they set out to conquer them in purely sexual, emotionally uninvolved encounters. Their sexual stance was consistent with the masculine socialization which had trained them to take a similar attitude toward life's many challenges. By adopting this approach to their heterosexuality, they were able to retain dominant self-images at the same time as they were able to claim the validation of their femininity, and therefore their femaleness, which is normally attributed to women who engage in heterosexual activity.

Two of the five women in this group reported that they had had major relationships with men considerably older than themselves, and one woman married a man who was abusive to her, as her father had been to her mother. One of these women had her first romantic relationship at the age of twenty-one with an older married man. He began the affair with her while she was dressing as a man and working for him in a male-dominated trade. This woman was the same person who had implied sexual abuse by her father and had spent the three years prior to this affair passing as a man. Another woman, who had been fatherless and had adored her older brother, later married a man considerably older than herself. She said that the men she was attracted to were "pretty" or "not macho" like her older brother. The third woman, who had called her father her "first love," married a man whose treatment of her was reminiscent of her father's disdainful conduct toward her mother. It would seem that all of these three women were attracted to men who bore some similarity to the men who had helped to shape their gender roles while they were young.

These five women, four who had always been heterosexually oriented and one who was heterosexual for approximately fifteen years, each found ways to continue to express her masculinity in her heterosexual relationships. They were attracted to men who reminded them of the male role models they had followed in their youths, or to men who were the type of men that they themselves aspired to be, or they were sexually predatory in their relationships. Older men and hypermasculine men offered them a sense of confirmation of their gender role choices. These men allowed them to see themselves as sufficiently feminine to be attractive to men at the same time as they provided a stamp of approval for their femininity and an arena for their masculinity. The men who bore similarities to the role models of their youths gained special power as authenticators of their gender role choices through that connection. The men who were hypermasculine carried an extra ability to bestow masculine approval in two ways. On the one hand, the sexual attentions of such men implied that the women who inspired those attentions were as femininine as the men were masculine. From another angle, the fact that hypermasculine men were interested in doing masculine activities with these women meant that although these gender blending females had proven their womanhood through their heterosexuality, they were still sufficiently masculine to play on the "big boys' team."

Three of these women also told stories which demonstrated an aggressive, unemotional sexual predation. This is a logical progression in persons who have been socialized by family and peers to masculine behavior patterns and for whom competition and aggression has always been a major part of their lives. Sexuality grows out of, and into, a personality which has already passed through many extremely strong social and psychological experiences. As such, the form that their sexuality took had to somehow be reconcilable with their already existing personality traits. These masculine women did not suddenly become feminine merely because society decided that it was time for them to do so. Instead they responded to social expectations by negotiating compromises between their own intrapsychic needs and social conventions. They found ways to express both their sexuality and their masculinity either by becoming romantically attached to their masculine ideals, or by sexually conquering men. In both circumstances, they affirmed their femininity and femaleness through the social meaning given to their heterosexuality by the dominant gender schema.

Of the eleven who were exclusively lesbian at the time of their interviews, four had had heterosexual relationships serious enough to include marriage or engagement to be married, or to last four years or more. Two additional women had dated desultorily during their latter teens and early twenties, and four of the eleven had engaged in periods of aggressive promiscuity with men. All of these women were searching for ways to reconcile their youthful boyishness with their growing sexuality and the gender role demands of the society in which they lived. They experienced the same kinds of socialization influences toward heterosexuality as their female peers, and most responded to those pressures by willingly trying to conform to the heterosexuality which was expected of them.

Only three of the women who later became exclusively lesbian said that they had regularly dated as teens or young adults. Three other women spoke of serious relationships with men, but two of those women denied having ever been involved in dating or having any particular interest in men. It seemed as though at least three of these six women became involved with boys or men only as a formality. One woman, who had been engaged to be married, recalled her adolescent attitude toward dating:

> I wanted to grow up and play hockey. I never had any wish to get married and have kids except for there was one stage when everybody, all your girlfriends, were talking about boys and stuff. So I had to talk about it, although I didn't really believe it myself. I thought that maybe that might be fun. . . . I was never really romantically interested in boys. . . . Boys, really—they were there—there was always the kind of comradery and brotherhood kind of thing, but never the whole idea of sex or anything like that.

Nonetheless she tried to play along with the heterosexual assumption and became engaged to be married. One day she realized that she was not the type of woman who could be happy as a wife:

> This was girl stage number two, and I felt, not because I needed to, but because I had to be a girl. That also means that you have to date boys, right? I was engaged and living with this guy and I woke up one night and I said, "This isn't going to work. It doesn't seem like this is the way things should be." I had been having these dreams about women, right?

Apparently, her relationships with men had little impact on her self-image, because she later claimed to have been a lesbian since she was two or three years old.

Two other women similarly recalled that they had dated during their teens and early adulthood because it was what was expected of them. One woman said, "I wasn't really interested in boys. . . . It was validation. It was expected. If you didn't have one, you would have been looked on with a great deal of suspicion." She managed to confirm her femininity by always having "a boyfriend somewhere, usually living in another city." This freed her from having to date the local boys, in whose company she could continue to enjoy her favorite masculine pastimes. Another woman did not date much because she was not asked out very often. She said that she preferred the company of boys more for "hanging out" than for dates, but that she did date because "I figured I was supposed to, so I did a little bit." She avoided the whole situation as much as possible by tying up her emotional energy in impossible longings. "Usually what I did was I had a crush on some boy that was going out with some friend of mine," thereby obscuring the fact that she had no real desire to participate in heterosexuality. Thus, although these women ostensibly engaged in heterosexual periods, they seemed to be doing so only as a legitimizing formality and out of some sense of obligation. They dated as a bow to social convention.

Three other of the women who later became lesbian did have long-lasting relationships with men. One of these three is the woman who became predatory toward men after she left her husband of many years. Both of the other two women were bisexual while they were involved with the men in their lives. One of these two women began her sexual career quite young. She first experimented with lesbianism with another young girl when she was twelve years old. The girl's mother found them kissing in bed together and threw up on the spot. Apparently that was enough to deter the girl from further experimentation for a few years.

Two years later she began a relationship, with a boy her own age, which was to last for four years. During that time she also briefly became sexually involved with another girl around her own age. Although she was devastated when her relationship with the boy ended, the description she gave of their relationship sounded less than romantic and more like one that two boys who were best friends would have: "He was the neatest guy. He was really neat. We did all our sports together. He treated me like a human being. We shared everything and we worked on our bikes together. He taught me how to work on cars. I taught him how to play basketball." But their relationship was not an asexual one:

> We were doing everything we could without sexual intercourse by the time we were fifteen or sixteen. . . . It was actually pretty neat because . . . we didn't worry about it too much. When we were seventeen we started talking about it. . . . I went to my mother and she told me, "Don't do it if you don't want to."

Soon after that the relationship started to deteriorate because she could no longer hold her boyfriend's interest against the incursions of more feminine girls. He, for one, was ready to stop hanging around with the boys. She felt hurt and rejected and entered into a highly promiscuous heterosexual phase after the breakdown of their relationship:

> I was rippling jealous. . . . It was like my territory was being overthrown. Like when I was alone with the boys, they really treated me like one of the guys. And what happened, I guess, was that when [the other girls] came along, they weren't as tomboyish as I was, so they got treated like girls. And the contrast became very apparent to me. . . . And then I started getting upset about being not pretty at that point.

She reacted to this rejection by entering a period of her life in which she frantically tried to validate her heterosexual desirability by having sexual encounters with numerous men: "I had been with over a hundred guys in two years and none of them were anywhere near his calibre. All they cared about was fucking." After two years of disappointing sexual relations, she came to identify herself as a lesbian without ever quite giving up her attraction to boys. At the time of her interview she still said "I like boys, I don't like men."

A third woman, who was later to become exclusively lesbian, also had a four-year relationship with a man. She had gone to a gender segregated Catholic school and so had had little contact with boys outside of her large family while she was growing up. As a teen, she had accompanied her girl friends on their date hunting trips to the local pub but claimed disinterest in boys herself. Her interest in men began when she was first asked out on a date at age seventeen. She dated men for seven years, until she was twenty-four years old, when she began her longest lasting heterosexual relationship. That relationship overlapped with the last four years of a seven year lesbian relationship which she kept hidden from everyone except another lesbian couple. During her interview, she spoke little of her heterosexual life or the men she had loved, except to say that she still loved both of the men she had fallen in love with over the years, and that she was "really into" the man she had seen for four years. Despite her love for more than one man, and her four-year relationship, she still said, "When I look back now, I realize that I was always a lesbian." She seemed to have denied her years of heterosexuality, since she had accepted a lesbian identity one year earlier.

All of these six women made some effort to conform to what they felt was appropriate for and expected of young women of their age. They absorbed the messages being directed at them from family, friends, the schools, and the media, which told them that, as girls maturing into women, they should become interested in boys or men. They tried to conform to the demands of the dominant gender schema, as communicated to them through their generalized and significant others. One by one, they found that heterosexuality did not suit them the way it did other young women.

Three of the women who were to become lesbian went through heterosexually promiscuous stages. One of them was the woman who had been married and later became predatory. Another was the young woman who became so "rippling" jealous of other more feminine girls. The third woman, who had been sexually abused by an older brother while quite young, never had any desire to be involved with men thereafter. In fact, her expressed attitude toward men was that "they should all be drowned at birth." Nonetheless, when she first announced to a group of her friends that she had discovered, to her delight, that she was a lesbian, they counseled her to "give it a try with men before you make a decision like that." She took a very narrow interpretation of their suggestion and obediently set out to "try" men: "So I did. That very day I went picking men up. For about a month, all the time, slept with them all the time. And I didn't like it, I really didn't like it. By then I had figured that out." Having proven to herself that she did not find satisfaction in heterosexual sexuality, she happily became exclusively lesbian.

All of these three women who experimented with heterosexual promiscuity had felt hurt and anger at men when they embarked on their course of promiscuity. They expressed their rage by objectifying and sexually using men for their own ends. They, as women who had a strong command of masculinity and a limited facility with femininity, chose to deal with their anger and frustration in a typically masculine fashion. They used and discarded their gender "opposites." Their promiscuity also served as a final testing ground before they abandoned their heterosexuality. They took their inability to find satisfaction in sexual relations with men as definitive proof that they were not really heterosexual after all. It seemed as if they believed the myth that "great sex" with "Mr. Right" would turn them, once and for all, into "real" women. When they failed to find that redemption, they were forced to face other possibilities: either they were lesbian women, or they were not really women at all.

Several of these women recalled being taught, and absorbing, negative and derogatory stereotypes about lesbian women. They thought of lesbians as mannish women who were not "real" women, or they thought lesbians were women who wanted to be men. When these women first began to have crushes on their girl friends and teachers, they had to confront the possibility that they might be lesbian; they had to decide if they were enough like their images of lesbian women to accept the title.

All of the eleven women who were lesbian at the time of their interviews had had to come to terms with their own negative conceptions of what lesbians were like. Most of them had impressions of lesbians which they had formed before the tenets of either gay liberation or feminism were pervasive enough to affect their beliefs. One woman, who never experimented with heterosexuality and had crushes on girls and women for close to ten years before she actually started to have sexual relations with other women when she was about twenty-four, described her image of lesbians in high school, "I looked like a lesbian. . . . They look tough. They don't look frilly . . . They don't wear makeup. They don't go out with boys." She thought that she might be a lesbian and wanted to talk with her mother about it, but she never did because she feared that her mother would want to change her into someone more feminine:

> Many times I nearly told my mother. I would drink with my mother and I would tell her how depressed I was, and how I didn't have any friends. And I wanted to tell her that I was a lesbian, but I thought she'd make me burn all my jeans, and make me start carrying a purse, and curl my hair. Which is probably what she would have done because that's the cure, you know?

This woman, as many other members of society, clearly equated lesbianism with a lack of femininity.

The woman who had been engaged to be married reported that she first started being attracted to other girls and older lesbian women around the age of thirteen or fourteen, but she took no action on her feelings for several years because she was not yet ready to accept the label for herself.

> I guess in about grade nine I started noticing that I was attracted to these women. There was always the old favorite, the phys. ed. teacher. . . . and all the phys. ed. teacher's friends. And they were all these, they were the kind of women I liked to be with. They cursed and they didn't take crap from anybody. And so I really had this

crush on a couple of them and I would follow them around and do all the things for them. There was this one woman in particular who I didn't—I had never heard the word lesbian—but a friend of mine came up to me and said, "You have to watch out for her. She's a lesbian and people will start to think that you're one." I couldn't understand, if that's the way people are—I'm going to talk to whoever I want to talk to.

She was quite a bit older than me. She had quite a reputation around town for being quite a bad girl. And she was what you'd call a bull dyke, I guess that's what she was. She used to get drunk in the bars and fight all the men and they were scared to death of her. But they all thought she was great, you know, as a friend. The thought of ever having sex or being, falling in love with a woman, never crossed my mind. It was more like, "I want to be your friend." I didn't want to grow up and be like her because, who she really was, like when you sat down and talked to her, was a really gentle person. But because of her upbringing, she was always portrayed as being forceful and mean. If she wanted something, the only way she knew how to get it was to take it or fight for it.

Her first images of lesbian women were based entirely on her experiences with particularly masculine women. She was fascinated by their strength but had not translated that attraction into sexual terms. She had not yet learned that it was possible to be a lesbian and be as masculine, or feminine, as she might wish to be.

One of the women who had a four-year relationship with a man was repulsed by lesbian women only a year or two before she began her first lesbian relationship. She said:

I knew about lesbians. I was scared to death of lesbians. I joined the police at 18. There was a policewoman on one of the divisions who took a shine to me. She would always want to hang about around me. . . . And I was scared to death of this woman. She used to come up to me and put her arms around me. And I hit her one time.

We'd had this social for policewomen where I'd been, and my place wasn't too far away so they'd been using my record player. And at the end of the social I was loading up my record player and she walked out with one of my speakers. And I went to take the speaker from her, and I took it and I turned around to put it into my car. And as I turned around and she went to put her arms around me to kiss me and I hit her.

She said of the lesbian women that she knew at the time:

I was avoiding them. I didn't want anything to do with them. I didn't want to be anywhere around them. They were a whole bunch of fucking dykes, you know? . . . They used to go around wearing men's clothes, and men's shoes, and men's shirts, and men's jackets. . . . I wore jeans all the time, but I didn't wear men's clothes.

She too felt that, whatever she was, she was not a lesbian because, in her mind, lesbians were women who wanted to be men.

Another woman's story displays this attitude about lesbian women most graphically. While still in her teens this woman found herself attracted to both boys and girls. She had closer and more intense relations with the boys that she knew, but she did find herself briefly sexually involved with one of the girls in her group of friends. Her lesbian affair prompted her to look at her life in a new light. She had never felt quite right as a female, and her sexual attraction to a member of her own sex, on top of her well-developed masculinity in other areas, was enough to make her doubt her very femaleness.

> When I was fifteen, I went to my brother who used to sit up, smoke cigarettes. I'd drink tea and he'd drink coffee and we'd sit in the kitchen. And he came one time, this was sort of a regular hangout in the house. And I said, "I don't know what to do." I had read this article about that tennis player Rene who had had a sex change and for the first time I started thinking, "Ah hah! Maybe this is the problem!". . . I had this thing with Jennifer. I got very mixed up and I said, "OK, I like cars, I want to be a doctor, and I like girls. What's the problem?" So I thought I had a problem, and I thought, "I'm supposed to be a boy."
>
> And then I started remembering when I was a kid, when my brother used to joke that I was supposed to be a boy. He'd say, "She's supposed to be a boy, look at her muscles, . . . look at her jaw, she's got this big jaw. And look at her shoulders. I've never seen any girls like that.". . . I think I thought it was kind of neat. I thought it was OK. Because for me, being a boy was strong and being a girl was pretty. Like for me, a girl was a sissy and a boy was strong, so it didn't really bother me. But then it started getting confusing because I met other girls who were athletes but who were pretty. And they still got boyfriends all the time. . . .
>
> So, at fifteen when I saw this article about a sex change, I went to my brother and I said "I want to have a sex change." And he said, "Why? That's crazy. Why do you want to do that?" And I said, "Because I like girls, and I like playing football, and I like mechanics and cars, and I want to be a doctor." And I went through all these society labeled things. And he turned to me and said, "Don't be a stupid jerk and start cutting up your body so society will accept your interests. Do what you want. If you want to like girls, you want to fix cars, you want to be a doctor, do it anyway. Who cares?" And it was the first time I felt really strong about being different because I knew I was different, and it wasn't just the sexuality.

At the time of her interview, she had not yet resolved the feelings that had arisen for her in her teens. She found that she was unable to completely resolve her ambivalence about her femaleness by becoming a lesbian. Even later, after her conception of lesbianism became more sophisticated, she still did not see herself as entirely belonging among women of that type either. Her well-developed masculinity continued to cause her to feel that she was part male.

Another of these women's teenaged lesbianism also caused her to seriously consider a sex change. She was sexually and romantically involved with another young woman for five years between the ages of twelve and seventeen. They were the only lesbian women they knew at the time, but they did not think of themselves as lesbians, rather, they saw themselves as boyfriend and girlfriend. The relationship ended when the gender blending woman's partner died. Had it not ended when it did, the gender blending woman said that she might have gone on to become a man. Happily, her whole outlook on herself changed when she later discovered a community of lesbian women in a nearby city. Up until that point, the only way she had to understand herself was by comparison to a traditional gender schema. Against that measure, she seemed more like a man than a woman. When she discovered other women like herself, she realized that she could indeed be a woman and be as masculine as she felt suited her temperament:

> I didn't know who I was, or what I was, or anything else like that. So when I went to the city, somebody brought me to a gay bar, and I saw all these people, and I got to meet people. And I realized, "Hey, I'm finding out who I am!". . . I found out what gay was. I found out who I was and I realized there's a whole bunch more people out there that were like me. So then I started to change.

This woman found that a lesbian identity saved her from believing that she was a man in a woman's body. She found that being lesbian offered her another option somewhere between man and woman: the "mannish woman."

The eleven women who became lesbian took advantage of two aspects of popular conceptions of lesbians to save themselves from the threat that their masculinity posed to their womanhood, and hence to their femaleness. Thinking from within the cognitive framework of the dominant gender schema, they were confronted with the logical possibility that their lack of femininity meant that they were not "real" women. They had grown up as tomboys, as had many other girls, but when the other girls began to become more feminine and develop romantic and sexual interests in boys, they found themselves acting like the boys they knew. They persisted in their desires to be masculine or boyish, and they started having crushes on other girls. They were merely proceeding in the direction that their socialization had thus far sent them. They became masculine women whose sexual and romantic desires conformed to masculine patterns.

This turn of events pushed two of these women to think that they might have to alter their bodies to become males. They found themselves unable, at the time that they considered changing sexes, to identify with lesbian images. The only other possibility open to them, within the logical boundaries of the dominant gender schema to which they subscribed, was that they must be some aberrant form of men. The others searched for less dramatic solutions. One woman remembered:

> I was deciding that there was something wrong with me. I didn't know what lesbians were, and didn't know that that was it, but there was something wrong with me in relation to how things were supposed to be, and I didn't fit. And I didn't want to fit, but I didn't want to be alone either. I thought that there might be something else, but I didn't know what it was.

The commonly held stereotype of lesbians as "mannish women" offered them an explanation of their own predilections for masculinity, at the same time as it allowed them to retain identities as women. They were thus freed to be masculine women without being forced to think of themselves as men.

Those women who had the benefit of discovering a lesbian community also discovered the confirmation of their womanhood that comes from the simple fact of a community of opinion. Thus, those who found a community were able, to a large degree, to neutralize that aspect of popular misconceptions about lesbian women which claims that lesbian women want to be men. They were able to check the stereotypes they had learned in their youths against the lives of a community of real women. They found that whether "butch," "femme," or neither, lesbians were clearly and indisputably women. Identifying themselves as lesbian women was not a perfect solution, but it was preferable to being enough of a misfit to want to turn into a man. As lesbians, they were freed from the imperative that women must be feminine. As one woman said, "It was like coming home."

Searching for a Fit

Sexuality became an issue for all fifteen of the gender blending women interviewed, either as a way of countering the anomalous gender message inherent in their masculinity, or as a confirmation of that masculinity. The gender schema which dominates in North America allowed them to be as masculine as they wished while they were still pre-pubertal. Before they reached reproductive age, there was no loss to patriarchy in their learning to enjoy masculine pursuits. Once they began to reach adulthood they were expected to leave behind their youthful "tomboyishness" and become feminine adults. A major component of that adult femininity revolved around the requirement that they should be heterosexually active so that they might perform their appointed support roles to men and to patriarchy.

This requirement was problematic for all of them in their own ways. Heterosexuality hinges on female attraction to men and women's ability to incite desire in men. Most of these women had developed an appreciation for men and masculinity, but many of them had failed to sexualize that attraction. They were women who were interested in masculinity as a set of qualities which they wanted to participate in rather than reflect. Those who became heterosexually oriented were confronted with the problem of their behavior being too masculine to invoke appropriate desires in men. Those who became lesbian found that their masculinity made them attractive to other women.

Most of the women in this study at least tried to be heterosexual. The four women who remained heterosexual at the time of their interviews found that the very fact of their heterosexuality was sufficient proof of their femininity to give some stability to their feminine self-images. Nonetheless, these women continued to encounter some difficulty in finding partners whose masculinity was not threatened by the magnitude of their own. Two women, at the time of their interviews, had settled down with hypermasculine men in whose reflection they seemed feminine, and with whom they could freely exercise their own masculine tendencies. Unfortunately, one of these women continued to be sufficiently masculine that her encounters with other people still caused her to question whether she had been correct in abandoning her desire for sex-change surgery. The other two heterosexual women continued to seek a comfortable balance between their own aggressiveness and the general sexual skittishness of men when approached by forthright and commanding women.

Those women who became lesbian were forced to confront their own stereotypes, misconceptions, and ignorance about lesbianism. In some cases, their misconceptions caused distinct problems for the women who held them. In others, their stereotypes offered them a way out of their difficulties. Those women who held the ignorant and erroneous belief that women who love other women want to be men, found themselves temporarily trapped in the belief that they were transsexuals. In both of the cases where this occurred, the desire for a sex change was partially or entirely ameliorated by the adoption of a lesbian identity.

Those women who thought of lesbian women as "mannish women" were able to find some solace in a lesbian identity. For them, being lesbian allowed them to integrate their masculinity into an identity which bestowed upon them the title of mannish *woman*. But for many, the identity of lesbian was still not completely satisfactory, because of the myth that lesbians are somehow not "real" women. Those women who were able to find their way into a lesbian community were pleased to discover that lesbians were not only masculine women but every other kind of women as well. Thus, lesbianism in isolation did not alleviate the gender role strain felt by these women, but a lesbian identity in a lesbian community proved to be very helpful in this regard.

The sexuality of these fifteen women was a logical outgrowth of their upbringings within a society dominated by a patriarchal gender schema. They built their sexuality upon their identities as active and often dominant people. At the same time, they shaped them according to the definitions made available to them by the dominant gender schema. Thus, their gender role development prescribed the themes that would prevail in their sexuality, and the dominant gender schema proscribed the sexual options available to them for the expression of those themes. The choices they made within these frameworks then reflected back, filtered through the responses that others made to their behaviors, and through their own personal interpretations of the dogma of the dominant gender schema, to either bolster or undermine their gender identities.

In the process of finding a sexuality that they felt reflected their self-identities, these women could not ignore the expectations of the people among whom they lived. They had to find ways to achieve harmony between their "I's" and their "me's" without offending their sense of priorities as symbolized in their generalized and significant others. Each woman had to find a sexuality which conformed sufficiently well within the dominant gender schema that she and others could understand her to fit within a preexisting cognitive gender schema category. Each woman had to do so while still remaining true enough to her individual gender identity so as not to threaten her basic sense of self. Those women who had failed to successfully find this balance continued to have doubts about their core identities as females.

SUNNY

Living with Gender Blending

Who? What? Where? When? How?

Many women have had the experience of being mistaken for a boy or a man by a stranger. For most of them such misidentifications are rare and as such can easily be dismissed from their minds as simple careless observances. Infrequent but more regular incidents can have a cumulative effect, sensitizing the persons who are mistaken to the attentions they receive from strangers, but not necessarily working to undermine their gender-confidence. Frequent and persistent mistakes can cause the women who are mistaken to come to believe that the mistakes happen to them because of something aberrant in their own natures.

The gender blending women interviewed for this study had been mistaken for men or boys for a minimum of five years. Seven of the fifteen women reported that they had been mistaken for boys or men throughout their entire lifetimes, another six had been assumed to be male by strangers for ten years or more, and the remaining two women had been sufficiently gender blending to be mistaken for five and six years. Eight women said that they were first mistaken for boys before the age of twelve. Four of those eight said that the mistakes were intermittent during their youths, and the other four recalled that they were thought to be boys "all the time." All eight of the women who had been mistaken for boys during their youths had played male roles in their own fantasies or in the games that they played with other children. Three of these eight women were those who had seriously considered sex-change operations at some point in their lives, and the other five had all expressed definite desires to be boys while they were children.

Most of the women who had been mistaken for boys when they were children remembered taking little note of the incidences. Six of the girls who were mistaken for boys when they were young either said that they had not cared or that they were pleased and flattered by the errors, while only two remembered being disturbed by the mistakes. Three of the six women who were unperturbed by being thought boys were girls to whom it happened very frequently. One woman recalled:

> I dressed up like a boy and I know I didn't mind, and I think I might have been pleased, when people mistook me for a boy. . . . I didn't want to be identified as a girl. Boys just had it good. Girls tended to have to come in early, they were weaker (supposedly, we all know they're stronger, now that we've read up on it, but when I

was a kid I was told that girls were weaker). Girls didn't have muscles. . . . People called me son in stores and stuff. I felt good about it.

Her only parent was unconcerned about the "phase" she was going through and defended her right to appear as masculine as she pleased.

> The main story I remember because my grandmother was so upset. Somebody came up to her, she was calling me, and said, "Are you calling your little grandson? He just ran around the corner." Which wouldn't faze my mother, but my grandmother freaked out. "Dress her up! She'll be a homosexual!" My mother told my grandmother that it was just a phase, and not to bug me.

As it turned out, both her mother and her grandmother were wrong. It was not just a phase which she would grow out of, and she did not become a homosexual.

A second woman, who thought "a girl was a sissy and a boy was strong," remembered that her mother had to correct people when they complimented her on her "nice looking son." She said, "As a kid I got mistaken for a boy all the time and my mother used to have to turn around and say 'It's my daughter.' . . . I don't think it bothered me when I was little. I don't remember it bothering me. I don't think I liked it, it just was."

A third woman, who was mistaken for a boy "constantly, all the time" when she was a child, expressed similar sentiments:

> I just thought that if people would think I was a boy, that it probably happens to everyone. . . . It didn't matter because I really didn't know that there was a whole lot of difference between girls and boys. I didn't know that there was supposed to be— boys were better and girls were not. . . . When I was a little kid, it wasn't that much of a problem then. I was never aware of it being a problem when I was a little kid.

The three other women who shared this nonchalant attitude reported that they had only occasionally been mistaken for boys during their childhood.

Two women remembered being unhappy about being thought a boy when they went out into public places. One of these two women said that she began to be mistaken for a boy at about ten years of age, when she first cut her hair short. After her haircut, she said that she was mistaken "all the time." She had a best girl friend at the time who was also mistaken for a boy, and she remembered being angered by the mistakes when they happened to her friend. She got into fist fights, which she usually won, with both boys and girls who called her a boy.

> It bothered me a lot when it first started happening. I would say something, or my friends would say something, like, "I'm a woman" or "I'm a girl." I couldn't figure out why they would think I was a guy. I didn't have much of a chest then either, but neither did all my friends. May went through the same thing, my best friend, so it helped because we were the same way all the way up. She was always mistaken for a guy and so was I. So we would just joke about it and stuff like that. For the first while, yeah, I guess I was angry.

A few years later, this woman seriously considered the possibility of a sex-change operation, but she abandoned the idea in her late teens. By the time of her interview, she had come to take responsibility for other people's errors. She said at her interview, "It's not their fault."

The other woman who was displeased by being mistaken for a boy as a child, had a slightly different feeling about it. She sensed, from a young age, that her desire to become a boy was "bad." When others thought that she was a boy, or that she was acting very much like a boy, she felt that they had been able to see her "bad" wish to become a boy, and she felt chastised by their recognition of her transgression. She vividly remembered the pain she felt as a result of two such incidences.

> I got mistaken for a boy when I was little. I had some really crummy experiences. Want to hear them? Well, when I was in kindergarten we had to do self-portraits . . . but I didn't know what a self-portrait was and neither did anybody else, so the teacher said, "It's a picture of yourself, with your favorite clothes on." But that's what got me into trouble. So everyone else put on their crinoline party dresses in their pictures and I put on these brand new brown corduroy pants with the plaid flannel lining and this striped shirt that was brown and yellow. . . . and I got totally ridiculed by the entire class, by these stupid little five year olds. . . . I was the only girl in the self-portraits wearing pants.

The second incident happened when she was five years old. She was leaving church one Sunday dressed in her "church dress and white shoes and bonnet" when an elderly woman remarked, "Oh, here's the little one who should have been a boy!" She remembered her reaction to that comment: "I felt like a piece of shit! . . . I knew it wasn't right . . . I wanted to be a boy and once again it was as if it was being pointed out to me that, like, this was really bad news, that I'm a bad person for wanting to be a boy." At the time of her interview, she continued to take being mistaken for a man or a boy as "criticism," but she felt less responsible for provoking people to do so.

By the time these fifteen women who were to become adult gender blending females were in their teens, all but two of them had been mistaken for boys or men. Four of these thirteen women reported that the mistakes either first started or became more frequent between the ages of twelve and fourteen. Some women were mistaken on a daily basis, while others experienced mistakes only every few months. One of these women, who had been occasionally mistaken as a child, became emotionally disturbed at puberty, when her father, with whom she had been very close, rejected her. She came to think of herself as very ugly, and when other people began to mistake her for a man, she developed a strong desire to become one. She said, "I wanted to have a sex change partly because people thought I looked like a guy before I even tried to look like a guy. Like that's part of the reason I wanted a sex change." She went on to live as a man from the ages of eighteen to twenty-one, during which time everyone thought that she was a man.

Another woman, who began to be mistaken during her early teens, remem-

bered that people drove by her on the street and called out of their car
windows, "Are you a boy or a girl?" and that others stopped her on the street
to ask her the same question. She said that in her teens such incidents occurred
about once a month and that they made her feel "very uncomfortable" and
"angry" because she "couldn't figure out what was going on." A third woman,
who had been occasionally mistaken as a child, recalled that the mistakes
became more frequent as she passed puberty. In her teens she said that she was
mistaken for a boy approximately once a month, most often by shopkeepers.
She felt especially embarrassed when her friends witnessed the error:

> I was with some friends. I was a teenager . . . we went into this store and the
> shopkeeper—it's always the stupid shopkeepers, they see thousands of people in a
> week, you'd think they could figure it out! So this woman in the store thought I was
> a boy . . . and I was so embarrassed in front of my friends. . . . I thought my friends
> would judge me. . . . Probably I felt responsible, because I liked girls.

She was the same woman who had felt humiliated because she had always
thought that her boyishness was "bad," and as a teen she felt that her
attraction for other girls was likewise bad. She interpreted the mistakes as her
"badness" leaking out so that others could see it.

A fourth woman, who had also been occasionally mistaken for a boy in her
youth, recalled that her career as a gender blender escalated in her early teens.
She had never felt that she really belonged in her family or in her society, and
her increasing gender attribution problems only contributed further to her
sense of being misplaced. She told a story about being detained for several
hours at a border crossing because the officials were confused by the photo-
graph in her passport. This experience made a deep impression on a twelve
year old girl.

> When I was twelve would've been when it actually started, because I used to have
> long hair. And I had my hair cut when I was twelve and I had it cut really short.
> That was the style at the time. I wasn't being unusual. . . . I went to get my haircut
> from school and it was compulsory uniform and so I had my shirt and tie and
> sweater on. . . . I had my hair cut and went straight from the hairdresser down to
> have my passport photograph taken.
>
> The first time I went across the border was when I was twelve with this passport,
> with this passport photograph in it. I ended up going across with my older sister.
> And I had no problems getting into the country, but coming out what happens is
> that they have like these pill boxes and it's a railway station and they have this long
> line and you have to put your passport in like this little letter box and you have to
> walk down to the end and get your passport out. We were there hours and neither
> one of us could speak the language. And eventually we went and found this woman
> who could speak it who went and took us to an official. Then we went into this
> official-looking room and we had to wait. And somebody came in to speak to us. It
> turned out that when they were looking at me they could tell that I was a woman
> but on my passport I looked like a man or a boy and they had been making all these
> enquiries to find out exactly what I was, and if I was me.

Neither she, nor her older sister, nor the immigration officials found the episode amusing. The woman speculated about her feelings at the time: "I was probably pissed off. I used to get really angry about it in those days. I think that helped with that whole solitary feeling that I had in those days. It helped with feeling so different." As she grew into an adult, such mistakes became so frequent in her life that she came to expect to be mistaken for a man as often as she dealt with people whom she had never met before.

Three women were first mistaken for men or boys, or started to be mistaken more often, while in their later teens. One of these women began to be mistaken around the age of eighteen and had been experiencing mistakes for about six years at the time of her interview. She seemed to be relatively unfazed by the mistakes, which happened to her only once every few months and which were self-corrected so rapidly that they made little lasting impression on her. Another of these three women said that she also first began to be addressed as a man or a boy around the age of eighteen. For her too, the mistakes were infrequent at that time, and they made little impression on her until some years later when they greatly increased in frequency.

The third woman was first mistaken for a young man when she was eighteen years old and living away from home for the first time. She had recently cut her hair short and was experimenting in front of a mirror with different ways of combing it. When she realized that a particular style made her look very masculine, she decided to see how far she could go with it.

> The first time that I realized that I could pass was when I was living . . . in a rooming house near the university. And it was pretty much the first I'd been off for any length of time where no one would know if I ever disappeared. So I was a bit concerned about walking around on the streets at nights. . . .
>
> I had a jacket that could've looked like a leather jacket, and I had short hair. And I put the jacket on and I sort of greased my hair back and put my hands in my pockets and I really startled myself because I looked like such a young punk. . . . I really looked like a guy. . . . It worked. Nobody hassled me. . . . I thought it was a great joke. I was really chuckling away to myself. And also I thought I felt a lot of freedom. This was great. I could pass. I didn't have to worry about it.
>
> I used it to my benefit, . . . I would take longer steps and hunch my shoulders up. . . . Once I decided that it would work I put on this "I'm not afraid" business and took big steps. You know there's a posture that you use to show that you're casual in the situation, and that's what I did.

She made use of her new discovery whenever she needed to go out onto the streets at night where she felt that she might be in some danger if she were perceived to be a woman alone. Later, what had begun as a consciously manipulated protective device became unconsciously habitual behavior. She then found that she was thought to be a man far more often than she wished to be.

Four women who had been mistaken for boys when they were children continued to be mistaken for boys while they were teenagers. One of them, who had been mistaken for a boy or a man about once a month all her life, said that in her teens her favorite clothing were army fatigues and that she was often mistaken when dressed that way. The other three women had been mistaken for men or boys more often than not for their whole lives. Two women said that as teens they had experienced problems with authority figures as a result of their mixed gender role behavior. One woman and her best friend sometimes had difficulties in high school when they first encountered a new teacher in a classroom.

> I had one teacher who looked at the name and then looked at me and then looked at the book three times, right? And then she started to get really embarrassed. You could just see it on her face. And then she apologized later, she just said, "I'm really sorry." She was really red and everything. . . . It would just be like a new teacher or something and they would always get embarrassed, and so we'd get embarrassed because they got embarrassed. And it wasn't anger any more. It happened all the time. We just got used to it.

The same woman also told a story about being stopped by the police and almost arrested for using false identification because the officer did not believe that the teenager standing before her was the young woman she claimed to be.

> There was this one policewoman in town, she's about six foot six inches, just huge, and a lot of people were afraid of her, but I wasn't. We crusied up and down the main drag in town all the time. We got pulled over and she asked for my ID. And she said, "I think I'll have to take you down to the cop station." And I said, "Is there a problem?" She said, "Well, I don't believe that this is your ID, you're using false ID." And I kind of stepped out of the car and she said, "Why are you using a female's ID when you're a male?" And I said, "Ah ha! Who'd be stupid enough, if they're the opposite, like for me to have a female's ID, for a male to have a female's ID?" So she said, "Either you take off your jacket or you come down to the police station." So I didn't want to go down to the police station, all I needed was for my parents to find out, so I took off my jacket.
> She kind of felt a little embarrassed and then she said, she made some comment like she wasn't going to be wrong about me thinking she was wrong about the whole thing. Like, you know, you should dress like a woman or something. Yeah, it was my fault, not hers. So she kind of just walked away.

The other woman who had been mistaken by a police officer told this story: "I got pulled over by the police one time and they wanted to search us. And there was three girls and myself. And I refused. I wouldn't let him and he said, 'What's the matter son? You got no guts?' And he pushed me up and my jacket opened and he saw my breasts. He said, 'Sorry' kind of thing and let us go. It shook him." Such mistakes continued to be daily occurrences in both of these women's lives to the time of their interviews. As a result, they had become so accustomed to being mistaken for men or boys that they were surprised when strangers correctly recognized them as females.

These two women also found that their masculine appearance made them attractive to other girls in their high schools. One said that when she met new girls at school, they would often assume that she was a boy and remark to the person who had introduced them that she was "cute." When corrected, the girls who had made the mistakes would often "stay away from me for a while and then I'd become friends with them later." The other woman told a similar story:

> One woman followed me around for a week because she thought I was a boy. It was a student and she wanted me to ask her out on a date. Then she would walk by me and look at me and I finally turned around and I said something. She went, "You're a girl!" I said, "Yes." And she was horrified. We became friends after that. She really had to question herself. She was shocked that she thought a woman could be so attractive.

Both of these women began to have lesbian relationships while still in their teens, although one of them also became engaged to be married. It seems likely that the kind of attention that they received from other girls contributed both to their willingness to experiment with lesbian relationships and to the entrenchment of their masculine self-images as the type of people who females find sexually attractive.

Their teen years were a period of rapid physical and emotional growth. Adolescence brought with it a searching for identity. As children transforming themselves into adults, they had to learn and become adept at the gender roles expected of adult women and men. They judged their successes and failures by their reflections in the eyes of others, and they likewise sensed what was expected of them on the basis of feedback they received from others. The tendencies toward masculinity in the gender role behaviors and gender identities of these gender blending teens were further consolidated by the messages they received from people's responses to them during this sensitive, high-growth period.

Six of the women interviewed said that they first began to be mistaken for men, or that the frequency of the mistakes increased, in their early twenties. All of these six women reported that they were mistaken for men or boys several times each week, and two of them were mistaken for a man or a boy more often than they were recognized, by strangers, as women. All six linked the mistakes to the time when they first cut their hair short. For all six of them, the decision to cut off their long hair was related to their sexual choices. For the heterosexual women, the decision to cut their hair was a rejection of a symbol of the feminine passivity that had allowed them to be hurt in their emotional relationships with men. For the lesbian women among these six, the cutting of their previously long hair was also symbolic. In their cases, it was a gesture claiming membership in a lesbian community.

Both of the two heterosexual women, among the six for whom the mistakes either began or increased during their early adulthood, tied the incidents to unhappy experiences in their love lives. One was the woman who had been beaten and raped by her husband. She cut off her hair and entered her "male phase" shortly after she left him. She said, "It started back when I started being assertive, OK? All the time I was unassertive, I would fit like the feminine type. But as soon as I was assertive I became 'Sir,' a man, to the people around." The other heterosexual woman said that people mistook her for a boy or a man far more often after she cut her hair short in her early twenties. She thought that her disappointment in a relationship which had just ended might have prompted her to make a dramatic change.

> I guess I did it in my senior year or just after I graduated. I also had a heartbreaking love affair. I don't know if that's related. It might have been. I fell madly in love with this fool from Winnipeg and tried to convince him to come out here, which he wouldn't do. So I decided I would go to Winnipeg, and I sold my beautiful '56 Chev and—what a fool! No man is worth a '56 Chev!—and went to Winnipeg. . . . And that didn't work out, so I came back. . . . I felt very in limbo and I think I might have been just trying to startle myself or make a change.

After she cut her hair she went from being mistaken for a boy or a man approximately once a month to being mistaken more than once a week. At the time of her interview she was mistaken often enough that she expected to be mistaken at least once on any day in which she had to deal with strangers in public places.

Three other women reported that the increases in the frequency of their being mistaken for boys or men coincided closely with their cutting their hair when they became active as lesbians. A fourth woman said that, although she had been occasionally mistaken for a man during seven or eight of the years that she had been lesbian, it was not until she found a community of lesbian-feminists and cut her hair that the mistakes increased to the point where they became a daily problem for her. Each of these woman found that although she had, at most, been mistaken for a boy or a man a few times a year before her hair cut, when she cut her hair short the mistakes increased to at least "a few times a week."

Most of the errors which occurred were simple and not very colorful. Clerks in stores and servers in restaurants were the most likely persons to mistake these women for boys or men. Usually, they simply were addressed as "Sir." In some cases, the persons who made the mistakes realized their error on their own and embarrassedly apologized. In some cases the women corrected them, and in others the mistakes were allowed to stand uncorrected. Sometimes the persons in error responded with some hostility to the women who looked so masculine to them. Sometimes, only the gender blending woman ever knew that a mistake had happened at all.

One woman said of the mistakes by clerks and servers that "there's really no story that goes along with it." She felt that mistakes of that sort were just commonplace events in her life as a gender blender.

> It's just when you go to buy something from a store and they say "Yes sir?" Or taking someone out for dinner and they think that you're the boy and you're taking a girl out for dinner, and so that's really embarrassing. The manner in which they kind of treat you. They'll take the woman's coat, that you're with, right? And they'll pull out her seat and seat her, and you'd have to seat yourself. And then they'll, there's this kind of catering sometimes to women, and I just sit there. And at

the end of it, they'll turn to you and say, "Are you ready to order sir?" And I'll say, "Sure." I don't know the right line to use on those occasions.

She reported that in most such instances, the clerks and servers who dealt with her never did figure out that they had made a mistake.

The gender blending females in this study had many masculine interests. One result of those interests was that they often were in places, and doing things, where men were more commonly found. Clerks who had to deal with them in those situations were often accustomed to finding men in front of them. The clerks' habituations may have contributed to their overlooking of gender cues which were not in alignment with their expectations. One woman's story of her interchange with a clerk in a hardware store was typical of many women's tales.

> I went to this hardware store. And I was working doing cabinet making, so I had my jeans on and my leather apron and my work shirt. . . . And I walked in and the guy said "Yes, sir?" and I said "It's madam actually." And he said "Oh, I'm sorry, you can't tell these days." And I said "Well you could probably tell if you looked. The problem with you salespeople is that you don't care who's here buying things off you providing they put their money on the counter." He was really apologetic and I was really angry.

The clerk in that store was probably more attentive to gender details for a period of time after such an interchange because one woman, on one occasion, took the time to make an issue of his inattentiveness. Many of the women interviewed, however, said that they usually did not take the time to bother to correct such mistakes.

Some gender blending females had problems when they had to produce identification in order to secure services to which they were entitled. Only the women with the most masculine appearances had problems in this regard. Other, less masculine, women were usually mistaken for only a few moments at the beginning of an exchange. Thus, the clerks who controlled access to the services they desired would usually have discerned that they were dealing with a masculine woman by the time identification had to be produced. Identification was therefore only a problem when clerks were still under the impression that they were dealing with a man or a boy when it came time to examine the woman's identification. In some cases, the misunderstandings were quickly cleared up, as in this woman's story: "Common incidents would be like cashing a check and they'd ask for my ID, and they'd say 'This isn't your ID. This is a girl's ID.' . . . My voice would rise in shock and I'd squeak out 'This is indeed my ID!' And they would agree. . . . They'd get embarrassed." Sometimes it took a little longer to clear the confusion, as is illustrated in this woman's story about a problem she had in a bank.

> Like at the bank just yesterday. I went down to the bank, my green card says Miss on it and the clerk said, "There must be a problem with this." And I says, "Is there a problem?" And she calls the manager over and she starts in on about this. I didn't

hear this, but I guess she said, "This young man has Miss on his card." And I said, "Is there a problem?" And she said "Well, this Miss shouldn't be here." And I said, "Why not?" She said, "Why do you have Miss on here?" And I said, "That's because I'm a woman." And she kind of just stood there for a second. And I said, "Would you like to see some more ID?" And she says, "No, that's fine." She gives me my money and that was it.

The story another woman told about the time she tried to collect welfare in Toronto was more disturbing. The government employees who were in charge that evening told her that they could only give her lodgings for the night in a shelter for single men. When she protested that she was a woman and produced her identification to prove it, they would not believe that the identification was hers. She was thus denied access to the welfare services that she needed at the time.

Many women spoke of incidents in which their vocational choices contributed to their being mistaken for men or boys. In some cases, the women merely worked in occupations which were usually populated by men. In those cases, the people they came into contact with expected a male to be doing their job, and the masculinity of the gender blending female was sufficient to cause casual observers to see a man under those circumstances. In other instances, the women were either doing jobs that required them to wear a uniform or work clothing which somewhat obscured indicators of their femaleness.

Two women said that, although they were mistaken for men or boys at various times, they were mistaken more often when they were in uniform or work clothes. Another woman talked about using her masculine appearance as a ruse to get hired at jobs where she believed that she would not have been hired if the employer had known that she was a woman at the time of her original job interview. One woman, who worked servicing electrical hand tools and light industrial machinery, found that the combination of her occupation and her facial hair provided such strong indicators of masculinity to most observers that she was rarely recognized as female on the job site.

> I started to be in a situation where they were expecting a boy and because I wasn't blantantly obvious as a girl, sometimes they would continue to expect that I was a boy. Except that I did wear just T-shirts and no bra so sometimes they could tell I was a girl. But I'd be in situations where I'd be delivering some piece of equipment to a construction site, and in that case I would think that it was best that they didn't notice that I was a girl and I wouldn't point it out. . . . It started to be more often than not. . . . By the time I started working in the small engine shop, I wore a shop coat. By that time I had more facial hair. I had a mustache for sure. And even though I had my name on my shop coat, their first response was to think I was a guy.

Another woman recalled that one of her earlier experiences with being mistaken for a young man was when she was working as a gas station attendant.

> Once when I was pumping gas . . . I was wearing GI pants and no bra (I have 34B breasts) and a T-shirt. It was fairly apparent. I mean bouncing around there filling

this guy's car. And so this guy came in to use the phone and he was talking to me, "May I use your phone?" "Yes, it's right here." And he says, "So, where are we?" and I say, "We're at the corner of such and such and you get there this way." "Well, this fellow says . . ." And I'm going, "Woman!" And he didn't hear me, and then he asked me another question, "Well, he says . . ." I was standing there going, standing right in front of him with my chest at his eyes. He never figured it out. You know, I worked in a garage, therefore I was a boy. And it didn't matter how many breasts I had. I was still a young boy. Maybe if I'd had a pink bow, he probably would've thought I was gay.

A few years later when this same woman was working as a rock musician, she found that the androgyny then in vogue among male rock performers worked against her in a similar way. She was annoyed that even though she wore makeup and ostentatious clothing, she was still thought to be a male musician by some members of her audiences.

It became a big deal when I was working at gigs, all the time, all the fucking time! I'd get people dance by and talk to themselves as to what sex I am. People will walk up to me on stage and say, "Excuse me," and I'd say, "Yes?" expecting "Can you play Bobbi McGee?" And they'd say, "Are you a boy or a girl?" And I'm sitting down on my break, and somebody comes up and says, "Listen, I have a bet with my friends over there. You're a girl, aren't you?" I'm sitting there with makeup on my face and, I don't know, I don't see that it should matter. But at first, I was amazed at their stupidity. I was playing fairly sleazy gigs, at first I thought, "Well, maybe these people are drunk, or brain damaged." . . . And then I got, I quit being amazed, and started being amused. And then I quit being amused and started being really pissed off. And now I'm still there. I get angry.

As experiences of this type became more and more frequent in the lives of these women, or as they continued to happen over a number of years and in a variety of circumstances, the women found it increasingly difficult to slough them off as meaningless annoyances.

The single most common and repeatedly mentioned venue where these gender blending females had difficulty with their gender status was in public washrooms. Many women reported that it was not unusual for them to be directed to the men's room when they asked where the toilet was in a public place, and occasionally they would be told the direction to both the women's and the men's rooms by people who were unsure where it would be appropriate to direct them.

Nine women also specifically mentioned that their right to use women's washroom or changeroom facilities had been challenged by other women. Each of these women was hurt and humiliated by these rejections by other women. In some cases, the women actually felt themselves to be in danger of being physically accosted by offended women; in others they were threatened with action by security personnel or the police. Most commonly, other women using the facilities just looked at a gender blending woman in a curious way. One woman's story was typical of many: "I've sort of come out of washrooms at the same time as women have been going in, and they stop and look at the sign on the door. And I'll say 'Yeah, it's the right place,' or something like that." Sometimes other women challenged their use of public lavatories. One woman, who had a low-pitched speaking voice, remembered the first time that ever happened to her. She was entering the women's washroom when another patron told her that "the gentlemen's is next door." She described her reaction to that pronouncement:

> Embarrassment. My stammer came back. Everything. I said I wasn't a man. She said, "Well, you certainly sound like a man and look like a man!" She just kept it up, with all the other people in the washroom just looking at me. I left without pissing. There was so many of them and I just couldn't deal with it. I mean it was hard to leave too because that was losing face, but, I don't know. I just couldn't. I didn't know what to do. I felt horrible, like a creep.

Other women found that their welcome was even less cordial. One woman said that she had so much difficulty in women's washrooms that she tried using men's rooms to see if she fared any better there. She reported that she had never been challenged or even noticed in men's lavatories, but she related the following about her experiences in women's washrooms.

> I've been chased out of washrooms. Old ladies with umbrellas, a cleaning lady with a broomstick. Like I don't have a chance. I walk in there, and all of a sudden—a couple of times they just banged me on the head. And I'd go running. . . . They actually hit me on the head. No questions asked. Wham! Then I'm out of there and they go on and on. Like one of the old ladies who chased me out with an umbrella, she going up and down saying boys aren't supposed to be in women's washrooms. I didn't have a chance to say anything.
>
> The only time it made me angry was one time I walked in with shorts and a T-shirt. And somebody said, "Don't you realize you're in the wrong washroom?" I looked at the door and said, "This is the ladies' washroom." And they looked at me and I said, "I think I'm in the right washroom." I walked into the washroom. And then I got angry because I thought, "I'm wearing shorts and a T-shirt, what do they want me to do?"

In one woman's case, what they wanted her to do was to supply them with tangible anatomical evidence that she was in fact female. The woman with the deep voice found herself face to face with male security officers one time when she refused to vacate a women's washroom. She had just checked her luggage through at the airport, had smoked some marijuana, and had gone to use the toilet before boarding her flight. She almost did not make it on board her aircraft before departure time.

> Part of the story was that I was stoned, which sort of explains some of my actions. . . . I was walking into the washroom and a woman was just coming out and she said, "Oh, you've got the wrong washroom, this is the ladies.' " So I was really charming and said, "No, it's true I don't look very ladylike, but I was dressed pretty comfortable for traveling," and then I walked by her. I went into the next stall . . .

and went to piss. . . . I was in the cubicle but I was in there a long time. I thought, "Oh good, they're gone." I heard some voices again and then I was just about to come out, with my hand on the latch, and I heard this male voice right outside of the door saying, "Come out of there please." And I open the door and there's these two guys in uniform. Airport security police. "These woman have complained and you'll have to come with us." At first I thought it was about dope. But then when he said that, I said, "I haven't made a mistake, They've made a mistake. I'm in the right washroom. I am a woman." And they didn't believe me. I mean they obviously don't believe me. "Come on. Come on." I'm without my ID. I start rummaging in my bag but I couldn't find it. No ID. "I think you should just come with us." By then I was thinking . . . I just wanted to get on my plane. I had a shirt over my T-shirt. So I undid the outside shirt and opened it up. And I pulled down my T-shirt and stuck my breasts in their fat faces. So I stuck my breasts in their fat faces and then he just went "Oh, that's alright, she's not a man." No apologies, nothing! And the women all just went about their business. They didn't apologize or nothing.

I felt freaked out. I felt totally freaked out. I felt like I wanted to cry and I wanted to scream. Except that I was too freaked out. I got as far as "you fuckers" to these women, and then my voice, I mean I knew I was going to cry and I wanted to lambaste them. I got on the plane and I was just freaked out. I was just thinking, "I can't go on like this any more."

The embarrassment and humiliation had become overwhelming for her that day. She, like others of these women, wished to spare herself from further episodes of this sort but felt at a loss as to how to accomplish that relief.

Seven women disconcertingly found that their particular balance of gender characteristics was such that strangers would think them effeminate men, or men who were trying to pass as women. The women who experienced these misidentifications found them particularly frustrating because they felt that their efforts to appear as women must be hopelessly inept and useless if they only resulted in them appearing to be gay men, transvestites, or transsexuals.

Two women reported that when they wore dresses, makeup, and jewelry, people thought that they were transvestite men wearing women's clothing. One of these two women was exceptionally tall, and the other was of moderate height but muscular. Both of these women concluded that their being mistaken was due to their physical attributes. The woman who had lived as a man for three years found that after she had resumed living as a woman, people made comments questioning her femaleness when she was in public places. She said that there was a rumor going around the small suburban community where she worked as a housekeeper that she was a male-to-female transsexual. One day when she was buying groceries, she said that she heard one elderly woman say to another, "We know that she used to be a boy but we don't know who she used to be, what her name used to be." She complained of hearing people making similar comments about her when she went to the beach in the summertime, and at her local pharmacy. She found these mistakes ironic and daunting, considering that in the past she had wanted very much to be a man and that at the time of these mistakes she had finally accepted that she was, and would remain, female.

More commonly, lesbian women who frequented establishments which catered to both gay men and lesbians found that gay men mistook them for one of their own. Five women reported that gay men "come on" to them either on the streets or in gay bars. The women said that most of the time they just made no response to the men's inviting looks and the incidents ended there. In some instances the misunderstandings went on a little longer. One woman told this "hilarious story."

> I was in a gay bar last summer. I was visiting my family and I knew there was a club there so I stopped in to have a drink one night because I wanted to take a look at it. I was sitting and writing in my journal in this bar and I just wanted to have a drink and look around and then go home. And this man came by and he noticed that the cigarettes I smoke are Chinese cigarettes and he said, "Oh, these are Chinese, aren't they?" And I said, "Yes." And he said, "I spend lots of time in the Far East." And so, we sort of talked for a bit while he was standing there and then he said, "Do you mind if I join you?" And I said, "No go right ahead. Have a seat." So he sat down and we were talking for about five minutes longer and he said, "Oh, by the way, my name is George." And I said, "My name is Margaret." And he said, "Well, that's a first one for me." And I looked at him and I said, "Well, what do you mean?" He said, "Well, I've never met a man before whose name is Margaret." And I said, "But I'm not a man!" And he said, "Oh, but you're very masculine." I said, "On the contrary, I really disagree with you and I think that you're very rude." And I left.

Another woman had a whole evening of similar experience not long before the time of her interview. She said that such incidents left her feeling "agitated" and that she finds them "bothersome" especially when they continue in a seemingly endless run as they did on this particular evening.

> Like there was this one bar in particular I walked into and these men thought that I was a cute little boy, right? And they asked me to go to this other bar across the street. I was working for Gayblevision and I was putting up posters and I was on my way over there any ways, and I was with my girlfriend. So we went over there and they sat me down and they said, "You could've been the prettiest boy," and they kept bringing their friends over and introducing me, and saying, "Don't you think she could've been a pretty boy?" So, I thought, "I have to leave." So, I went upstairs and there was this woman sitting up there and I stopped and I was talking to her and I could see out of the corner of my eye, I could see this man. He was looking at me and I thought, "Oh, no. Like here it comes." And he swished over and he wrapped his arm around me, and he touched my breast. And it was like his hand caught on fire! And he ran away, but he came back and he says, "I'm really sorry. I thought you were this guy I picked up last week." And I said, "Oh yeah. Sure. Tell me another story." I'd just about had enough.
> That's when the waiter came over and he says, he used some kind of name to talk to me, specifically, like "sport" or something. And he had this rip in the bottom of his pants. And he wanted me to feel through. And I said, "Hey, look. This has really been fun but I can't do this." Right? And he says, "No, it's a lot of fun!" Right? And I said, I had to stop and explain to him that I was really a woman but it still didn't matter to him. He was wearing an athletic supporter and he wanted every-

body to know it. His boyfriend came over and gave him hell because I was a woman. He had realized I guess. The whole night, men had thought I was a man.

She left at the end of that night feeling extremely harassed by an excess of unwanted attention erroneously directed at her in the mistaken impression that she was someone who she wasn't. She was disturbed because she felt that it meant "a kind of lack of identity. People weren't really looking at me and seeing me. They were seeing something else. . . . How dare somebody outside not notice who I really am?"

By the time these women had reached adulthood they had each had to accept that being mistaken for a boy or a man was a part of their lives. Their experience of such mistakes ranged from occasional fleeting errors made at a glance, to interchanges lasting an hour or more. For two women, the inconvenience they experienced was minor and so had little effect on their identities as women and as females. For the others, the persistence or the frequency of the errors demanded of them that they make some adjustments either in how they presented themselves in public, or in how they saw themselves. The thirteen women for whom being mistaken for a boy or a man was frequent and persistent were faced with a conflict between their personal senses of themselves as women and the public's vision of them as men or boys. They had to find resolutions to their "I/me" conflicts.

Individual Solutions

All of the fifteen women who participated in this study were mistaken for men or boys often enough to have claimed those mistakes as a regular feature of their lives. They had to find ways to live as comfortably as possible with the fact that some people, some of the time, thought that they were men. As the frequency of the mistakes varied over the years that they experienced them, and the number of years that they continued to persist accumulated, their individual response to the errors also varied.

The techniques that they used to deal with the mistakes fell into two broad categories. On the one hand, it was necessary for these women to find ways of dealing with the persons who mistook their gender. On the other, they had to rationalize, in their own minds, the reasons for the errors in ways that left their self-esteem as intact as possible. The simplest and least emotionally demanding strategy for dealing with the situations in which the mistakes occurred was an entirely passive one. In many instances, the women who were mistaken for men or boys merely continued about their business, making no efforts to correct the mistakes. Either of two outcomes resulted from such a strategy. In some instances, the persons who had made the misidentifications recognized their errors and made apologies or other comments indicating that they had realized their mistakes. At other times, the exchanges in which the mistakes occurred continued to completion with the mistake remaining uncorrected and unacknowledged.

A second approach used by many women was to correct persons who mistook them for boys or men. This method, of course, was unnecessary in those instances where a mistake was recognized spontaneously by the person who made it. Those women who used this technique sometimes gently corrected strangers' errors; at other times, they were aggressive and hostile in their confrontations. Although a gentle correction was no guarantee of a friendly response, neither was aggression sure to elicit negativity in return.

Most of the women in this study found that the frequency of their being mistaken for men or boys fluctuated over the years. Six women said that the mistakes happened often enough in their lives that they had come to expect to be thought to be a man or a boy whenever they met new people. Thus, nine of these women found that they were generally unable to predict when and where the mistakes would occur, or how members of the public would respond to them in situations where it became known that a mistake had occurred.

Six of the fifteen women interviewed said that people who mistook them for boys or men sometimes, or often, figured out by themselves that they had made a mistake. Usually they quickly recognized their mistake upon hearing a woman's voice, or by looking directly at the person they were dealing with. The reactions of the people who had made the mistakes were most often apologetic, which sometimes proved to be more of an inconvenience than the mistakes themselves had been.

Three women specifically complained that the commotion that people made when they realized their mistakes was more embarrassing to them than the mistakes were. One woman said, "To the extent that it bugged me, it bugged me because it mattered to them." Another felt that the people who made the mistakes only made themselves look more foolish by their exaggerated apologies: "They'd get really flustered, and they would blush, and they would stutter, and they would apologize, which I found stranger than them actually mistaking me for a man. I didn't think it was such a big deal. They'd created more fuss with their apology than they ever did by saying, 'What can I do for your, Sir?' " A third woman, who was well over six feet tall, felt sorry for the people who mistook her for a man and tried to minimize the discomfort of the people who made the mistakes: "I usually make a joke of it . . . I think it's probably more embarrassing for them because they probably think they've done something very drastic. I mean, they're insulting my femininity, or they're doing something very heavy which really doesn't bother me." When the mistakes were infrequent and apologies were immediately forthcoming without the women themselves having to correct people, the gender blending females were able to believe that the mistakes were the result of other people's inattentiveness or ignorance, or both.

More commonly, the women had to point out that a mistake had happened, or the situation passed without the strangers ever knowing that they had interacted with a woman. Nine of the women said that they had gone through periods wherein they rarely pointed out that mistakes had occurred. Five women said that they regularly corrected people, and one woman said that people always figured out for themselves without her having to interject any information about her gender. Those women who said that they rarely corrected people who mistook them for boys all arrived at that position after having first gone through periods during which others recognized their mistakes, or during which they experimented with pointing out to people that they had misidentified them as men or boys. The experiences they had when correcting people convinced them that it was easier and less painful for them to let the mistakes pass unnoticed by anyone but themselves.

The nine women who rarely corrected people's mistakes about their gender repeatedly had unpleasant experiences with being mistaken for men or boys. The sum of those experiences convinced each of them that if she could not be immediately obvious as a woman, it was more advantageous to her to be a man throughout whatever interaction she was to engage in with a mistaken stranger. Three women described stages that they had gone through in the process of deciding how to respond to being mistaken for boys or men. At first they were "amused" or "amazed" when they had no idea why this was happening to them. During that time they generally corrected people's mistakes. Then they began to feel somehow responsible for the mistakes as they persisted and became more frequent. During that phase they most often corrected people and felt some embarrassment about the mistakes. Eventually the whole thing became "tedious" for them, and they finally became angry that this happened to them. In this final stage, they stopped correcting people and found that "passing" for men or boys was the path of least resistance. One woman, speaking from the last stage, said, "I'm not embarrassed so much any more. It gets to be bothersome because I keep having to explain to people about, 'Oh, yes. I do look like a boy. I am not.' And then proving it. People asking me to prove it, which I think is really disgusting." Another woman, who said she was mistaken for a man or a boy "pretty much every time I go out . . . practically every day . . . just about any time I meet somebody who didn't know me or who I was," described her reasons for not correcting people this way:

> Usually I don't say anything . . . because it happened so many times that if I said something every time it would bother me a lot. . . . The guy is just somebody who's trying to sell me something. There's no sense in carrying on a big conversation right there. He's just going to say I'm sorry and walk away. . . . If I constantly corrected people, I wouldn't want to go out any more. It would just be annoying for me.

Apparently, she was less annoyed by being thought a man than by being forced to engage in a somewhat intimate conversation about her gender with a complete stranger with whom she merely wanted to have a simple impersonal transaction. In certain circumstances, she said that she left people uncorrected because she felt some compassion for the predicament of those who mistook her for a boy or a man. She tried to save them the embarrassment of exposing their misjudgment.

I don't know what to say. You talk to somebody for an hour, and I don't want to get them angry, I don't want to hurt them. It's just that I'm a woman. I'm not a guy. But I guess I have a hard time saying that sometimes. It depends who it is, I guess. I guess I'd hate to be in their shoes. Trying to put myself in their shoes, and I've been talking with them and thinking they're the opposite sex, and then they tell me. Like if I was talking to somebody and I thought they were a woman, or a guy, and all of a sudden it clicked that, "Oh, my god. They're the opposite sex!" What would I say, or how would I feel? And then I guess I don't want to put them in that position. I try to make it easier for them.

It's not their fault. I know that I don't dress in dresses and have curls in my hair, or whatever, wear makeup and stuff. So it's not their fault. Like the way I am carrying myself, and stuff, is how I feel comfortable. So I don't want them to feel really bad, put them on the spot, so I try to make it easier however I can.

She realized that she had chosen not to participate more fully in femininity and accepted that there were consequences which accompanied her choices.

A third woman went through a long and difficult process as the mistakes escalated while she increasingly allowed her facial hair to grow out. In the beginning,

it wasn't that regular, but it would surprise me when I would go to my own bank and they would say to me, "Yes, sir?" . . . My first response was that I didn't know who they were talking to. And then after I realized that they were talking to me, mostly I just thought, "How strange." . . . I didn't really start to take it on. I thought, "Well, you stupid asshole, what's the matter with you?" . . . Usually I was so nonplussed that I wouldn't even bother to correct them.

Later, when the mistakes became a regular part of her everyday life, she unhappily discovered that it was easier to be thought a man than a woman who looked like a man.

When it first started to happen regularly, like every day, I started to take it on. Like I was a freak, and I had to learn to live my life as a freak. Something that everybody could stare at whenever they wanted to, and comment about whenever they wanted to. . . . Well, if they thought I was a man from beginning to end, then I wasn't a freak. The freak was in the mistake. So I didn't correct them. I just sort of shrunk a little bit inside of myself, but I didn't correct them.

The effect that this realization and strategy had on this woman was debilitating. She became anxious about going out into public places, lest she be mistaken for a man again. She said that even when she got "dressed up real femme" she felt "really self-conscious, like I'm in a masquerade and nobody else is." The net effect was that even if she did not correct people and tell them that she was a woman, there were still times when she could not avoid feeling like "a freak."

There was quite a long time there when I wasn't regularly employed and I didn't go out of the house. Because the longer I would stay in, the easier it was to stay in. And

I just didn't want to deal with it. Sometimes I'd feel so fragile that I would feel that I couldn't cope with it if it would happen one more time, so I just wouldn't go out.

This series of mistakes, over and over again, has really altered the way I deal with the world. Some people just pass through in a lot of situations which cause me a great deal of anxiety. Like using the bathroom in a public place. I have been told lots of times I'm in the wrong place. I've also been washing my hands in the sink and seen somebody beside me staring at me in the mirror. Now, I think that's how you treat a freak.

A major complaint of all of these women was that they were not able to pass freely about their business in the world, unperturbed by other people's intrusions into their psychic privacy. They rightfully felt that they should be able to conduct themselves in public without being forced to discuss their gender, sex, or sexuality with clerks in stores, servers in restaurants, or passers-by on the streets. Five women reacted angrily to the mistakes and often confronted, with some hostility, the people who mistook them for boys or men. One of these women said that she found it insulting and rude when clerks in stores mistook her gender and that when this happened, she responded in kind.

If I'm in a bad mood and if it's a store, I'll make a rude comment and walk away without making whatever purchase I'm making and I'll just say something to the effect, "If you're not interested enough in me as a customer, to see me as an individual, then I don't need to buy this." And if I really need what I'm buying, or it's the only place I can get it, I'll just, I won't respond and I'll just pay them. And if I have to talk—when people take that second look, they definitely see that I'm female and they generally apologize. . . . Sometimes I think that people do it as a put down. But it's usually fairly subtle and I can't really come up with ten different incidents right now where I feel it's subtle.

I was in the Love Shop one day. A friend of mine was looking at all the toys, and one of the people who worked there came up, it was a man, and he said, "Yes sir, can I help you?" And I turned around and said, "Well, if you can't figure out what gender I am, how can you help me with my sexuality?" And he sort of sputtered and walked away. Well, I was quite huffy. I thought it was a pretty bizarre place for it to happen. . . . My sort of line is that if I'm rude to people, maybe they'll be a little more careful with the next person who doesn't fit a prescribed role.

Unfortunately, aggressively correcting people did not always achieve the desired results of being treated as a woman and sensitizing clerks and servers to recognize less feminine females as women. Another woman, who was out for a meal with a male companion, was addressed as "Sir" by the waitress. When she said to the woman "It's madam, actually," the waitress reacted as if she were "some kind of weird effeminate faggot," and the gender blending woman became embroiled in an argument with her male companion over the episode. A third woman preferred to use snappy one-liners. When people first mistook her gender and then realized their mistakes, she would respond to their exclamations of "Oh, you're a girl!" with retorts such as, "So what. Are you going to refuse to serve me?" or "Get your eyes checked four eyes!" She reported that this technique was usually successful at stymying any further discussion about her gender.

Each woman found her own ways of dealing with the problems she had with mistaken gender attributions, but none found a way to eliminate the difficulties entirely. For some women, an elusive satisfactory solution seemed to lie in making themselves readily visible as women. Others seemed to prefer to avoid problems by passing as men whenever they went out in public. Most ended up forced to some uneasy compromise by the conflict between their own personalities and preferences, on the one hand, and the expectations and assumptions of members of society, on the other.

Choosing Complicity

All of the women to whom these mistakes happened needed to make sense of these occurrences in ways that would allow them to retain secure senses of themselves as women, as females, and as "normal" people. In order to do so they had to see their own behavior as within the realm of social acceptability, and label the actions of the persons who mistook them for men or boys as aberrant. Basically, their logic took them through four steps. Firstly, many of them simply took the position that they were doing nothing out of the ordinary. They saw their behavior as within the range of normal and assumed that the errors occurred because other people failed to be sufficiently observant to recognize those feminine gender cues that they did present. They took the attitude that it was not their fault that the mistakes occurred and so they had no reason to either question themselves further or effect any change in their own appearances or behavior patterns. Secondly, they entered into a critique of femininity, often using feminist criticisms of femininity to justify their minimal femininity as a rational and progressive response to patriarchal oppression of women. Thirdly, they relied on this criticism of femininity to support their contentions that they had taken every reasonable step to make themselves obvious as women. They argued that if other people could not see that they were women based on the cues that they offered to the public, then that was because of failings in the social system which defined women so narrowly and unfairly. They claimed that it was impossible for them to become consistently recognizable as women without resorting to extreme and oppressive forms of femininity. Fourthly, all of these women found that their ambiguous gender status gave them certain privileges and freedoms which are normally available only to men in their society. In the final analysis, each of them had decided that she was willing to pay a price to gain those freedoms and privileges.

All of these fifteen gender blending females were left with the task of rationalizing why they had not taken the steps necessary to halt the mistakes once and for all. Each woman, when asked, was able to come up with reasons why she was mistaken for a boy or a man, but the women were also eager to offer reasons why the mistakes were due to circumstances beyond their control. They believed, as the dominant gender schema had taught them, that because they were female they were essentially and indisputably women. This left them with some confusion as to why these mistakes should happen to them, even though they recognized that they were, in some ways, not "distinctively feminine." One woman summed up this cognitive dilemma nicely:

> I couldn't understand why people were such jerks and why they couldn't see who I really was, and why they just naturally assumed that I was a boy. It never occurred to me that it was because of what I was wearing, or my hair style, because I thought a girl looks like a girl no matter how her hair is—Like her face, her features. And it's like still, now, when people do that, they don't really look at your face.

Armed with the belief that the physical fact of femaleness is both a necessary and sufficient condition for legitimate claim to womenhood, these women were able to cite many of their masculine characteristics at the same time as most of them were able to lay the blame for the errors squarely with the negligence of the people who failed to observe what they believed to be the indelible signs of their femaleness and hence, of their womanhood.

Eight women thought that the reason for their being mistaken for men or boys was partly because of their physical characteristics, which were socially defined as masculine. One woman said that she had "a face like a boy." Two others thought that their facial hair was a deciding factor. Another two cited their low-pitched speaking voices, and three women thought that the fact that they were either tall or big boned and muscular made people see them as men or boys. Five women said that they thought that the way they moved contributed to their gender being mistaken. Likewise, seven women suggested that self-confidence and self-esteem were dispositions that made them seem more like men in the eyes of others. Finally, all of the women interviewed said that they wore their hair in short simple style, only one woman wore makeup with any regularity, and all preferred to dress in what they considered to be gender "neutral" clothing. They seemed to believe that their neutral clothing was the same as many other women wore and thus should not cause them to be seen as men or boys, but three women correctly recognized that a "neutral" appearance does not necessarily translate into looking like a woman just because it is done by a female person. As one woman put it, "because I don't go through the antics to make that female, it becomes male by default."

These fifteen women, as adult members of society, were aware that if they were to increase the femininity of their appearances they would become less likely to be mistaken for boys or men. When asked what they had done, or would be willing to try, to cause them to be more consistently recognized as women, twelve of the fifteen women replied that they were willing to make few or no changes to themselves for that purpose. They justified their position by saying that they were happy being the way they were, other than the problem with their gender being misattributed; or that they had already gone as far as they thought was reasonable and that society was now at fault. The crucial assumption inherent in their stance was that increased femininity would be injurious to their self-esteem and inimical to their natures.

The gender blending women repeatedly said that they could not be comfortably themselves if they were to increase the femininity of their appearances. One woman said,

> I won't wear dresses and I won't wear makeup, or carry a purse and act more feminine. My boyfriend told me that's the reason I'm being bugged by people, and I know that it is, but I just refuse to do that. I wouldn't feel comfortable wearing a dress. I couldn't sit like I'm sitting now. Like you've got to walk a certain way. And makeup's such a bloody nuisance.

Another argued that if she were to change her appearance enough to be consistently known as a woman, she wouldn't be the same person any more: "If I was wearing a dress or if there was something different about me, people would know that I'm a woman. And that's why it bothers me, is that I would have to be different for someone to see that I'm a woman. They should just look. I don't think I look like a man." A third woman said, "I'm not stupid. I could wear a skirt if I wanted to. I'd be uncomfortable, but I could force myself. I've done it for periods of my life. . . . If you want to be part of the gang, you wear the appropriate costume. But the most important thing in my life is to be absolutely comfortable with myself." For her, that meant wearing "the kinds of clothes I wore as a kid . . . tomboy clothes." Still another woman simply said that she would not make any changes to herself in an effort to decrease the mistakes, "because to change it I would have to change me, and I feel like I like me the way I am."

Perhaps more telling were the comments about femininity made by eight of the fifteen women, which indicated that they felt that extreme femininity was an absurdity and that only extreme femininity could make them look like women in the eyes of strangers. One woman remarked that she thought that any woman was well rid of femininity, implying that femininity was tantamount to consensual sexism.

> I think that some of the things that are attributed to femininity are really a lot of shit. And so becoming more in control of my life, and putting forth my ideas, and looking people in the eye, and not apologizing for everything, when I don't really mean it, could be considered becoming more masculine, but I look on it as unlearning a lot of negative things. . . . The epitome of femininity to me is what drag queens pretend to be, and I find that really quite repulsive. Femininity to that extent isn't what real people are. It's all a big game. So why should I want to play that game?

Another woman was equally critical even of a degree of femininity that she was willing to participate in for special occasions, such as a night out at the opera.

> I really felt play acting. I think the gay movement's got the right word for it when they say "in drag." I mean to this day I will refer to, if I go to the opera in a dress, I

will say I'm going in drag. But it's neat, as long as you recognize it as a costume, it's fine.

You explain to me, objectively, how standing two inches above your natural heels' placement, how wearing things which constrain you, nylons which dig into your body, bras which harness you, and clothing which seems to fundamentally pull out at every layer, and then walk around as if your shoulders are two inches closer together than they actually are—how physically free is this? It is not! It is signs of oppression!

Unlike many of the people she and the other gender blending women met in their everyday lives, she was able to make a distinction between femininity and femaleness: "Instinctively, I would say that I'm not very feminine, because feminine means oppressed . . . but if you said to me. 'You're not very female,' I would deeply resent that. . . . I know that I am a woman. I have no desire to be a man." She rejected femininity but retained a strong identification with her femaleness and her womanhood despite the confusion that her appearance and manner sometimes caused other people.

Three other women also suggested that femininity was like being "in drag," but they were not as general in their characterization of femininity as masquerade. They expressed the opinion that if they were to attempt to eliminate being mistaken for men or boys from their lives, they would have to resort to an extreme form of femininity which would leave them feeling and looking foolish. One woman said that she was at a loss as to what to do: "I can't think of anything that isn't ridiculous. I also can't think of many things that would particularly work. . . . I suppose I could wear dresses, but then I think I would just look like a man dressed in drag." If her appraisal were correct, then wearing dresses, which would only change her from looking like an unremarkable man into looking like a man in a dress, would not be a solution for her. A second woman took a similar point to view: "I know a way to be called madame. If I dress up and put on high heels, or makeup, or things like that, they will call me madame. But I'm not going to be a transvestite to myself." The third woman, who was twenty-nine years old at the time of her interview, and whose "fondest dream is to own a three-piece suit," likewise felt that she would be untrue to herself if she were to don a dress. "There are certain things I wouldn't do. . . . The last time I wore a dress was when I was seventeen. . . . I would just feel outrageous . . . I would feel like I was in drag . . . ridiculous." These women felt that dresses were the only solution to their dilemma, and they rejected them on the grounds that they were uncomfortable or inappropriate to their lifestyles.

Three other women also seemed to think they would have to resort to excessively feminine dress and demeanor if they wished to look like women all the time. Certainly their assumptions of what would be required of them to meet that standard were an exaggerated vision of femininity which would appeal to few women on an everyday basis. One woman said that she might wear "clothes that aren't quite as androgynous as the ones I seem to wear," but that she would not go so far as to become "fashionable": "I guess what is too far, is becoming fashionable, in the way that fashion goes for women. I'm not really interested in stiletto heels, nylons, and short skirts, or any of those things because I feel strongly about freedom of movement and being comfortable at the same time." She seemed unable to imagine sensible and comfortable clothing which was neither masculine nor neutral. She expressed an anachronistic view of femininity and an exaggerated concept of how much femininity would be necessary for her to appear as a woman. Clearly, few other females need to wear stiletto heels and short skirts to merely be recognizable as women.

A second woman implied that any woman who was "not into wearing high heels and mincing down the street to impress whoever happened to be looking out the window at us" would, like her, be prone to being mistaken for a man. Again, this suggests that extreme and sexualized femininity is the only antidote for being thought a man or a boy by strangers. A third woman was resentful that she could not just be herself and still be recognized as a woman. She too believed that she would have to go to distasteful extremes to clearly distinguish herself as a woman.

> I'm angry that it happens but I don't want to have to change who I am or make myself physically uncomfortable, as in high heels or a dress. . . . If you're going to be seen as a woman in this society, you have to wear very distinctive female clothing or have distinctive female hair, which doesn't just mean long, it has to be also styled or curled. Or lots of makeup and jewelry. And I'm not willing to do any of those things. . . . You know, I don't see that I've done anything—I haven't tried to go out and look like a boy. . . . I knew from the beginning that if I wore the right clothes, it wouldn't be a problem. I knew that if I wore slinky pink pants instead of black cords. I knew that I would have to be overt, dress more like a hooker.

One is left wondering whether these women believed that average women, in the course of their normal everyday lives, look like transvestites and prostitutes.

All but one of the fifteen women who participated in this study expressed sympathy for the principles of feminism, yet when their opinions of more feminine women are examined it seems that they were not very supportive of the choices those more feminine women had made with respect to their own gender. Nine women made comments which suggested that either they felt that women who participated in anything more than minimal femininity were foolish, or that they preferred not to be associated with the "antics" of women in general. Although they sometimes couched their comments in feminist terms, they seemed to be saying that they shared the assumption of the dominant patriarchal gender schema that to be feminine and a woman was less desirable than to be masculine and a man. Thus, in part, their unwillingness to change their appearances so as to make themselves more readily recognizable as women stemmed not only from a sense of discomfort with the trappings of femininity but also with their sense of the stigma attached to being a woman in a patriarchal society. As one woman put it, "I hate being treated or seen as a female. I'd rather be seen as kind of a human being."

Their view of women and their lot was not an enticing one. They had absorbed the message, taught to all members of society, that women are not as good as men, and they had somehow managed to dissociate themselves from what they considered to be typical women. As one woman put it, "Let's say being mistaken for a 'typical female' bothers me a lot more than being mistaken for a man." Sadly, their view of "typical females" was tainted by misogyny.

One woman, who said that "women can be shit-holes too," called women who were stereotypically feminine by the derogatory name "fem-bots" because she thought they were "very effectively brainwashed" into a robotlike acceptance of femininity. She said that although she knows she is a women like the women she works with, "I don't see myself as one of them." She went on to admit, "I understand where men get that attitude. . . . In a lot of ways I'm very sexist against women." Another woman, in explaining why she thought that she was mistaken for a man or a boy, described what she felt was characteristic of most females.

> Generally, women don't talk loud. They don't flail their arms around when they're talking. They don't laugh out loud. They don't walk with the full length of their leg, they walk from their knees, not their hips. They aren't boisterous. They don't take command. They're pretty wimpy, generally, I think. I think I'm not! I don't sort of hold back, or defer. In the store, [if] there's a line of ten women . . . eight of them are wimpy.

The same woman who had referred to feminine teenaged girls as "ineffectual little bo-bo's" said that most people expect women "to be empty-headed . . . to be a little bit airy, like their hair-dos." Her own opinion of the women she worked with was not much more complimentary:

> They're really hard to comprehend because they're willing to be clerical workers for all their lives. . . . And the way that they dress, the amount of money they spend on clothes so that they can look a certain way, and the shoes that they wear, the total obsession with the way they look, how thin they are. . . . It's dumb! It's very exasperating to be around them! . . . I want them to have richer, fuller lives!

One woman claimed that she had held such opinions when she was younger but that now that she had become a feminist she had moved on from her previously misogynous position:

> I'm a feminist, and I think women are better than men, and I have no reason to want to be a man. . . . Because I had a big personal catharsis when I woke up one day and realized (I was twenty-seven, twenty-eight), and realized that I never wanted to be a woman. I always felt that I was weaker, stupider, and had less opportunity, which was certainly true. So I enlightened myself.

But seven years later, at the time of her interview, she was still being mistaken for a boy or a man as often as several times a week. Clearly, she still retained some reason to continue to dissociate herself from looking like a woman when she went out in public.

Many of the comments that these women made about femininity and more feminine women inferred an underlying criticism of a patriarchal social structure which confines women within a limited sphere. But while nine women made condemnations of femininity, only three of them generalized their comments to a higher social level. One woman placed the blame for her predicament squarely on the shoulders of society. She felt that she should have the right to be however she felt most comfortable with herself. "The source of my problem is society's attitude. I mean, lots of people's attitudes towards the way they think women should look. It's not my problem. Really, it's their problem, but I'm the one who gets the shitty end of the deal it seems." Another woman succinctly said that her appearance was "a political statement," and a third lamented, "Why should I have to be overt to be assumed to be a woman? Why does the norm have to be male?" A fourth woman defiantly stated, "I feel hurt by it, and I take it as a criticism . . . but I also feel like the rest of the world is fucked." Thus, these women felt that their rights to self-definition were abridged by the immoderate social restraints normally imposed on persons who would be seen as women.

Over time, their ambiguous gender status placed strain on the self-images of these women. They found themselves in situations where their choices seemed to be to expose themselves to ridicule and embarrassment by disclosing that they were women, or to comply with the expectations of others and act like the men they were assumed to be. The attractiveness of choosing to appear to be men was bolstered, for these women, by the obvious preferential treatment that many of them encountered as men. The contrast they discovered between the public censure of masculine women, and the ease with which men quietly move through social interchanges, acted as a powerful reinforcer of masculinity for these women.

The two main advantages to their gender blended status mentioned most often by the women were being free to move safely through the world without fear of sexual violence from men, and being treated more respectfully as men than they were as women. Ten women cited the feeling of safety on the streets at night, or safety from the threat of rape, as a valuable benefit of their masculine appearances, and six women said that they felt that they received more deferential treatment as men than they did as women. Two women also felt that it gave them an advantage in male-dominated work situations, and three women felt that being mistaken for a man was an advantage for them as lesbians because it allowed them to publicly express affection with their lovers without attracting undersirable attention.

One woman recalled the epiphany she felt the first time she walked the street at night as a man. The contrast between her experience as a woman and her first glimpse of life as a man was compelling.

I was walking down the street and men were looking me straight in the eye with this incredible amount of respect. I didn't know what the fuck was going on. I was walking down this street on the way to this meeting, and I was going, "What's going on with these men?" Like it was totally different, and I said, "You know what? You know what happened?" I told everybody and I said, "This feels like being in another world, it was like being a human being." I couldn't believe the sensation. What a power trip. It was wonderful. So I started to learn, hey, if I looked like a guy no one is going to hassle me.

Another woman recalled the graphic contrast between the way she passed men on the street at night and the attention that a more feminine woman walking ahead of her attracted.

I remember a classic in Toronto one night coming down College Street. There was this woman about half a block ahead and she was close enough that I could—every man that passed her, either looked at her or something, or every second man, every greaser on College Street, every third car slowed down and looked at her. She was pretty casually dressed and she was slight. . . . It was about eleven or twelve at night and there was cafe bars along College with greaser men standing outside. And I watched that woman run the gauntlet. I mean she was trying to have a daydream, there was no way. It was like interrupted three times a block and mine never were. I had come to take it for granted until this particular night when I saw this woman get harassed by this guy. I wondered if he was going to say anything to me. Of course, he didn't. There was this obvious contrast. I was invisible on the street.

Other women mentioned using their ability to pass for a man as a protective camouflage when they hitchhiked. One woman said that in one instance she had not intended to be mistaken for a young man but that she was very glad that she had been when she found herself in a car with three other male hitchhikers and a drinking driver: "This guy who was driving was giving everybody beer and I said 'No, thanks.' And then he started saying weird things like, 'Too bad there aren't any chicks on the road we could pick up and have a good time.' " She decided that the best policy was to keep her voice low, say as little as possible, and get out of the car at the next stop. Another woman similarly took advantage of the fact that she looked like a man when dressed in particular outfits.

I used to hitchhike home from the hospital and the other nurses used to freak out that I'd hitchhike home. But I'd wear a toque and a down jacket and work boots. No man in his right mind would think I was a woman, and when someone had stopped (a woman would never stop to pick me up, unless it was a dyke, which happened twice, which was great), but the men would stop, thinking I'm a man, and sometimes not find out until I got out of the car, sometimes not find out ever. But I believed that if they think I'm a man, and they're stopping to pick up a man, they can't be into that much kinky.

Fortunately for her, she never did meet any men who were "kinky" enough to cause her any harm when they realized their error.

Several women also mentioned that they were struck by the amount of respect that they received from strangers when they were perceived as men. One woman said that she was always thought to be a man rather than a boy and that when she was addressed as a man it was "sometimes the only respect I got." Other women highlighted the contrast between the way they were treated by people who incorrectly thought them to be men and by people who thought they were women. One woman commented that men were assumed to be competent whereas women were not. "In that way it's really positive, because it's awful to be treated like a girl by the general population. They think you're dumb. They think you don't know anything. They think they have to explain every little thing to you, even if you know more than they do. I don't like that." One woman also very clearly realized, as a result of her experiences being mistaken for a man, that men have many more advantages than women.

> I guess a lot of it is that men are so in control of the world, and this is an awful thing to say. I don't think I will, I can't, I can't say this. I'm shocked that I even think it. But what I was going to say is, is that men, in this world, are so dominant that everything seems to go towards them, that sometimes to be mistaken, to look like a man, can be an advantage . . . if by accident you can look like a man you have more chances than if you look like a woman.

The greater respect that these women experienced when mistaken for men further encouraged them in both their masculinity and their choices to allow the mistakes to stand uncorrected. They opted for the increased social status and mobility that being mistaken for a man or a boy afforded them.

Other women were in a position to contrast the "civil inattention"[1] granted to men with the demeaning sexualized attention they received when trying to pass quietly about their business as women.

> Now here's another interesting thing that happens. I noticed this last summer, because I work out on the street, and because it's really hot, I wore a lot of T-shirts last summer. . . . And I found that there were a lot of men who stared at my breasts. And that was just as bad, as far as I was concerned, as having somebody mistake me for a boy. So again, it's a bind for me. I feel also very strongly about male attention that is obviously focused on sexual characteristics as I do about being mistaken for a man.

The same woman who had discovered that men looked at her "with an incredible amount of respect" when they thought she was also a man, treated her quite differently when it was obvious that she was a woman.

> When I look like a woman, men hassle me. I can't stand it! I absolutely can't stand it! The first time I dressed up in the city was to go to a job interview in the summer, and I almost killed this guy. I was so angry, and I got so upset because I was wearing this tight T-shirt, and it was boiling out, so I took off my sweater. And he was just staring at my tits like, "Really nice," you know? And I'm going "Fuck off! Get away from me!" I just couldn't stand it. And I got home and I ripped the clothes

off, like get away from me. I can't stand it that just the difference in clothing will protect me or create a completely different scene, you know?

I like being feminine on the outside but I don't like doing it in public very much because when I do I just get too many hassles from men. And I just don't want to deal with that. I don't want them looking at my tits. I don't want them, you know, "Hey there." I refuse to go through that I HATE that! I get really angry.

She concluded that being a woman was a liability: "Sometimes I hate being a woman. . . . I want it to be easy. Men got it made in this world. They can go anywhere, they don't have to be afraid. They can get any job they want. . . . I don't want to be a man, but I don't like the way I get treated as a woman." These women read a clear message from their experiences. As women, they were vulnerable to sexual objectification, trivialization, and violence. As men, they were assumed to be capable actors with full rights to privacy and respect. It seemed an entirely logical choice, to many of them, to take advantage of the benefits of looking like a man in public.

Ten of these gender blending females had also worked, at some time, in areas of employment strongly dominated by men. Two women specifically stated that their masculine appearances had been helpful to them in their chosen occupations. One woman said that the fact that customers often thought that she was a man protected her from sexual innuendo and assumptions of feminine incompetence. The second woman said that she used her ambiguous appearance to help her get jobs.

> The jobs that I am interested in are usually traditionally male jobs. . . . Usually I'd never write my full name on an application form if I'm applying for a job that is traditionally male. So it's a big advantage for me because I do a lot of those jobs, trades things. When I'm talking I usually don't say anything either, when I'm having an interview or something. There's nothing on my resume or application that says whether I'm male or female. They assume what they want to assume.
>
> I've gotten a few jobs where they thought I was a guy and then they realized. Like during the interview, they would find out that I'm a female. I'd usually tell them, and after we'd talked and they'd found out what I'd done. Well, one job in particular, he said he didn't want to hire me because he was looking for a man for the job. And I just said to him, "I would really like to do this job. Give me a chance. Let me work for a week and if you don't think that I'm capable of doing it, you don't have to pay me. But if you think I can do it, you've got yourself an employee and you haven't lost anything. You've still got somebody working for you." And he hired me after that, and he considered me a very good employee. And he actually came up to me later, after I quit, and said that he was really glad that I opened his eyes because he was an older man who thought that boys should do boys' jobs and girls should do girls' jobs.

This same woman also used her masculine appearance as an insurance policy against sex discrimination.

> That's why my resume doesn't say male or female because a lot of the jobs, usually they want males. And what can you do? . . . If I'm applying for a job and they know

I'm a female, they can easily say, "I've hired somebody else." And I can't do anything about it. But if they hire me and they think I'm male and then I say I'm female, if they fire me, I've got a suit against them. I can easily take it and say, "Listen, I had this job until you knew my sex." And I have no problem getting them. And usually by then they think I can do the work. I'm not going to apply for it unless I think I can do it.

Unfortunately, this woman did not find it as easy to choose to be thought of as a woman when it suited her purposes.

Three of the lesbian women cited their ability to pass for a man or a boy as an advantage which afforded invisibility to their lesbian relationships. They found that, because strangers assumed them to be heterosexual couples, they could freely engage in lesbian affection in public places without becoming the object of ridicule or curiosity. One woman said that she enjoyed the freedom that looking like a boy gave her: "Like when Cynthia and I walk down the street, we hold hands and nobody looks at us twice because they think I'm a guy. So there's another advantage right there. I guess I wanted to be known as a guy so that I could hang around with my girlfriends." Another lesbian woman had an exciting and satisfying adventure when she decided to make use of her ability to look like a man to live out a sexual fantasy that she entertained.

When I was twenty-one, twenty-two . . . I met this woman at a coffee house who was dressed to the nines, but totally off. . . . I was at this coffee house wearing typical shirt, vest, and pants, the uniform, right? And so was everybody else. And this woman shows up in a white silk top with a very tight bra so that her breasts were what I used to call rocketheads sticking out at me, and these tight, tight pants, which I swear to god she couldn't breathe in, and these high heeled leather boots which came up to here, like right up to here. I mean, she was attractive, but she wasn't. Like, I mean, . . . she was something. But anyways, she was blonde, hair out to here, gobs of makeup, black and blue and just like wow!

I was also on the welcoming committee at this drop-in group so I was always finding people sitting alone and I was sort of known for bringing people in who were feeling lonely because that was how I felt when I first came. So I went up to her and she sat down with me and we started talking, and we listened to the poetry, and then we talked a bit more after. . . . She was a secretary and was a stripper and worked in this nightclub called the Strip. So we visited and talked and when she left she said, "You can always come by the Strip, and maybe after work we could go out somewhere. It would be nice to see you again." So I said, "Bye" and sort of blew it off.

And one of my fantasies has been to go to a straight bar, and pick up a straight woman, and have her believe that I'm a man. What I did was, it was after a while, not a week after but like two months later. . . . I told everyone that I had this fantasy and I'm going to go to this bar and pick up this woman. . . . So I put on this silk shirt and a tie and a vest. I didn't bind my breasts or anything, but my vest was tight enough so it wouldn't look like I had breasts, and a jacket, and dress pants, and big Frye boots, and a big winter coat, and a fedora, and my hair was really short, this big ring that I always wear, and some big gloves. I got into a taxi and I went to the

Strip. But the taxi driver knew I was a woman and I was going "Oh, shit. It's not going to work." I couldn't get the voice, you know?

So I came in, I was really nervous. But I just stuck my nose up in the air. "Hey, this is no problem. I've been doing this all my life. What's the difference. Now I just know I'm doing it, that's all." . . . So they sat me down in front . . . and Suzanne was on the dance floor with nothing on. This woman was in her high heels and she was dancing away. . . . She was dancing right in front of me. Her legs were right in front of me. And I was standing there with this hat on going, "I don't believe this." I sort of looked up and she looked at me and she smiled and she started dancing even more. "Oh my god. Here's her crotch right in my face." And all these other guys are wondering, "What are you doing over there? Come on over here!" They're all waving their dollar bills and then this other woman saw me and she says, "Hey, stop dancing in front of her. It's a woman. Stop." So Suzanne pretends, "Oh, yeah. I'm not supposed to be doing that." And she goes off. . . .

And then she got off the dance floor and she came by holding all her stuff she had stripped off. Still stark naked, she came over and gave me this big kiss and said, "I'll be out in five minutes," and went into the change room. Fuck, I was dying. My pants were soaked. So she came out of the dressing room . . . and she was just dressed to kill. And so I took her by the arm and we went outside, and I helped her walk on the ice. I hailed a cab and we got into the taxi, and the taxi driver this time thought I was a man. And she asked me what I wanted to do, and I said, "Let's go to this place that's still opened." And she said "How about your place? Do you have any booze there?" I said, "Yeah, I've got some sherry." So we went to my place, we drank sherry and took off all of our clothes and made love for about six hours. It was wonderful!

But the next day, it was great! I put her in a pair of jeans, running shoes, and a T-shirt. She took off all of her makeup and she went out with me and my dyke friends, down the street where we used to hang out looking at records, and she got mistaken for a man. And she almost had a heart attack. She couldn't believe it. I said, "Life is wonderful, You can be whatever you want." It was really neat.

Experiences such as this one, no doubt, acted as a powerful reinforcer of her masculinity. But not all of her experiences with being mistaken for a man were so contrived, or so satisfying.

Four women spoke of negative sides to the more prized aspects of their blended gender status. Two women were pained to discover that when they were enjoying safety and freedom of movement on the streets at night, not only were other women not sharing their right to move freely through their world, but by looking like men themselves they became the very people who more feminine women feared. The same woman who so enjoyed making use of her masculinity in sexual conquest suffered for the contribution her presence made to other women's feelings of danger on the streets at night.

And then I started thinking about how when I see women at night. I've seen the women who see me and just look really scared and walk to the other side of the street. And I think like "Hey, if a guy came and raped you I'd probably kill him, you know, and you're worried about me?" And it really hurts because they can't see it and they see it and they see me and they think there's a man and go to the other side of the street and run away from me. It just really hurts a lot and it makes me really sad.

Another woman told a similar story of women avoiding her at night: "There have been times that I have noticed, that I have been walking down the street at night and a woman who has been walking in front of me crosses the street. When that happens I feel like calling out, 'Don't worry. It's just me, and I'm a girl too. It's OK.' But yeah, I have noticed women on the street be a little leery of me." A third woman reported that although her appearance insulated her from sexual violence from men, men who mistook her for one of them were more likely to want to engage her in nonsexual male-male violence.

> I have gotten into fights with men because they thought I was a guy. That's a disadvantage, but an advantage in the fact that the chances of me getting raped are very small. That has come up a couple of times where I've been beaten up and I know that if the guys had known I was a woman, they probably would have done a lot more.

Still another woman ironically found that as she came to feel better about herself as a person, and as she began to understand and sympathize more with the life course choices of other more feminine women, she became less and less acceptable to them. This was a very difficult development for her to come to terms with.

> Washrooms are the worst place, because everywhere else it doesn't matter. And I think the part that's humiliating and freakish and that makes it a kind of weird parallel is that since I've become a feminist, I've gotten really clued into women. I mean I was tuned into them before, but I even tuned into women who are totally unlike me. I mean I see us as being all part of this, so I developed this affinity for all those straight women that I never had before because I had some sense of why they were like that. So there I was, like me actively loving women all the time, and going into a space that's a special place for women, the only place they can be without men and the only place they can be real outraged if there's a man in there, and I was excluded from that. So the very same things that made me look like a man, also made it matter to me more.

Nonetheless, most of these women felt that the advantages outweighed the disadvantages. Not all of them were willing to state this unequivocally but only six of them gave a clear "yes" to the question "Do you want it to stop?" They lived in a public world which disdained femininity and they had had firsthand experience both of that disdain, and of the benefits which society affords to masculinity.

As well, all of these women had found communities of support in which their masculinity was at least benignly tolerated, if not actively validated. All of the heterosexual women in the group reported some support for the ideas of feminism and found support for their masculine predilections in the writings of feminists. One woman found some support from her lovers, but her only contact with feminism was through books she had read. The three other heterosexual women lived and worked among people who espoused feminism. Their companions and coworkers supplied them with a community of permissive support for their gender choices. One woman credited feminist support as an important factor in her comfort with herself as she was. "The thing is that I've got a terrific support network, through my companion, through my family, through people like that who do not give me too bad a time about the way I dress." She worked in a place which had a relaxed dress code, and she socialized among people who endorsed her choices. She was therefore able to discount the opinions of strangers as largely irrelevant to her self-definition.

The majority of the women in this study were lesbians who socialized and found many of their most significant relationships within communities of lesbians. Stereotypically lesbians have been typecast as masculine women, and historically, lesbian communities have condoned a percentage of lesbian women taking on the "butch" role. Certainly this is not true of all or even most lesbians, but one woman seemed to be speaking the truth when she said, "I think that for the most part lesbians are supportive of women who look even more like men than I do." The lesbian women thus found a sheltering haven for their lingering boyishness in the social mores of lesbian communities.

All but one of the lesbian women were also feminists and as lesbian-feminists they had theoretically relegated "butch" roles to history. Still, lesbian and lesbian-feminist communities do not generally encourage femininity and do quietly condone masculinity. One woman summed up the lesbian-feminist position this way: "We sort of dress in what's comfortable, in a way a uniform of wearing butchy clothes but we don't wear them because we want to be like men, but because we want the privilege of dressing comfortably." Another woman recalled that her episodes of being mistaken for a man increased in frequency after she became acquainted with lesbian-feminists because such social norms gave her permission to abandon many of her previous attempts at femininity. "I had all these wonderful new friends and I was getting pretty constant positive reinforcement that I was just fine. And so when I was with them I felt totally normal." She had acquired new friends who shared her experience of being mistaken for a man, helped her to view it as normal, and provided her with a more congenial set of peers to populate her generalized and significant others. She recounted this story about one morning when she joined a friend at a restaurant for breakfast. The waitress approached them and asked: " 'What would you gentlemen like for breakfast?' I said nervously 'Oh, ah, we're not gentlemen' and Jasmine said 'We're not even men!' and threw her head back and laughed all over the restaurant. She was a great role model for me." These lesbian women shared their lives and world with other women who tolerated or rewarded them for their masculinity.

Thus, these fifteen gender blending females were able to enjoy many of the privileges of men and circumvent some of the most odious aspects of being a woman in a patriarchal society by critiquing and dissociating themselves from femininity. They successfully sustained their attachment to masculinity by limiting the constituency of their significant and generalized others to communities of persons who shared or supported their critique of femininity and accepted their masculinity as an attractive and rational response to an unfair social order.

Managing Stigma

Gender is neither static nor neutral, and gender is never socially meaningless. People's gender identities, and the gender attributions made by others, color all aspects of social exchange. The gender blending women in this study learned to be adept at, and take pleasure in, many aspects of masculinity. As children, they learned from their family members, peers, the schools, and the media that men and boys were more privileged and prized than women and girls. They were taught, and adopted, many of the mannerisms, prejudices, and preferences of the people whom they most admired, and when they imagined their future lives as adults, they foresaw themselves in roles and positions of power and prestige. In the worlds of their childhoods, such people and places were the domain of men.

In the broadest of terms, these gender blending females could be said to have been raised to become adults who would communicate their femaleness poorly. Their home environments taught them to see men as socially superior and women as powerless and ineffectual. They learned from their parents, grandparents, and siblings to associate the behaviors and attitudes of masculinity with power, respect, and authority, and to associate the behaviors and attitudes of femininity with weakness, incompetence, and servility.

Adolescence brought to them new and increased demands for feminity. As children, their boyish pursuits and aspirations had been benignly tolerated as harmless tomboyishness. When they reached adolescence they were expected to leave that stage behind and start acting like the young women their bodies were changing them into. They were expected to turn away from their identification with boys and boyish pleasures, and join the sisterhood of women. They were asked, in many ways, to transform themselves from active "subjects" of their own lives and fantasies into passive "objects" of the passions and aspirations of others.

For many of them, this was their first initiation into feeling shame and embarrassment at being female. They felt that they were being asked to "lower" themselves to a diminished status. They felt shame and embarrassment both for being forced to become part of a group whose social inferiority was obvious to them, and for the loss of face they suffered before their male friends who were not being so curtailed. They rebelled against and mourned for the lost possibilities that their femaleness then came to mean to them.

Most tried, for a time, to become more feminine and to comply with many of the demands which were placed on them as teenagers. The limited success that they had with their forays into femininity only served to sharpen their sense of shame in their femaleness. They felt that they were not able to be "proper" females even when they consciously made the effort to be pretty, feminine, and heterosexual. Some women simply retreated from the challenge until young adulthood; a few took refuge in the stereotype of the lesbian as a "mannish woman" and adopted that as their persona.

In their late teens and early adulthood, those gender blending females who had not already learned it, discovered that being female meant being subject to sexual victimization at the hands of men. This realization served to further consolidate their resolve to distance themselves from femininity and womanhood, wherever they saw it as a liability to them. In short, they dealt with their femaleness as a stigma[2] which required careful management lest they become discredited by the inadvised disclosure of the fact of their having been born as females. One woman put it plainly when she said, "The people I know, they know I'm a woman. Everybody out there in the world doesn't have to know I'm a woman."[3]

As women they were members of a stigmatized group in society. They were assumed to be incompetent in areas where they excelled and to be interested in pursuits they spurned. They were expected to be heterosexually flirtatious and seductive where they felt more comfortable being aggressive and conquering. As women, they had little right to psychic privacy in public places and were vulnerable to sexual assault at any time. As men or boys, they discovered, they were saved from the danger of masculine hostility against women, *and* they were able to enjoy a taste of the respect and privilege normally reserved for men in North American society. The combination of the stigma of being female in a patriarchal society, the lure of masculine safety and privilege, and the misogyny that they had learned in the company of men, sent an irrefutable message to these women. They chose to take advantage of, and in some cases actively encourage, the misconceptions of strangers in public places whenever they thought it would work to their advantage.

Like all persons who carry a stigma, their options for managing their stigma fell into two categories. In some instances, their femaleness was unconcealed or unconcealable, in which case they were persons who were already discredited, and their challenge lay in managing that information in a way which would cause them the least privation. In other situations, they were able to conceal their femaleness and thus were in the position of being discreditable. As discreditable persons they were faced with the necessity of deciding when, if, and how they might, or might not, allow their stigma to become disclosed.[3] In either situation, they faced their femaleness as an insurmountable impression management problem. When they presented themselves in public as feminine females they felt that they were discredited on the basis of their own, and society's, misogyny. When they presented themselves as masculine women, they had to deal with the double stigma of being female and of being a failed female, or a "mannish" woman, in a patriarchal society. When they passed as men, they were able to temporarily avoid being treated as persons discredited for being female. But, by choosing this last impression management option, they courted the danger of both their femaleness and their duplicity being exposed, thereby leaving themselves subject to discreditation on two accounts.

Thus, there was no way for them to effectively circumvent the fact that in a patriarchal society, femaleness is a stigmatized and secondary status. They attempted to avoid this unavoidable fact by taking advantage of inconsistencies and vagaries in the dominant gender schema which allowed them to garner some masculine privileges and respect through a passive complicity with misogyny. They were able to pass as men, without actually having to take responsibility for attempting to misrepresent themselves to others, because of the common assumption of the genericness of all things associated with maleness.

The dominant gender schema teaches us to think, and see, using a male-based standard. When members of a patriarchal society receive ambiguous or confusing gender messages, they cognitively judge them by comparison to a male standard. If there are a minimal number of male cues and no strong counterindicators, maleness is assumed. In North American society, maleness is used as a standard of purity; femaleness, as a stigmatized condition, must bear the mark of "other." Thus, when gender blending females refused to mark themselves by publicly displaying sufficient femininity to be recognized as women, they were in no way challenging patriarchal gender assumptions. Their ruse brought them momentary relief from the shame they felt at their membership in the stigmatized class of female, but at the price of feeling "freakish" in their hearts and at the cost of their womanhood. When they demanded to be recognized as women, no matter how masculine they might have appeared to others, they did challenge the assumption that females must be feminine in order to be women. Those women who used this tactic paid the price of being doubly discredited each time they used it, but they were able to retain the comfort of their moral integrity and their membership in the sisterhood of women. The choice was not an easy one to make.

ANNA

SEVEN

Gender in Context

The gender blending females in this study learned well the tenets of the patriarchal gender schema which dominates North American society. They learned that their female sex was supposed to be the irrefutable fact which made them into women and that, as women, they were supposed to behave in a feminine fashion. They also learned, early in their lives, that femininity was patriarchy's way of marking a portion of the population for a secondary status in the service of men.

At the same time as they were learning that femaleness was a stigmatized condition in their society, they were also learning to be proficient at, and take pleasure in, the ways of masculinity. By accident, they discovered that if, as adults, they practiced the degree of masculinity to which they had become accustomed as youngsters, they could neutralize some of the stigma of their femaleness as well as enjoy some of the privileges usually reserved for men.

This realization served to reinforce their tendency to masculinity in three ways. Firstly, their masculinity was an accustomed stance which had been with them since their childhoods. They had little desire to change their habits and were thus pleased to find reasons to support their continuance of that behavior. Secondly, the contrast between their status as women, on the one hand, and the freedom and respectableness they acquired when mistaken for men, on the other, only confirmed and solidified their awareness of the stigmatized condition of womanhood. Their sense of femininity as a contaminant to be avoided was thus enhanced. Thirdly, they simply found joy in the sense of power that walking the streets with the freedom of men imparted to them. That sense of freedom of movement and security of person, on an everyday individual basis, gave them a feeling of exhilaration unmatched in their experience of femininity. They learned that, as men, they were free to do the things they enjoyed most, where they wanted to, and when they wanted to. As women, they felt humiliated, constrained, and vulnerable to sexual attack and violation. Their choice was to buy their public dignity and freedom at the price of their womanhood.

Problematically, their awareness of these social and intrapsychic dynamics was largely unconscious. They therefore were able to make the choices they did while maintaining that they made no effort to induce people to mistake them for men or boys. But since they believed that their femaleness made them women, they could see little reason for the mistakes to occur. Thus, they were

145

left with the problem of rationalizing to themselves and to others why they were so often thought to be men.

Their explanatory efforts took refuge both in their partial acceptance of the dominant gender schema and in their partial rejection of it. In dismissing their being mistaken for men or boys as careless inobservance on the part of members of the public, they resorted to the "truism" that because they were adult females, they were also women. In their minds, that was a simple fact of nature which could neither be disputed nor denied, but could be overlooked by negligent observers. Having thus embraced one of the underlying assumptions of the dominant patriarchal gender schema, they then went on to criticize the specific cultural application of those assumptions.

They argued that the requirements of femininity were too restrictive and that the distinctions between the genders were unnecessarily pronounced. There was no need, they asserted, for such dramatic marking of females with cultural signs of their femaleness if their biology alone made them women. They wanted to be able to live like men, not suffer the vulnerability and powerlessness of women, and still be women to themselves, their friends, and loved ones—that is, wherever it was safe and convenient. To the degree that they accomplished the strategic camouflaging of their femaleness, they took advantage of a discrepancy between the way the dominant gender schema leads members of society to believe gender is created and substantiated, and the way it actually is communicated, attributed, and maintained in the course of normal everyday social interactions.

Gender Identity and Gender Attribution

In the normal dramaturgy of everyday life, few people give much thought or attention to the workings of their own personal gender schema or to those of the persons with whom they interact. Nonetheless, the dominant gender schema functions as an underlying basis of most interpersonal interactions. But, because there are considerable small-scale variations in the ways that individuals interpret that gender schema, there are also variations in the ways that people understand and perform their gender roles. Therefore, there must be a constant, usually unacknowledged, negotiation of the situationally specific working definitions of gender role norms and behaviors whenever persons socially interact

Persons must therefore engage in impression management techniques to communicate to others, by means of gender role characteristics and behaviors, the gender and sex which they wish to have attributed to them. Although this happens under normal circumstances more or less continuously, it also happens largely unconsciously on the parts of most social actors. As a result, few people are aware of exactly what cues they are giving off, or receiving, in any given situation. What people *are* aware of are the social "facts" of gender identity and gender attribution. In other words they know what gender they are and the genders of the persons with whom they interact. This knowledge tells them how they ought to behave and what they ought to expect from others.

This negotiation of gender in everyday life does not faithfully reflect the ideological rationale of the dominant gender schema.[1] Gender is socially constructed, recognized, and attributed in roughly the reverse of how most people believe it is accomplished. The dominant gender schema teaches members of society that their genders are the natural results of their physical beings, and that their gender roles are likewise natural outgrowths of the demands of their bodily predispositions. Gender roles, rather than being the results of biological imperatives, actually function as cues to sex and gender. Persons become socially recognized and accepted as members of genders on the basis of their gender role behaviors, not on the basis of their sexes. In the normal course of everyday life, primary sex characteristics are rarely exposed for public view. Sexes are attributed on the basis of gender attributions.

The gender attribution process in everyday life works roughly as follows: Persons display gender role behaviors in the process of presenting themselves as creditable human beings. Those gender role cues usually form a more or less cohesive whole from which others attribute the gender status intended by the actor. Following from the assumptions and logic of the dominant gender schema, that gender attribution is then used as the basis for the attribution of the corresponding sex. If a person exhibits a predominance of gender role characteristics normally assumed to be the result of the biological demands and limitations of a particular sex/gender status, that person will be attributed membership in that category without the necessity of biological evidence in support of such an attribution. Thus, in everyday gender information processing, gender roles act as indicators of genders, and genders act as indicators of sexes. Rather than sex causing gender to happen and gender causing gender roles to happen, gender roles cause genders to be attributed and gender attributions cause sexes to be attributed.

⌈The dominant gender schema provides a basis for a sexist society by propagating an ideology of an innate, and entirely pervasive, sex determined social structure.⌋ This schema conditions members of society to see a clear unbroken causative link leading from physical sex to gender status to gender role, and encourages people to see and govern all human situations through a binary matrix of male and female. In the course of normal everyday life, people use the dominant gender schema to help them make gender attributions as follows (see Figure 2):

1. All people are assumed to be either male or female, men or women, masculine or feminine.

2. Physical characteristics, mannerisms, and personality traits of others are interpreted as masculine or feminine on the basis of the dominant gender schema.

3. Observed gender cues are instantaneously and unconsciously weighed,

and a gender status is attributed, i.e., feminine people are seen as women, masculine people are seen as men.

4. Once a gender status has been attributed to a person, the corresponding sex is attributed, i.e., men are males, women are females.

5. The assumption of that sex and the causation postulated by the dominant gender schema then combine to provide explanations for any lingering misaligned gender cues. Seemingly inappropriate gender role cues are thus interpreted in ways which support, rather than call into question, both the attributions made and the biological determinism of the dominant gender schema. For example, a prominent chest on a person assumed to be male might be explained away as large pectoral muscles, or simply fat on the upper body.

FIGURE 2. GENDER ATTRIBUTION PROCESS

GENDER ROLE → GENDER ATTRIBUTION → SEX ATTRIBUTION

Thus, in a patriarchal and sexist society, people may change the gender and sex statuses attributed to them by altering the gender role characteristics they communicate to others. The combined effects of the weight of social stigma and the lure of greater social status can be powerful enough to induce members of society to do so.

Sex and gender identities are formed both by individuals' internalization of the dominant gender schema and as a result of the gender attribution process. In other words, persons' gender identities are a product of what they know about themselves and what others tell them about themselves. This is a dynamic interaction process which is largely dependent on the success of the gender impression management techniques used by social actors. Persons must be able to convey gender cues in ways such that other people will be able to interpret them as actors intend them to be understood.

Persons' physical sexes, interpreted in terms of their own individual understandings and acceptances of the dominant gender schema, provide them with the basis for their sex identities. Their sex identities similarly direct people to accept corresponding gender identities. Hence, physical sex characteristics give rise to sex identities and, indirectly, to gender identities. Identification with a gender category, seen in light of the dominant gender schema, gives instruction as to what gender role behaviors are appropriate for individuals to use and which to avoid. If actors use the appropriate techniques successfully, they are attributed membership in the gender and sex with which they identify, thereby reinforcing their own gender and sex identities. If persons exhibit gender role behaviors which are not interpreted by others as indicators of the gender and sex which they intend to convey, they will be attributed membership in the only other gender and sex cognitively available within the dominant patriarchal gender schema. When this happens often enough to consciously register as a pattern in a person's psyche, that person's gender and sex identities can become weakened and confused (see Figure 3).

FIGURE 3. GENDER IDENTITY FORMATION

Individuals cannot create social meanings independently of the larger society within which they live. Social norms and conventions determine the boundaries within which individuals may legitimately negotiate gender meanings, and those limitations affect the gender role presentations that social actors choose to use in their interchanges with others. Due to the wide range of gender role behaviors available, and the wide range of interpretations possible, gender role identity, cueing, and attribution form a dynamic negotiation process. Thus the gender attribution/gender impression management/gender identity formation and maintenance process forms a unit of dynamic exchange within the constraints of a larger gendered social vocabulary. The full picture of giving gender social meaning on the microsocial level in everyday life is roughly as follows (see Figure 4):

1. Persons have the physical attributes of a biological sex.

2. The facts of their sex characteristics give them sex identities as members of a sex category.

3. Sex identities give rise to corresponding gender identities.

4. Those gender identities dictate a permissible range of gender role behaviors.

5. Social actors attempt to communicate their gender and sex identities to others through displaying gender role behaviors appropriate to their gender identities and understandable to their audiences. Actors thus attempt to cue their desired gender attribution from their audiences.

6. Actors constantly monitor the responses of others to their gender displays and adjust their gender role behaviors in ways designed to illicit their desired attributions.

7. When this process is successfully completed to the actors' expectations, they are attributed by their audiences with the desired gender and sex attributions and their gender and sex identities are reinforced. When the cueing is unsuccessful, a misattribution occurs and actors' gender and sex identities are not reinforced or are weakened.

FIGURE 4. GENDER IDENTITY/ATTRIBUTION CYCLE

SEX   GENDER IDENTITY → GENDER ROLE

SEX IDENTITY   GENDER ATTRIBUTION

Thus, gender is a social product, produced and maintained by individuals in dynamic interactions and given meaning through the cognitive framework of the dominant gender schema.

Gendered Individuals in Gendered Societies

Gender can only be properly understood through an examination of its functioning on both macrosocial and microsocial levels. Ideologies shape social institutions on the macrosocial level. Social institutions shape individuals' intrapersonal gender schemata, which in turn constrain how people perceive themselves and those around them. Microsocial level interpersonal interactions feed back into intrapersonal gender constructs, which then aggregate back to shape social institutions and mass ideology (see Figure 5).

The dominant gender schema (V1) holding sway in a society acts as the rational basis for the gendered substance and structures of social institutions (V2). Social institutions transmit social ideology and norms to members of their societies differentially by attributed gender (V8), training them to conform to and uphold the rational basis for gender distinctions in their society by molding their personal gender schemata (V3) to reflect the dominant gender schema. Groups of individuals, born into societies, are bestowed membership in sex categories (V4) on the basis of the social meanings given to primary sex characteristics by the gender schemata of their societies as applied by individual members. They then accept sex identities (V5) which are schematically consistent with the evidence of their sex organs. Sex identities in turn dictate gender identities (V6) in accordance with personal understandings of societies' gender schemata. In other words, the dominant gender schema is the theoretical underpinning for gender-based segments of major social institutions which inform persons' beliefs about gender. Persons' beliefs about what is appropriate and normal for members of each sex are the result of socialization processes in such social institutions as the home, peer groups, schools, workplaces, and the media. Such socialization processes, directed at individuals, are mediated by the gender attributed to the persons being socialized.

Gender on the microsocial level must be looked at from the point of view of the self both as an "I" and as a "me." Thus both identity and attributions by others contribute to the making of gendered meaning on the microsocial level. The belief systems which persons learn through their socialization (V3) give meaning to biological evidence and thereby allow them to form clear identities (V5) as persons having either of the two sex statuses (V4), e.g., to believe that if they are equipped with penises, they are males. Gender schemata further mediate individuals' identities so that persons who have particular sex identities may know what genders are appropriate for them to belong to and identify with (V6), e.g., females should identify as girls or women. Gender identities, under the influence of personal gender schemata, in turn form the basis for gender role behaviors (V7), e.g., men are supposed to act in masculine ways. When persons act in accordance with the generally understood gender prescriptions, they are attributed membership in genders by other persons who observe their behaviors (V8), e.g., when someone seems to be feminine, they are attributed with being a woman or a girl. Those who make such attributions also make attributions of sex statuses (V9), e.g., persons attributed with

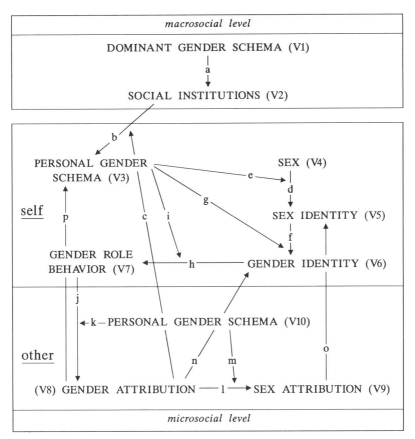

FIGURE 5. THE SOCIAL CREATION OF GENDER

being men are also attributed with being male. The attributions of others, made under the influences of their own personal gender schemata (V10), serve to either reinforce or undermine the gender (V6) and sex identities (V5) of those about whom attributions are made.

Thus, the process of gender functions on three levels. On the macrosocial level social forces exert their influences in one direction only. The system is basically a recursive one wherein the dominant gender schema limits and defines the structures and functioning of major social institutions. On the microsocial level the system must be viewed on two planes: that of individuals, and that of the others with whom they interact. On the level of the individual self, the system is again one-directional, or recursive, wherein gender schemata give meaning to biological facts so that those facts become the rationale for gendered behavior patterns. But when persons meet, their interactions affect both their perceptions of themselves (V6, V5) and their personal gender schema (V3). Therefore on the microsocial level, gender is the result of a complex and subtle system of cueing, interpretation, and feedback between individuals and is thus highly non-recursive both in an immediate and a long-term sense.

The entire system of macrosocial and microsocial levels taken together is non-recursive when looked at in a longer temporal view. Over time, feedback and interaction at the microsocial level creates change in the people who make up social institutions. The aggregation of such changes in the individuals who populate those institutions alters the face of social institutions. Tenacious and disruptive large-scale changes can and do create strains in social institutions which inevitably force movement in the ideological constructs used to support and rationalize their existence. Thus, the accomplishments of radical social change movements of one era become the basis of social institutions and ideological conservatism of another.

Gender Blending and Social Change

The gender blending females in this study were mistaken for boys or men because they used the gender attribution process to their own ends. When they presented themselves to the public in ways which displayed their masculinity while obscuring their femininity, members of the public saw enough masculinity to attribute them with being men or boys. They made these attributions from within the cognitive framework of the dominant gender schema which trains members of society to observe gender with a patriarchal bias, and which values maleness more highly than femaleness. The patriarchal system also demands that the persons who must be contained and controlled are the ones who must distinguish themselves. Therefore, when these gender blending females failed to clearly mark themselves as women, they were mistaken for men because (1) they exhibited some characteristics which normally are interpreted as cues for manhood, (2) they had not clearly signaled to others that they wanted to be recognized as women, and (3) they were mistaken for men or boys by strangers who either wanted to give no offense or were fearful of sexual assault.

The persons who mistook their gender were reading cues which either instructed them to attribute manhood or sent unclear messages to them. When members of the public are presented with contradictory gender cues they tend to solve the conflict this creates in their own minds by applying the gender attribution process in as schematically logical and inoffensive a way as possible. They tend to attribute manhood and maleness because of the patriarchally induced tendency to see maleness as basic and femaleness as a variation on maleness. The dominant patriarchal gender schema, favoring men and maleness over women and femaleness, specifies that women must mark themselves as "other," requires few cues to identify maleness, and needs many to identify femaleness. When gender cues are not unequivocally feminine, people therefore have a tendency to see men.[2] When people wish to give the benefit of the doubt to a person whose gender is ambiguous, they tend to attribute manhood and maleness because those statuses will be correct if persons are males, and patriarchally backhanded compliments if they are females. Gender is as much in the reading as in the telling, and in a sexist society the vocabulary is limited. Members of society can see two, and only two, genders. All persons must be one or the other.

Women, in particular, as stigmatized people who are always aware of the possibility of sexual assault in patriarchal societies, and who often feel themselves individually less powerful than men, need to be cautiously protective of the few places where they have the socially sanctioned right to exclude men and boys. When confronted with a person of ambiguous gender in a possibly dangerous situation, the most prudent attribution for women to make is one of manhood and maleness. If their attribution proves to be incorrect, they have been overly cautious. If they attribute womanhood and femaleness incorrectly, the consequences could be dire. Thus, women in washrooms and on nighttime streets often attributed manhood to these gender blending females.

Many of the gender blending women interviewed for this study maintained that their unfeminine conduct and appearances were by way of a protest against sexism and patriarchy. Patriarchal social structures are based on the assumption that maleness, and all that is associated with it, entitles its incumbents to social superiority. Those women who rose to this challenge by refusing to mark themselves with femininity while still claiming their womanhood did indeed move against patriarchal hegemony. Those gender blending females who insisted that they be recognized as women posed a threat to patriarchal conceptualizations of womanhood and femaleness. As one woman said, "Bucking the system is a social necessity. Variation is the way of evolution."

Sex and gender discrimination requires that genders categories remain at all times distinct, that the sex and gender statuses of all members of society be seen as immutably linked, and that persons' genders always be clearly in evidence. When these requirements are met it is possible to establish and maintain a hierarchical social structure based on male dominance. When peoples' gender role behaviors cause them to be attributed with social genders which do not schematically match their sexes, the foundation of sexism is undermined.

A gender schema that would more accurately describe the present situation and that would allow for a less sexist future might be based on the concept of gender blending. Such a conceptualization of gender would start from the recognition that sex identity, sex attribution, gender identity, gender attribution, and gender roles can all combine in any configuration.[3] In such a schema, sex would not be assumed to be related to behavior in any way beyond the mechanical concerns of reproduction of the species. Genders would become social statuses available to any persons according to their personal dispositions and their exhibited behaviors. Members of society might be taught to value adaptability and flexibility rather than obedience to gender roles, so that the most respected and socially valued personality types would be those which were able to make use of any behaviors which served their purposes in any situation. Under such a schema, the goal of mature personality development would be to reach a balance of gender characteristics. Men and women, masculinity and femininity, would be seen as immature stages in the process of reaching a blended gender identity and display.

A gender blending schema could serve as a transitional step between the present patriarchal sexist gender schema and a future state wherein the concept of gender would become obsolete and meaningless. Gender, as we now think of it, is an artifact of sex. Were gender to become divided from sex, it would begin to lose its meaning and it would become impossible to use gender as the basis for sex discrimination. Were gender blending to become a goal and increasingly a reality in society, the social entities we now call women and men would become archaic and the basis for gender as a meaningful concept would become irreparably eroded. Were people to become no longer distinguishable on the basis of sex, were all gender choices open to all people, were there to cease to be a cognitive system which measured the world in gendered units, the material basis for sexism would cease to exist.

Notes

Introduction

1. Galen V. Bodenhauser and Meryl Lichtenstein, "Social Stereotypes and Information-Processing Strategies: The Impact of Task Complexity," *Journal of Personality and Social Psychology* 52 (1987), pp. 871–80.

I. Where It All Begins

1. Incorrigible beliefs are those concepts which people believe so strongly that nothing can cause them to question their veracity. At one time the idea that the world was flat was such a belief. H. Mehan and H. Wood, *The Reality of Ethnomethodology* (New York: John Wiley and Sons, 1975), p. 9.

2. R. Bleier, "Social and Political Bias in Science: An Examination of Animal Studies and Their Generalizations to Human Behavior and Evolution," in *Genes and Gender II: Pitfalls in Research on Sex and Gender*, ed. R. Hubbard and M. Lowe (New York: Gordian Press, 1979), pp. 49–69.

3. A. A. Ehrhardt, "Maternalism in Fetal Hormonal and Related Syndromes," in *Contemporary Sexual Behavior: Critical Issues of the 1970's*, ed. J. Zubin and J. Money (Baltimore: Johns Hopkins University Press, 1973), p. 113; A. Lev-Ran, "Gender Role Differentiation in Hermaphrodites," *Archives of Sexual Behavior* 3 (1974), pp. 391–424, esp. p. 391; R. J. Stoller, *Sex and Gender: On the Development of Masculinity and Femininity* (New York: Science House, 1968), p. 83.

4. Gunter Dorner, "Sexual Differentiation of the Brain," *Vitamins and Hormones* 38 (1980), pp. 325–81, esp. pp. 360–69.

5. Charles H. Doering, "The Endocrine System," in *Constancy and Change in Human Development*, ed. O. G. Brim Jr. and J. Kagan (Cambridge, Mass.: Harvard University Press, 1980), pp. 229–71, esp. p. 251.

6. Ibid., p. 251.

7. Ibid., p. 238.

8. C. J. Dewhurst and R. R. Gordon, *The Intersexual Disorders* (London: Bailliere, Tindall and Cassell, 1969), pp. 111–13.

9. J. Money and A. A. Ehrhardt, *Man and Woman, Boy and Girl: The Differentiation and Dimorphism of Gender Identity from Conception to Maturity* (Baltimore: Johns Hopkins University Press, 1972), pp. 105–108.

10. Ibid., p. 109.

11. Dewhurst and Gordon, pp. 58–60.

12. Money and Ehrhardt, pp. 105–14.

13. When females are born with more than two X chromosomes they likewise share a tendency toward low IQ with increasing numbers of chromosomes, but show no other physical or behavioral abnormalities. Dewhurst and Gordon, pp. 114–16.

14. Dewhurst and Gordon estimate that as many as half of all males having more than one Y chromosome are over six feet tall. See Dewhurst and Gordon, p. 116.

15. W. M. C. Brown, P. A. Jacobs, and W. H. Price, "Sex Chromosome Aneuploidy and Criminal Behavior," in *Genetic and Environmental Influences on Behavior*, ed. J. M. Thoday and A. S. Parkes (New York: Plenum Press, 1968), pp. 180–93, esp. p. 185.

16. Mosaic chromosome arrangements can be any combination of XX, XY, XO, XXY, XYY etc.; mosaic combinations are notated as XX/XY, XO/XY, XX/XXY, XY/XYY etc. Mosaics are often hermaphrodites whose physical characteristics are a mixture of normal female and male characteristics. See Dewhurst and Gordon, pp. 116–20.

17. Suzanne Kessler and Wendy McKenna, *Gender: An Ethnomethodological Approach* (New York: John Wiley and Sons, 1978), p. 78 note.

18. Dewhurst and Gordon, p. 12.

19. Androgens and estrogens are thought to inhibit the action of one another while estrogens and progestins can enhance each other's actions. These effects act in relation to relative quantities of the hormones involved and there may be minimum quantity thresholds that must be surpassed for the effects to occur. See R. D. Lisk and L. A. Rueter, "Hypothalamic and Sexual Behavior: Progesterone Modulation of Estrogen Sensitivity," in *Current Studies in Hypothalamic Function: Metabolism and Behavior*, vol. 2, ed. W. L. Veale and K. Lederers (New York: Karger, 1978), pp. 183–94, esp. pp. 190–91; A. C. Petersen, "Hormones and Cognitive Functioning," in *Sex Related Differences in Cognitive Functioning: Developmental Issues*, ed. M. A. Wittig and A. C. Petersen (New York: Academic Press, 1979), pp. 189–214, esp. pp. 191–92.

20. J. A. Rosko, "Fetal Hormones and Development of the Central Nervous System in Primates," in *Regulatory Mechanisms Affecting Gonadal Hormone Action*, ed. J. A. Thomas and R. L. Singhal (Baltimore: University Park Press, 1977), pp. 138–68, esp. p. 162; M. J. Baum et al., "Hormonal Basis of Proceptivity and Receptivity in Female Primates," *Archives of Sexual Behavior* 6 (1977), pp. 173–92, esp. p. 184.

21. Lisk and Rueter, pp. 190–91; Petersen, p. 192.

22. John Money, *Love and Love Sickness: The Science of Sex, Gender Difference and Pair Bonding* (Baltimore: Johns Hopkins University Press, 1980) p. 138.

23. Ibid., p. 137.

24. A. A. Ehrhardt and S. W. Baker, "Fetal Androgens, Human Central Nervous System Differentiation and Behavior Sex Differences," in *Sex Differences in Behavior*, ed. R. Friedman et al. (New York: John Wiley and Sons, 1974), pp. 33–52, esp. p. 42.

25. Money and Ehrhardt, p. 10.

26. J. M. Reinisch, "Fetal Hormones, the Brain, and Human Sex Differences: A Heuristic, Integrative Review of the Recent Literature," *Archives of Sexual Behavior* 3 (1974), pp. 51–90, esp. p. 67.

27. Interview with Harry Harlow in A. Keller, *Sexuality and Homosexuality: A New View* (New York: W. W. Norton, 1971), p. 401.

28. Money, *Love and Love Sickness*, p. 25.

29. DES babies assigned as males require little or no corrective surgery. DES babies assigned as females usually require surgery to decrease the size of their clitoris and possibly to correct abnormalities of the labia. The assignment of such babies to the male or the female sex is largely based on the size of the clitoris, if it is large enough, in the opinion of doctors, to be serviceable as a penis, the infant is assigned as male. If not, the child is assigned as female.

30. Money and Ehrhardt actually refer to the progestin DES as androgenizing XX fetuses. See Money and Ehrhardt, pp. 49, 95; Ehrhardt and Baker, p. 35.

31. Money and Ehrhardt, p. 290.

32. R. Bleier, "Bias in Biological and Human Sciences: Some Comments" *Signs* 4 (1978). pp. 159–62; Bleier, "Social and Political Bias," pp. 52–53; Rosko, p. 162.

33. Male DES babies also suffer abnormalities of the urino-genital tract, most commonly undescended testes and infertility. See K. Nuefeld, "DES Exposure: What You Should Know," *HERizons* (March, 1983), pp. 20–23.

34. J. M. Reinisch and W. G. Karow. "Prenatal Exposure to Synthetic Progestins and Estrogens: Effects on Human Development," *Archives of Sexual Behavior* 6 (1977), pp. 257–88, esp. p. 262.

35. Money and Ehrhardt consider DES girls in their discussion of androgenized females. See Money and Ehrhardt, pp. 98 ff.

36. Reinisch and Karow, pp. 257–88.

37. AGS individuals assigned as males require hormone therapy as well. If untreated

they will experience premature puberty. Some also elect for minor cosmetic surgery to implant artificial testes in the empty scrotum.

38. Ehrhardt and Baker, pp. 40–44; Money and Ehrhardt, pp. 98–103.

39. Ehrhardt and Baker, p. 44.

40. V. R. Brooks, *Minority Stress in Lesbian Women* (Toronto: Lexington Books, 1981), pp. 27–28.

41. Ehrhardt and Baker, p. 43.

42. As a normal feature it seems a misnomer to refer to this cluster of behaviors as "tomboyism," a word which originally meant "a rude, boisterous or forward boy." See B. Fried, "Boys Will Be Boys: The Language of Sex and Gender," in *Women Look at Biology Looking at Women: A Collection of Feminist Critiques*, ed. R. Hubbard, M. S. Henifin, and B. Fried (Cambridge, Mass.: Schenkman, 1979), pp. 37–59, esp. p. 37.

43. A. Heilbrun and N. Thompson, "Sex-Role Identity and Male and Female Homosexuality," *Sex Roles* 3 (1977), pp. 65–79, esp. p. 71.

44. S. Oldham, D. Farnill, and I. Ball, "Sex-Role Identity of Female Homosexuals," *Journal of Homosexuality* 8 (1982), pp. 41–46.

45. C. Seavey, P. Katz, and S. R. Zalk, "Baby X: The Effects of Gender Labels on Adult Responses to Infants," *Sex Roles* 2 (1975), pp. 103–109.

46. Money and Ehrhardt, p. 9; Money and Ehrhardt report the interesting case of the entirely normal identical twin baby boy whose penis was irretrievably damaged in a circumcision accident. The parents and doctors of the boy decided to reassign him as a girl. Corrective surgery and a name change were undertaken and the baby subsequently grew up to be acceptably female as a young child but experienced gender role difficulties as an adolescent. The girl's twin brother showed no signs of femininity, thus allowing for a control of sorts. See Money and Ehrhardt pp. 118–23; Milton Diamond, "Sexual Identity, Monozygotic Twins Reared in Discordant Sex Roles and a BBC Follow-Up," *Archives of Sexual Behavior* 11 (1982), pp. 181–86.

47. C. N. Jacklin, "Epilogue," in *Sex Related Differences in Cognitive Functioning: Developmental Issues*, ed. M. A. Wittig and A. C. Petersen (New York: Academic Press, 1979), pp. 357–71, esp. p. 364.

48. R. Rose, T. Gordon, and I. Bernstein, "Plasma Testosterone Levels in the Male Rhesus: Influences of Sexual and Social Stimuli," *Science* (November 10, 1972), pp. 643–45.

49. Allen Mazur and Theodore A. Lamb, "Testosterone, Status, and Mood in Human Males," *Hormones and Behavior* 14 (1980), pp. 236–46; Arthur Kling, "Testosterone and Aggressive Behavior in Man and Nonhuman Primates," in *Hormonal Correlates of Behavior Volume 1: A Lifespan View*, ed. Basil E. Eleftheriou and Richard L. Sprott (New York: Plenum Press, 1975), pp. 305–23; J. Raymond, *The Transsexual Empire: The Making of the She-Male* (Boston: Beacon Press, 1979), p. 57.

50. D. H. Baucom, P. K. Besch, S. Callahan, "Relation between Testosterone Concentration, Sex Role Identity, and Personality among Females," *Journal of Personality and Social Psychology* 48 (1985), pp. 1218–26.

51. H. F. L. Meyer-Bahlburg, "Aggression, Androgens, and the XYY Syndrome," in *Sex Differences in Behavior*, ed. R. Friedman et al. (New York: John Wiley and Sons, 1974), pp. 433–53, esp. p. 444.

52. Petersen comments that in humans the link between stress and hormones "is a contingent correlation dependent upon the presence of a stimulating or provocative situation." See Petersen, p. 200; Doering et al. found that there was "a significant correlation between . . . average levels of self-perceived depression and the average concentration of plasma testosterone" in men. Human males may respond to depression as if provoked to action or as if defeated. These, and many other possible responses to depression might evoke different hormonal reactions. See C. H. Doering et al., "Plasma Testosterone Levels and Psychologic Measures in Men over a Two Month

Period," in *Sex Differences in Behavior,* ed. R. Friedman et al. (New York: John Wiley and Sons, 1974), pp. 413–33, esp. p. 430.

53. Kenneth E. Moyer, "Sex Differences in Aggression," in *Sex Differences in Behavior,* ed. R. Friedman et al. (New York: John Wiley and Sons, 1974), pp. 335–72, esp. p. 345.

54. K. Sano et al., "Results of Stimulation and Destruction of the Posterior Hypothalamus in Man," *Journal of Neurosurgery* 33 (1970), pp. 689–707; G. Schmidt and E. Schorsch, "Psychosurgery of Sexually Deviant Patients: Review and Analysis of New Empirical Findings," *Archives of Sexual Behavior* 10 (1981), pp. 301–23.

55. J. Panksepp, "Hypothalamic Integration of Behavior: Rewards, Punishments, and Related Psychological Processes," in *Behavioral Studies of the Hypothalamus,* ed. P. Morgane and J. Panksepp (New York: Marcel Dekker, 1981), pp. 289–431.

56. Panksepp, p. 304.

57. A. Siegel and H. Edinger, "Neural Control of Aggression and Rage Behavior," in *Behavioral Studies of the Hypothalamus,* ed. P. Morgane and J. Panksepp (New York: Marcel Dekker, 1981), pp. 230–40, esp. p. 230.

58. D. Gupta et al., "Hypothalamic-Pituitary-Testicular Feedback Mechanism during Mammalian Sexual Maturation," in *Hypothalamic Hormones: Structure, Synthesis and Biological Activity,* ed. D. Gupta and W. Voelter (Weinheim, Germany: Verlag Chemie, 1975), pp. 179–206, esp. p. 179.

59. Arthur P. Arnold and Marc Breedlove, "Organizational and Activational Effects of Sex Steroids on Brain and Behavior: A Reanalysis," *Hormones and Behavior* 19 (1985), pp. 469–98.

60. Gupta et al., p. 179.

61. Research done by J. M. Reinisch, R. Gandelman, and F. S. Spiegel indicated that there are differences in perceptual abilities between men and women and that these differences are linked to hormonal status. They cite examples in the perception of odors and sounds. They speculate that "at the most basic level it is possible that environmental stimuli have different 'meanings' for males and females. Thus, it may be that males and females are essentially quite different creatures whose perceptions of the world differ markedly, even when confronted with similar physical environments." See "Prenatal Influences in Cognitive Abilities: Data from Experimental Animals and Human Genetic and Endocrine Syndromes," in *Sex Related Differences in Cognitive Functioning: Developmental Issues,* ed. M. A. Wittig and A. C. Petersen (New York: Academic Press, 1979), pp. 215–39, esp. p. 234.

62. The shifting of dominance status during the aging process might be a partial explanation for the decrease in androgen secretion by both men and women as they age, the decrease in estrogen secretion in aging women, and the increase in estrogen secretion in elderly men. As women grow older in our society they do not move up the dominance hierarchy so far as to reach a position of dominance, but maturity often brings with it some feeling of control over one's life. Elderly men often retain much of the status of their youth but understand themselves to be losing status to younger men.

63. Transsexuals assigned at birth to the male sex will be referred to as male-to-female transsexuals. Transsexuals assigned at birth as females will be referred to as female-to-male transsexuals. These designations will be maintained regardless of their hormonal or surgical status.

64. R. Green, *Sexual Identity Conflict in Children and Adults* (New York: Basic Books, 1974), pp. 82–116; Stoller, *Sex and Gender,* pp. 89–92.

65. As the definition of transsexual excludes the question of chromosomal abnormalities, hermaphrodites and other persons of ambiguous chromosomal status are defined out of the transsexual group. See L. M. Lothstein, *Female to Male Transsexualism: Historical, Clinical and Theoretical Issues* (Boston: Routledge and Kegan Paul, 1983), p. 62.

66. G. Fulmer, "Testosterone Levels in Female to Male Transsexualism," Letter to the Editor, *Archives of Sexual Behavior* 2 (1973), pp. 399–400; Green, p. 38; J. Jones and J. Saminy, "Plasma Testosterone Levels in Female Transsexualism," *Archives of Sexual Behavior* 2 (1973), pp. 251–56; C. J. Midgeon, M. A. Rivarola, and M. G. Forest, "Studies of Androgens in Male Transsexual Subjects: Effects of Estrogen Therapy," in *Transsexualism and Sex Reassignment*, ed. R. Green and J. Money (Baltimore: Johns Hopkins University Press, 1969), pp. 203–11; I. Sipova and L. Starka, "Plasma Testosterone Values in Transsexual Women," *Archives of Sexual Behavior* 6 (1977), pp. 477–81.

67. Green, p. 38; D. Hunt, J. Carr, and J. Hampson, "Cognitive Correlates of Biologic Sex and Gender Identity in Transsexualism," *Archives of Sexual Behavior* 10 (1981), pp. 65–77; Jones and Saminy, p. 255; Midgeon et al., p. 209; Money and Ehrhardt, p. 231; Stoller, *Sex and Gender*, p. 66.

68. Fulmer, p. 399; Sipova and Starka, p. 477.

69. Green, p. 38; Midgeon et al., pp. 203–11; L. E. Seyler et al., "Abnormal Gonadotropin Secretory Responses to LRH in Transsexual Women after Diethylstilbestrol Priming," *Journal of Clinical Endocrinology and Metabolism* 47 (1978), pp. 176–83.

70. Seyler et al., pp. 176–83.

71. Midgeon et al., pp. 203–11.

72. Seyler et al., p. 181.

73. Ibid., p. 181.

74. J. Money, "Sex Reassignment as Related to Hermaphroditism and Transsexualism," in *Transsexualism and Sex Reassignment*, ed. R. Green and J. Money (Baltimore: Johns Hopkins University Press, 1969), pp. 91–113, esp. p. 102.

75. Seavey, Katz, and Zalk; J. D. Lichtenberg, *Psychoanalysis and Infant Research* (Hillside, New Jersey: The Analytic Press, 1983), pp. 3–27; Gupta et al., p. 179; N. Ross, "On the Significance of Infant Sexuality," in *On Sexuality: Psychoanalytic Observations*, ed. T. B. Karasu and C. W. Socarides (New York: International Universities Press, 1979), pp. 47–60, esp. pp. 48–49.

76. Keller, p. 401.

77. Money and Ehrhardt, pp. 4, 16, 18.

II. Learning to Be Gendered

The poem at the beginning of this chapter is by the author.

1. Seavey, Katz, and Zalk, pp. 103–109.

2. John Delk et al., "Adult Perceptions of the Infant as Function of Gender Labelling and Observer Gender," *Sex Roles* 15 (1981), pp. 527–34; Michael E. Lamb, Margaret T. Owen, and Lindsay Chase-Lansdale, "The Father-Daughter Relationship: Past, Present, and Future," in *Becoming Female: Perspectives on Development*, ed. Claire Kopp and Martha Kirkpatrick (New York: Plenum Press, 1979), p. 95.

3. J. Condry and S. Condry, "Sex Differences: A Study in the Eye of the Beholder," *Child Development* 47 (1976), pp. 812–19.

Adults do not reserve this sort of double vision to their experience of infants. Media Women of New York have summarized this approach, in part, as follows:

If

A Person Is:	Call Her:	Call Him:
Supportive	Bright	Yes-Man
Intelligent	Helpful	Smart
Innovative	Pushy	Original
Insistent	Hysterical	Persistent
Tough	Impossible	Go-Getter
Cute & Timid	A Sweetheart	A Fairy

See Media Women-New York. "How to Name a Baby-A Vocabulary Guide for Working Women," in *Sisterhood Is Powerful: An Anthology of Writings from the Women's Liberation Movement*, ed. Robin Morgan (New York: Vintage Books, 1970), pp. 590–91.

4. Lawrence Kohlberg and Dorthy Z. Ullian, "Stages in the Development of Psychosexual Concepts and Attitudes," in *Sex Differences in Behavior,* ed. Richard Friedman et al. (New York: John Wiley and Sons, 1974), pp. 209–22; Joesph H. Pleck, *The Myth of Masculinity* (Cambridge, Mass.: M.I.T. Press, 1981), p. 11.

5. Consider that "five year old children believe that if you put a dress on a man he could change into a woman. Adults know that this is not "true," but they believe that if you put a penis on a woman and remove her breasts, ovaries and uterus and give her androgens she could change into a man." See Kessler and McKenna, p. 107.

6. Sigmund Freud, "Group Psychology and the Analysis of the Ego," in *A General Selection from the Works of Sigmund Freud,* ed. John Rickman (New York: Liveright, 1921, 1957). pp. 169–209, esp. pp. 185 88; Sigmund Freud, "The Ego and the Id," in *A General Selection from the Works of Sigmund Freud,* ed. John Rickman (New York: Liveright, 1923, 1957), pp. 210–46, esp. pp. 219–21; Nancy Chodorow, *The Reproduction of Mothering: Psychoanalysis and the Reproduction of Mothering* (Berkeley: University of California Press, 1978), pp. 166–74.

7. Albert Bandura, *Social Learning Theory* (Englewood Cliffs, New Jersey: Prentice Hall, 1977).

8. Lawrence Kohlberg, *Essays on Moral Development* (San Francisco: Harper and Row, 1981); Carol Gilligan, *In a Different Voice: Psychological Theory and Women's Development* (Cambridge, Mass.: Harvard University Press, 1982).

9. Sandra L. Bem, "Gender Schema Theory: A Cognitive Account of Sex Typing," *Psychological Review* 88 (1981), pp. 354–64 and "Gender Schematic Theory and Its Implications for Child Development: Raising Gender-aschematic Children in a Gender-schematic Society," *Signs* 8 (1983), pp. 598–616.

10. Bem, "Gender Schema Theory: A Cognitive Account" and "Gender Schematic Theory and Its Implications."

11. Robin A. Fleischer and Jerome Chertkoff, "Effects of Dominance and Sex on Leader Selection in Dyadic Work Groups," *Journal of Personality and Social Psychology* 50 (1986), pp. 94–99; Deborrah Frable, "Sex-Typed Execution and Perception of Expressive Movement," *Journal of Personality and Social Psychology* 54 (1987), pp. 391–96; Linda Nyquist and Janet Spence, "Effects of Dispositional Dominance and Sex Role Expectation on Leadership and Behavior," *Journal of Personality and Social Psychology* 50 (1986), pp. 87–93.

12. Human brains continue to grow and develop well into life. Growth is 90 percent complete by the age of six years, with 60 percent of growth being completed by the age of two years. See Steven Rose, *The Conscious Brain* (New York: Vintage Books, 1978), p. 187; J. M. Tanner, *Foetus into Man: Physical Growth from Conception to Maturity* (Cambridge, Mass: Harvard University Press, 1978), p. 115.

13. Donald G. Stein and Ronald G. Dawson, "The Dynamics and Growth, Organization and Adaptability of the Central Nervous System," in *Constancy and Change in Human Development,* ed, O. G. Brim Jr. and J. Kagan (Cambridge, Mass.: Harvard University Press, 1980), pp. 174–77.

14. Dennis M. Parker, "Determinate and Plastic Principles in Neuropsychological Development," in *Brain and Behavioral Development: Interdisciplinary Perspectives on Structure and Function,* ed. John W. T. Dickerson and Harry McGurk (London: Surrey University Press, 1982), pp. 203–32.

15. The hypothalamus is capable of secreting hormone stimulating and inhibiting substances before birth and at the time of birth, but is not fully developed until early childhood. See Peter D. Gluckman, Melvin M. Grumbach, and Selna L. Kaplan, "The Human Fetal Hypothalamus and Pituitary Gland," in *Maternal-Fetal Endocrinology,*

ed. D. Tulchinsky and K. J. Ryan (Philadelphia: W. B. Saunders, 1980), pp. 196–232, esp. p. 216.

16. Newborn infant females respond more than males to sweet taste, touch, and light and tend to move their mouths more than males. Male infants tend to be better able to lift their heads and to startle more easily than females infants, who are calmer and sleep more than males do. By the age of six months brain wave pattern differences can be seen in the EEG's of male and female infants. See Anneliese F. Komer, "Methodological Considerations in Studying Sex Differences in the Behavioral Functioning of Newborns" in *Sex Differences in Behavior,* ed. Richard Friedman et al. (New York: John Wiley and Sons, 1974), pp. 197–208; Cherry Thompson, "Cortical Activity in Behavioral Development," in *Brain and Behavioral Development: Interdisciplinary Perspectives on Structure and Function,* ed. John T. Dickerson and Harry McGurk (London: Surrey University Press, 1982), pp. 131–67; Lichtenberg, p. 20.

17. Doering, p. 266.

18. Amy C. Baldwin et al., "Androgyny and Sex Role Measurement: A Personal Construct Approach," *Journal of Personality and Social Psychology* 51 (1986), pp. 1081–88; Thomas J. Payne, Jane M. Conner, and Gep Colletti, "Gender Based Schematic Processing: An Empirical Investigation," *Journal of Personality and Social Psychology* 52 (1987), pp. 937–45; Thomas A. Widiger and Shirley A. Settle, "Broverman et al. Revisited: An Artifactual Sex Bias," *Journal of Personality and Social Psychology* 53 (1987), pp. 463–69.

19. Pleck, pp. 6–8.

20. Sandra L. Bem, "The Measurement of Psychological Androgyny," *Journal of Consulting and Clinical Psychology* 42 (1974), pp. 155–62.

21. Pleck, p. 37.

22. Ibid., p. 37.

23. Inge K. Broverman et al., "Sex-Role Stereotypes and Clinical Judgments of Mental Health," *Journal of Consulting and Clinical Psychology* 39 (1970), pp. 1–7.

24. Harry Benjamin, *The Transsexual Phenomenon* (New York: Julian Press, 1966), p. 148.

25. Warren H. Jones, Mary Ellen O'C. Chernovetz, and Robert O. Hansson, "The Enigma of Androgyny: Differential Implications for Males and Females?" *Journal of Consulting and Clinical Psychology* 46 (1978), pp. 298–313.

26. Baldwin et al., pp. 1081–88; Widiger and Settle, pp. 463–69.

27. Broverman et al., p. 3.

28. Bem, "Psychological Androgyny," p. 156.

29. Donald H. Baucom and Bahr Weiss, "Peers' Granting of Control to Women with Different Sex-Role Identities," *Journal of Personality and Social Psychology* 51 (1986), pp. 1075–80; Jones et al.; Jacob L. Orlofsky and Connie A. O'Heron, "Stereotypic and Nonstereotypic Sex Role Trait and Behavior Orientations: Implications for Personal Adjustment," *Journal of Personality and Social Psychology* 52 (1987), pp. 1034–42; Janet Spence, Robert Helmreich, and Joy Stapp, "Ratings of Self and Peers on Sex-Role Attributes and Their Relation to Self Esteem and Conceptions of Masculinity and Femininity," *Journal of Personality and Social Psychology* 32 (1975). pp. 29–39.

30. J. McGuire, "Gender Specific Differences in Early Childhood: The Impact of the Father," in *Fathers: Psychological Perspectives,* ed. Nigel Beail and Jacqueline McGuire (London: Junction Books, 1982), pp. 95–125, esp. p. 107.

31. Lamb, Owen, and Chase-Lansdale, p. 95.

32. Ibid.

33. Anne Wollett, David White, and Louise Lyon, "Observations of Fathers at Birth," in *Fathers: Psychological Perspectives,* ed. Nigel Beail and Jacqueline McGuire (London: Junction Books, 1982), pp. 71–91.

34. McGuire, p. 101.

35. David White, Anne Wollett, and Louise Lyon, "Fathers' Involvement with Their Infants: The Relevance of Holding," in *Fathers: Psychological Perspectives*, ed. Nigel Beail and Jacqueline McGuire (London: Junction Books, 1982), pp. 126–43.

36. Michael E. Lamb, "Father-Infant and Mother-Infant Interaction in the First Year of Life," *Child Development* 48 (1977), pp. 167–81.

37. Michael Lewis and Marsha Weinraub, "Sex of Parent X Sex of Child: Socioemotional Development," in *Sex Differences in Behavior*, ed. Friedman et al. (New York: John Wiley and Sons, 1974). pp. 165–89; Howard Moss, "Early Sex Differences in Mother-Infant Interaction," in *Sex Differences in Behavior*, ed. Friedman et al. (New York: John Wiley and Sons, 1974), pp. 149–63; Ross D. Parke and Barbara R. Tinsley, "The Father's Role in Infancy: Determinants of Involvement in Caregiving and Play," in *The Role of the Father in Child Development*, ed. M. E. Lamb (New York: John Wiley and Sons, 1981), pp. 429–57.

38. Phyllis R. McGrab, "Mothers and Daughters," in *Becoming Female: Perspectives on Development*, ed. Claire Kopp and Martha Kirkpatrick (New York: Plenum Press, 1979), pp. 113–29; Parke and Tinsley, pp. 429–57; McGuire, pp. 103–4, 118; Beverly I. Fagot, "The Influences of Sex of Child on Parental Reaction to Toddler Children," *Child Development* 49 (1978), pp. 459–65.

39. McGuire, p. 101.

40. Michael E. Lamb, "The Development of Father-Infant Relationships," in *The Role of the Father in Child Development*, ed. Michael Lamb (New York: John Wiley and Sons, 1981), pp. 459–88, esp. p. 473; Lamb, Owen, and Chase-Lansdale, p. 97; Judith Langlois and A. Chris Downs, "Mothers, Fathers and Peers as Socialization Agents of Sex-Typed Play Behaviors in Young Children," *Child Development* 51 (1980), pp. 1237–47; Eleanor Maccoby, *Social Development: Psychological Growth and the Parent-Child Relationship* (New York: Harcourt, Brace, Jovanovich, 1980), p. 255; McGuire, pp. 101–12.

41. Lewis and Weinraub, pp. 165–89.

42. Lichtenberg, p. 49.

43. Lamb, Owen, and Chase-Lansdale, p. 97.

44. Doering, p. 266.

45. A stunted physical stature resulting from a deficiency of emotional warmth during childhood has been observed in orphans and severely neglected children. See Lytt I. Gardner, "Deprivation Dwarfism," *Scientific American* 227 (July, 1972), pp. 76–82.

46. Investigations into brain activity in newborn infants have shown no differences as measured by EEG monitoring, until sometime between six months and one year of age by which age infants have experienced six months or more of constant and intensive gender-role training from the adults around them. See Thompson.

47. Experiments with rats, cats, and monkeys have all demonstrated these effects. See Rose, pp. 218–20; Robert Ader, "Early Experiences and Hormones: Emotional Behavior and Adrenocortical Function," in *Hormonal Correlates of Behavior: Vol. 1: A Lifespan View*, ed. Basil E. Eleftheriou and Richard L. Sprott (New York: Plenum Press, 1975), p. 19; Stein and Dawson.

48. Margaret S. Mahler, Fred Pine, and Anni Bergman, *The Psychological Birth of the Infant: Symbiosis and Individuation* (New York: Basic Books, 1975), p. 4.

49. Thomas S. Weisner, "Some Cross-Cultural Perspectives on Becoming Female," in *Becoming Female: Perspectives on Development*, ed. Claire Kopp and Martha Kirkpatrick (New York: Plenum Press, 1979), pp. 313–32.

50. Jane Flax, "The Confict between Nurturance and Autonomy in Mother-Daughter Relationships and within Feminism," *Feminist Studies* 4 (1978), pp. 171–89.

51. Teresa L. Buck, "Familial Factors Influencing Female Transsexualism" (Unpublished M.S.W. Thesis, Smith College for Social Work, 1977), pp. 60–67; Robert

Stoller, "Etiological Factors in Female Transsexualism: A First Approximation," *Archives of Sexual Behavior* 2 (1972), pp. 47–64.

52. Margaret Mead, "On Freud's View of Female Psychology," in *Women and Analysis: Dialogues on Psychoanalytic Views of Femininity*, ed. Jean Strouse (New York: Grossman, 1974), pp. 95–106.

53. Chodorow, pp. 166–74.

54. Henry Biller, "The Father and Sex Role Development," in *The Role of the Father in Child Development*, ed. Michael Lamb (New York: John Wiley and Sons, 1981), pp. 319–58, esp. p. 325.

55. Biller, p. 342; Buck, pp. 60–67; Stoller, p. 50.

56. McGuire, p. 104.

57. Michael E. Lamb, "The Development of Father-Infant Relationships," in *The Role of the Father in Child Development*, ed. Michael Lamb (New York: John Wiley and Sons, 1981), pp. 459–88, esp. p. 473.

58. Lamb, Owen, and Chase-Lansdale, pp. 100–107.

59. Such a schedule of aperiodic reinforcement has been shown to produce stronger and more persistent behavioral effects than a consistent one. See Norma Radin, "The Role of the Father in Cognitive, Academic, and Intellectual Development," in *The Role of the Father in Child Development*, ed. Michael Lamb (New York: John Wiley and Sons, 1981), pp. 379–427, esp. p. 384.

60. McGuire, p. 101; Lamb, Owen, and Chase-Lansdale, p. 99; Biller, p. 341.

61. Maccoby, pp. 240–41.

62. McGuire, pp. 115–21.

63. Sara Ruddick, "Maternal Thinking," *Feminist Studies* 6 (1980). pp. 342–67.

64. Chodorow, p. 78.

65. Ibid., p. 59.

66. John Bowlby, *Attachment*. Vol. 1 of *Attachment and Loss* (New York: Basic Books, 1969), pp. 4, xiii.

67. Chodorow, pp. 167–74; Gilligan, p. 8.

68. Flax, pp. 174–75; Alice Rossi, "On *The Reproduction of Mothering:* A Methodological Debate," *Signs* 6 (1981), pp. 482–514, esp. p. 492.

III. Becoming Members of Society

1. Much research has been devoted to determining when gender identity becomes solidified in the sense that a child knows itself to be unequivocally either male of female. John Money and his colleagues have proposed eighteen months of age because it is difficult or impossible to change a child's gender identity once it has been established around the age of eighteen months. Money and Ehrhardt, p. 243.

2. Mary Driver Leinbach and Beverly I. Fagot, "Acquisition of Gender Labels: A Test for Toddlers," *Sex Roles* 15 (1986), pp. 655–66.

3. Maccoby, pp. 225–29; Kohlberg and Ullian, p. 211.

4. See Susan Baker, "Biological Influences on Human Sex and Gender," in *Women: Sex and Sexuality*, ed. Catherine R. Stimpson and Ethel S. Person (Chicago: University of Chicago Press, 1980), p. 186; Evelyn Blackwood, "Sexuality and Gender in Certain Native American Tribes: The Case of Cross-Gender Females," *Signs* 10 (1984), pp. 27–42; Vern L. Bullough, "Transvestites in the Middle Ages," *American Journal of Sociology* 79 (1974), 1381–89; J. Cl. DuBois, "Transsexualisme et Anthropologie Culturelle," *Gynecologie Practique* 6 (1969), pp. 431–40; Donald C. Forgey, "The Institution of Berdache among the North American Plains Indians," *Journal of Sex Research* 11 (Feb. 1975), pp. 1–15; Walter L. Williams, *The Spirit and the Flesh: Sexual Diversity in American Indian Culture* (Boston: Beacon, 1986).

5. Maccoby, p. 255.

6. Ibid., p. 227.

7. George Herbert Mead, "Self," in *The Social Psychology of George Herbert Mead*, ed. Anselm Strauss (Chicago: Phoenix Books, 1962, 1934), pp. 212–60.

8. G. H. Mead.

9. Hans Gerth and C. Wright Mills, *Character and Social Structure: The Psychology of Social Institutions* (New York: Harcourt, Brace and World, 1953), p. 96.

10. Consider, for example, the different interpretations of symptoms of physical illness given by western medical practitioners and shamanistic peoples: invasion by bacteria or viruses, versus invasion by evil spirits.

11. Weisner.

12. See Introduction for definitions of the terms "sex," "gender," "gender role."

13. Bem, "Gender Schema Theory: A Cognitive Account" and "Gender Schematic Theory and Its Implications."

14. Seavey, Katz, and Zalk.

15. Kessler and McKenna, pp. 145–46.

16. Ibid., pp. 149–50.

17. Ibid., p. 151.

18. Ibid., pp. 151–53.

19. Egoistic dominance is a striving for superior rewards for oneself or a competitive striving to reduce the rewards for one's competitors even if such action will not increase one's own rewards. Persons who are motivated by desires for egoistic dominance not only wish the best for themselves but also wish to diminish the advantages of others whom they may perceive as competing with them. See Maccoby, p. 217.

20. Judith Howard, Philip Blumstein, and Pepper Schwartz, "Sex, Power, and Influence Tactics in Intimate Relationships," *Journal of Personality and Social Psychology* 51 (1986), pp. 102–109; Peter Kollock, Philip Blumstein, and Pepper Schwartz, "Sex and Power in Interaction: Conversational Privileges and Duties," *American Sociological Review* 50 (1985), pp. 34–46.

21. Chodorow, p. 134.

22. Jon K. Meyer and John E. Hoopes, "The Gender Dysphoria Syndromes: A Position Statement on So-Called 'Transsexualism'," *Plastic and Reconstructive Surgery* 54 (Oct. 1974), pp. 444–51.

23. Erving Goffman, *Gender Advertisements;* (New York: Harper Colophon Books, 1976) Judith A. Hall, *Non-Verbal Sex Differences: Communication Accuracy and Expressive Style* (Baltimore: Johns Hopkins University Press, 1984); Nancy M. Henley, *Body Politics: Power, Sex and Non-Verbal Communication* (Englewood Cliffs, New Jersey: Prentice Hall, 1979); Marianne Wex, *"Let's Take Back Our Space": "Female" and "Male" Body Language as a Result of Patriarchal Structures* (Berlin: Frauenliteraturverlag Hermine Fees, 1979).

24. Karen L. Adams, "Sexism and the English Language: The Linguistic Implications of Being a Woman," in *Women: A Feminist Perspective*, 3rd edition, ed. Jo Freeman (Palo Alto, Calif.: Mayfield, 1984), pp. 478–91; Hall, pp. 37, 130–37.

25. Pleck, p. 139.

26. Goffman, *Gender Advertisements;* Hall; Henley; Wex.

27. Adams; Hall, pp. 37, 130–37.

28. See chapter 1.

29. See chapter 2.

30. Howard, Blumstein, and Schwartz; Kollock, Blumstein, and Schwartz.

31. Chodorow.

32. Ibid., p. 139.

33. Ibid., p. 207.

34. Adrienne Rich, "Compulsory Heterosexuality and Lesbian Existence," *Signs* 5 (1980), pp. 631–60, esp. p. 637.

35. Catharine A. MacKinnon, "Feminism, Marxism, Method, and the State: Toward Feminist Jurisprudence," *Signs* 8 (1983), pp. 635–78; and "Feminism, Marxism, Method, and the State: An Agenda for Theory," *Signs* 7 (1982), pp. 515–44.

36. Pleck, p. 140.

37. Ibid., p. 4.

38. Gilligan.

39. Erving Goffman, *The Presentation of the Self in Everyday Life* (New York: Doubleday, 1959), p. 35.

40. Aaron Cicourel, *Cognitive Sociology: Language and Meaning in Social Interaction* (New York: The Free Press, 1974), pp. 52–58.

41. Erving Goffman, *Frame Analysis: An Essay on the Organization of Experience* (Cambridge, Mass: Harvard University Press, 1974), pp. 22, 39.

42. Kenneth Leiter, *A Primer of Ethnomethodology* (New York: Oxford University Press, 1980), p. 5.

43. Harold Garfinkel, *Studies in Ethnomethodology* (Englewood Cliffs, New Jersey: Prentice Hall, 1967), p. 54.

44. Goffman, *Presentation*, p. 9.

45. Garfinkel, p. 181; Goffman, *Gender Advertisements*, p. 8.

46. Goffman, *Gender Advertisements*, p. 9.

47. Saul Feinman, "Approval of Cross-Sex-Role Behavior," *Psychological Reports* 35 (1974), pp. 643–48; Norma Costrich et al., "When Stereotypes Hurt: Three Studies of Penalties of Sex-Role Reversals," *Journal of Experimental Social Psychology* 11 (1975), pp. 520–30.

48. Jones, Chernovetz, and Hansson, pp. 310–11.

49. Pleck, p. 9.

50. Goffman, *Presentation*.

51. Erving Goffman, *Stigma: Note on the Management of Spoiled Identity* (Englewood Cliffs, New Jersey: Prentice Hall, 1963), p. 5.

IV. Growing Up Gender Blending

1. See "Theoretical Models of Gender Acquistion" in chapter 2.

2. See "Parental Influences on Infant Gender Development" and "Separating the Boys from the Girls" in chapter 2.

3. Zolinda Stoneman, Gene H. Brody, and Carol E. MacKinnon, "Same-Sex and Cross-Sex Siblings: Activity Choices, Roles, Behaviour, and Gender Stereotypes," *Sex Roles* 15 (1986), pp. 495–511.

V. Sexuality and Gender

1. Ethel Spector Person, "Sexuality as the Mainstay of Identity: Psychoanalytic Perspectives," in *Women: Sex and Sexuality,* ed. Catherine Stimpson and Ethel Spector Person (Chicago: University of Chicago Press, 1980), pp. 36–61, esp. p. 50.

2. Valerie J. Edwards and Janet T. Spence, "Gender-Related Traits, Stereotypes, and Schemata," *Journal of Personality and Social Psychology* 53 (1987), pp. 146–54; Person, p. 50.

VI. Living with Gender Blending

1. Erving Goffman, *Behavior in Public Places: Notes on the Social Organization of Gatherings* (New York: Free Press, 1963).

2. See "Gender Role Strain" in chapter 3.
3. Goffman, *Stigma*, pp. 4, 42.

VII. Gender in Context

1. See "Gender as a Cognitive Schema" in chapter 3.
2. See "The Male Standard" in chapter 3.
3. David Grimm had proposed an excellent matrix along these lines. See "Toward a Theory of Gender: Transsexualism, Gender, Sexuality, and Relationships," *American Behavioral Scientist* 31 (1987), pp. 66–85, esp. pp. 74–76.

Bibliography

WORKS CITED

Adams, Karen L. "Sexism and the English Language: The Linguistic Implications of Being a Woman." *Women: A Feminist Perspective.* 3rd ed. Edited by Jo Freeman. Palo Alto, Calif.: Mayfield, 1984.

Ader, Robert. "Early Experiences and Hormones: Emotional Behavior and Adrenocortical Function." *Hormonal Correlates of Behavior Volume 1: A Lifespan View.* Edited by Basil E. Eleftheriou and Richard L. Sprott. New York: Plenum Press, 1975.

Arnold, Arthur P., and Marc Breedlove. "Organizational and Activational Effects of Sex Steroids on Brain and Behavior: A Reanalysis." *Hormones and Behavior* 19 (1985), 469–98.

Baker, Susan W. "Biological Influences on Human Sex and Gender." *Women: Sex and Sexuality.* Edited by Catherine R. Stimpson and Ethel S. Person. Chicago: University of Chicago Press, 1980.

Baldwin, Amy C., Joseph W. Critelli, Larry C. Stevens, and Sue Russell. "Androgyny and Sex Role Measurement: A Personal Construct Approach." *Journal of Personality and Social Psychology* 51 (1986), 1081–88.

Bandura, Albert. *Social Learning Theory.* Englewood Cliffs, New Jersey: Prentice Hall, 1977.

Baucom, Donald H., Paige K. Besch, and Steven Callahan. "Relation between Testosterone Concentration, Sex Role Identity, and Personality among Females." *Journal of Personality and Social Psychology* 48 (1985), 1218–26.

———, and Bahr Weiss. "Peers' Granting of Control to Women with Different Sex-Role Identities." *Journal of Personality and Social Psychology* 51 (1986), 1075–80.

Baum, M. J., B. J. Everitt, J. Herbert, and E. B. Kererne. "Hormonal Basis of Proceptivity and Receptivity in Female Primates." *Archives of Sexual Behavior* 6 (1977), 173–92.

Bem, Sandra L. "Gender Schema Theory: A Cognitive Account of Sex Typing." *Psychological Review* 88 (1981), 354–64.

———. "Gender Schematic Theory and Its Implications for Child Development: Raising Gender-aschematic Children in a Gender-schematic Society." *Signs* 8 (1983), 598–616.

———. "The Measurement of Psychological Androgyny." *Journal of Consulting and Clinical Psychology* 42 (1974), 155–62.

Benjamin, Harry. *The Transsexual Phenomenon.* New York: Julian Press, 1966.

Biller, Henry. "The Father and Sex Role Development." *The Role of the Father in Child Development.* Edited by M. E. Lamb. New York: John Wiley and Sons, 1981.

Blackwood, Evelyn. "Sexuality and Gender in Certain Native American Tribes: The Case of Cross-Gender Females." *Signs* 10 (1984), 27–42.

Bleier, Ruth. "Social and Political Bias in Science: An Examination of Animal Studies and Their Generalizations to Human Behavior and Evolution." *Genes and Gender II: Pitfalls in Research on Sex and Gender.* Edited by Ruth Hubbard and Marian Lowe. New York: Gordian Press, 1979.

———. "Bias in Biological and Human Sciences: Some Comments." *Signs* 4 (1978), 159–62.

Bodenhauser, Galen V., and Meryl Lichtenstein. "Social Stereotypes and Information-Processing Strategies: The Impact of Task Complexity." *Journal of Personality and Social Psychology* 52 (1987), 871–80.

Bowlby, John. *Attachment*. Vol. 1 of *Attachment and Loss*. 3 vols. New York: Basic Books, 1969.

Brooks, Virginia. *Minority Stress in Lesbian Women*. Toronto: Lexington Books, 1981.

Broverman, Donald M., E. L. Klaiber, and W. Vogel. "Gonadal Hormones and Cognitive Functioning." *The Psychology of Sex Differences and Sex Roles*. Edited by J. E. Parsons. New York: McGraw Hill, 1980.

Broverman, Inge K., Donald M. Broverman, Frank E. Clarkson, Paul S. Rosenkrantz, and Susan R. Vogel. "Sex-Role Stereotypes and Clinical Judgments of Mental Health." *Journal of Consulting and Clinical Psychology* 39 (1970), 1–7.

Brown, W. M. C., Patricia A. Jacobs, and W. H. Price. "Sex Chromosome Aneuploidy and Criminal Behavior." *Genetic and Environmental Influences on Behavior*. Edited by J. M. Thoday and A. S. Parkes. New York: Plenum Press, 1968.

Buck, Teresa L. "Familial Factors Influencing Female Transsexualism." Unpublished M.S.W. Thesis, Smith College for Social Work, 1977.

Bullough, Vern. "Transvestites in the Middle Ages." *American Journal of Sociology* 79 (1974), 1381–89.

Chodorow, Nancy. *The Reproduction of Mothering: Psychoanalysis and the Reproduction of Mothering*. Berkeley: University of California Press, 1978.

Cicourel, Aaron. *Cognitive Sociology: Language and Meaning in Social Interaction*. New York: The Free Press, 1974.

Condry, J., and S. Condry. "Sex Differences: A Study in the Eye of the Beholder." *Child Development* 47 (1976), 812–19.

Costrich, Norma, Joan Feinstein, Louise Kidder, Jeanne Marecek, and Linda Pascale. "When Stereotypes Hurt: Three Studies of Penalties of Sex-Role Reversals." *Journal of Experimental Social Psychology* 11 (1975), 520–30.

Delk, John R., Burt Madden, Mary Livingston, and Timothy Ryan. "Adult Perceptions of the Infant as a Function of Gender Labelling and Observer Gender." *Sex Roles* 15 (1981), 527–34.

Dewhurst, Christopher J., and Ronald R. Gordon. *The Intersexual Disorders*. London: Balliere, Tindall and Cassell, 1969.

Diamond, Milton. "Sexual Identity, Monozygotic Twins Reared in Discordant Sex Roles and a BBC Follow-Up." *Archives of Sexual Behavior* 11 (1982), 181–86.

Doering, Charles H. "The Endocrine System." *Constancy and Change in Human Development*. Edited by O. G. Brim Jr. and J. Kagan. Cambridge, Mass.: Harvard University Press, 1980.

———, H. K. H. Brodie, H. Kraemer, H. Baker, and D. A. Hanburg. "Plasma Testosterone Levels and Psychologic Measures in Men over a Two Month Period." *Sex Differences in Behavior*. Edited by Richard Friedman, R. M. Richart, R. L. Vande Wiele, and L. O. Stern. New York: John Wiley and Sons, 1974.

Dorner, Gunter. "Sexual Differentiation of the Brain." *Vitamins and Hormones* 38 (1980), 325–81.

Dougherty, E., and C. Culver. "Sex-Role Identification, Ability, and Achievement among High School Girls." *Sociology of Education* 49 (1976), 1–3.

Dubois, J. Cl. "Transsexualisme et Anthropologie Culturelle." *Gynecologie Practique* 6 (1969), 431–40.

Edwards, Valerie J., and Janet T. Spence. "Gender-Related Traits, Stereotypes, and Schemata." *Journal of Personality and Social Psychology* 53 (1987), 146–54.

Ehrhardt, Anke A. "Maternalism in Fetal Hormonal and Related Syndromes." *Contemporary Sexual Behavior: Critical Issues of the 1970's*. Edited by J. Zubin and J. Money. Baltimore: Johns Hopkins University Press, 1973.

———, and Susan W. Baker. "Fetal Androgens, Human Central Nervous System Differentiation and Behavior Sex Differences." *Sex Differences in Behavior*. Edited by Richard Friedman, R. M. Richart, R. L. Vande Wiele, and L. O. Stern. New York: John Wiley and Sons, 1974.

Fagot, Beverly I. "The Influences of Sex of Child on Parental Reaction to Toddler Children." *Child Development* 49 (1978), 459–65.

Feinman, Saul. "Approval of Cross Sex-Role Behavior." *Psychological Reports* 35 (1974), 643–48.

Flax, Jane. "The Conflict between Nurturance and Autonomy in Mother-Daughter Relationships and within Feminism." *Feminist Studies* 4 (1978), 171–89.

Fleischer, Robin A., and Jerome Chertkoff. "Effects of Dominance and Sex on Leader Selection in Dyadic Work Groups." *Journal of Personality and Social Psychology* 50 (1986), 94–99.

Fleming, M., D. Cohen, P. Salt, D. Jones, and S. Jenkins. "A Study of Pre and Postsurgical Transsexuals: MMPI Characteristics." *Archives of Sexual Behavior* 10 (1981) 161–70.

Forgey, Donald. "The Institution of Berdache among the North American Plains Indians." *Journal of Sex Research* 11 (Feb. 1975), 1–15.

Frable, Deborrah. "Sex-Typed Execution and Perception of Expressive Movement." *Journal of Personality and Social Psychology* 54 (1987), 391–96.

Freud, Sigmund. "Group Psychology and the Analysis of the Ego." *A General Selection from the Works of Sigmund Freud*. Edited by John Rickman. New York: Liveright, 1957.

———. "The Ego and the Id." *A General Selection from the Works of Sigmund Freud*. Edited by John Rickman. New York: Liveright, 1957.

Freund, K., R. Langeuin, Y. Zajac, B. Steiner, and A. Zajac. "Parent-Child Relations in Transsexual and Nontranssexual Homosexual Males." *British Journal of Psychiatry* 124 (1974), 22–23.

Fried, Barbara. "Boys Will Be Boys: The Language of Sex and Gender." *Women Look at Biology Looking at Women: A Collection of Feminist Critiques*. Edited by Ruth Hubbard, Mary Sue Henifin, and Barbara Fried. Cambridge, Mass.: Schenkman, 1979.

Fulmer, G. "Testosterone Levels in Female to Male Transsexualism." *Archives of Sexual Behavior* 2 (1973), 399–400.

Gardner, Lytt I. "Deprivation Dwarfism." *Scientific American* 227 (July 1972), 76–82.

Garfinkel, Harold. *Studies in Ethnomethodology*. Englewood Cliffs, New Jersey: Prentice Hall, 1967.

Gerth, Hans, and C. Wright Mills. *Character and Social Structure: The Psychology of Social Institutions*. New York: Harcourt, Brace and World, 1953.

Gilligan, Carol. *In a Different Voice: Psychological Theory and Women's Development*. Cambridge, Mass.: Harvard University Press, 1982.

Gluckman, Peter D., Melvin M. Grumbach, and Selna L. Kaplan. "The Human Fetal Hypothalamus and Pituitary Gland." *Maternal-Fetal Endocrinology*. Edited by D. Tulchinsky and K. J. Ryan. Philadelphia: W. B. Saunders, 1980.

Gluksmann, A. *Sex Determination and Sex Dimorphism in Mammals*. London: Wykeham, 1978.

Goffman, Erving. *The Presentation of the Self in Everyday Life*. New York: Doubleday, 1959.

———. *Behavior in Public Places: Notes on the Social Organization of Gatherings*. New York: Free Press, 1963.

———. *Stigma: Note on the Management of Spoiled Identity*. Englewood Cliffs, New Jersey: Prentice Hall, 1963.

———. *Frame Analysis: An Essay on the Organization of Experience*. Cambridge, Mass.: Harvard University Press, 1974.

———. *Gender Advertisements*. New York: Harper Colophon Books, 1976.

Green, Richard. *Sexual Identity Conflict in Children and Adults*. New York: Basic Books, 1974.

————, and Robert Stoller. "Two Monozygotic (Identical) Twin Pairs Discordant for Gender Identity." *Archives of Sexual Behavior* 1 (1971), 321–27.

Grimm, David. "Toward a Theory of Gender: Transsexualism, Gender, Sexuality, and Relationships." *American Behavioral Scientist* 31 (1987), 66–85.

Gupta, D., K. Rager, K. Zech, and W. Voelter. "Hypothalamic-Pituitary-Testicular Feedback Mechanism during Mammalian Sexual Maturation." *Hypothalamic Hormones: Structure, Synthesis and Biological Activity.* Edited by D. Gupta and W. Voelter. Weinheim, Germany: Verlag Chemie, 1975.

Hall, Judith A. *Non-Verbal Sex Differences: Communication Accuracy and Expressive Style.* Baltimore: Johns Hopkins University Press, 1984.

Heilbrun, Alfred, and Norman Thompson. "Sex-Role Identity and Male and Female Homosexuality." *Sex Roles* 3 (1977), 65–79.

Henley, Nancy M. *Body Politics: Power, Sex and Non-Verbal Communication.* Englewood Cliffs, New Jersey: Prentice Hall, 1979.

Howard, Judith, Philip Blumstein, and Pepper Schwartz. "Sex, Power, and Influence Tactics in Intimate Relationships." *Journal of Personality and Social Psychology* 51 (1986), 102–109.

Hunt, D., J. Carr, and J. Hampson. "Cognitive Correlates of Biologic Sex and Gender Identity in Transsexualism." *Archives of Sexual Behavior* 10 (1981), 65–77.

Jacklin, Carol N. "Epilogue." *Sex Related Differences in Cognitive Functioning: Developmental Issues.* Edited by M. A. Wittig and Anne C. Petersen. New York: Academic Press, 1979.

Jones, J., and J. Saminy. "Plasma Testosterone Levels in Female Transsexualism." *Archives of Sexual Behavior* 2 (1973), 251–56.

Jones, Warren, Mary E. O'C. Chernovetz, and Robert O. Hansson. "The Enigma of Androgyny: Differential Implications for Males and Females?" *Journal of Consulting and Clinical Psychology* 46 (1978), 298–313.

Keller, Arno. *Sexuality and Homosexuality: A New View.* New York: W. W. Norton, 1971.

Kessler, Suzanne, and Wendy McKenna. *Gender: An Ethnomethodological Approach.* New York: John Wiley and Sons, 1978.

Kling, Arthur. "Testosterone and Aggressive Behavior in Man and Nonhuman Primates." *"Hormonal Correlates of Behavior Volume 1: A Lifespan View.* Edited by Basil E. Eleftheriou and Richard L. Sprott. New York: Plenum Press, 1975.

Kohlberg, Lawrence. *Essays on Moral Development.* San Francisco: Harper and Row, 1981.

————, and Dorothy Z. Ullian. "Stages in the Development of Psychosexual Concepts and Attitudes." *Sex Differences in Behavior.* Edited by Richard Friedman, R. M. Richart, R. L. Vande Wiele and L. O. Stern. New York: John Wiley and Sons, 1974.

Kollock, Peter, Philip Blumstein, and Pepper Schwartz. "Sex and Power in Interaction: Conversational Privileges and Duties." *American Sociological Review* 50 (1985), 34–46.

Komer, Anneliese F. "Methodological Considerations When Studying Sex Differences in the Behavioral Functioning of Newborns." *Sex Differences in Behavior.* Edited by Richard Friedman, R. M. Richart, R. L. Vande Wiele, and L. O. Stern. New York: John Wiley and Sons, 1974.

Lamb, Michael E. "Father-Infant and Mother-Infant Interaction in the First Year of Life." *Child Development* 48 (1977), 167–81.

————. "The Development of Father-Infant Relationships." *The Role of the Father in Child Development.* Edited by M. E. Lamb. New York: John Wiley and Sons, 1981.

————, Margaret T. Owen, and Lindsay Chase-Lansdale. "The Father-Daughter Relationship: Past, Present and Future." *Becoming Female: Perspectives on De-*

velopment. Edited by Claire B. Kopp and Martha Kirkpatrick. New York: Plenum Press, 1979.

Langlois, Judith, and A. Chris Downs. "Mothers, Fathers and Peers as Socialization Agents in Sex-Typed Play Behaviors in Young Children." *Child Development* 51 (1980), 1237–47.

Leinbach, Mary Driver, and Beverly I. Fagot. "Acquisition of Gender Labels: A Test for Toddlers." *Sex Roles* 15 (1986), 655–66.

Leiter, Kenneth. *A Primer of Ethnomethodology.* New York: Oxford University Press, 1980.

Lev-Ran, A. "Gender Role Differentiation in Hermaphrodites." *Archives of Sexual Behavior* 3 (1974), 391–424.

Lewis, Michael, and Marsha Weinraub. "Sex of Parent X Sex of Child: Socioemotional Development." *Sex Differences in Behavior.* Edited by Richard Friedman, R. M. Richart, R. L. Vande Wiele, and L. O. Stern. New York: John Wiley and Sons, 1974.

Lichtenberg, J. D. *Psychoanalysis and Infant Research.* Hillside, New Jersey: The Analytic Press, 1983.

Lisk, R. D., and L. A. Rueter. "Hypothalamic and Sexual Behavior: Progesterone Modulation of Estrogen Sensitivity." *Current Studies in Hypothalamic Function: Metabolism and Behavior,* vol. 2. Edited by W. L. Veale and K. Lederers. New York: Karger, 1978.

Lothstein, L. M. *Female to Male Transsexualism: Historical, Clinical and Theoretical Issues.* Boston: Routledge and Kegan Paul, 1983.

Maccoby, Eleanor. *Social Development: Psychological Growth and the Parent-Child Relationship.* New York: Harcourt, Brace, Jovanovich, 1980.

MacKinnon, Catharine A. "Feminism, Marxism, Method, and the State: Toward Feminist Jurisprudence." *Signs* 8 (1983), 635–78.

———. "Feminism, Marxism, Method, and the State: An Agenda for Theory." *Signs* 7 (1982), 515–44.

Mahler, Margaret S., Fred Pine, and Anni Bergman. *The Psychological Birth of the Infant: Symbiosis and Individuation.* New York: Basic Books, 1975.

Mazur, Allen, and Theodore A. Lamb. "Testosterone, Status and Mood in Human Males." *Hormones and Behavior* 14 (1980), 236–46.

McGrab, Phyllis R. "Mothers and Daughters." *Becoming Female: Perspectives on Development,* Edited by Claire B. Kopp and Martha Kirkpatrick. New York: Plenum Press, 1979.

McGuire, Jacqueline. "Gender Specific Differences in Early Childhood: The Impact of the Father." *Fathers: Psychological Perspectives.* Edited by Nigel Beail and Jacqueline McGuire. London: Juction Books, 1982.

Mead, George Herbert. "Self." *The Social Psychology of George Herbert Mead.* Edited by Anselm Strauss. Chicago: University of Chicago Press, 1962 (1934).

Mead, Margaret. "On Freud's View of Female Psychology." *Women and Analysis: Dialogues on Psychoanalytic Views of Femininity.* Edited by Jean Strouse. New York: Grossman, 1974.

Media Women-New York. "How to Name a Baby–A Vocabulary Guide for Working Women." *Sisterhood Is Powerful: An Anthology of Writings from the Women's Liberation Movement.* Edited by Robin Morgan. New York: Vintage Books, 1970.

Mehan, Hugh, and H. Wood. *The Reality of Ethnomethodology.* New York: John Wiley and Sons, 1975.

Meyer, Jon K., and John E. Hoopes. "The Gender Dysphoria Syndromes: A Position Statement on the So-Called 'Transsexualism'." *Plastic and Reconstructive Surgery* 54 (Oct. 1974), 444–51.

Meyer-Bahlburg, H. F. L. "Aggression, Androgens, and the XXY Syndrome." *Sex*

Differences in Behavior. Edited by Richard Friedman, R. M. Richart, R. L. Vande Wiele, and L. O. Stern. New York: John Wiley and Sons, 1974.

Midgeon, C. J., M. A. Rivarola, and M. G. Forest. "Studies of Androgens in Male Transsexual Subjects: Effects of Estrogen Therapy." *Transsexualism and Sex Reassignment*. Edited by Richard Green and John Money. Baltimore: Johns Hopkins University Press, 1969.

Money, John. *Love and Love Sickness: The Science of Sex, Gender Difference and Pair Bonding*. Baltimore: Johns Hopkins University Press, 1980.

———. "Sex Reassignment as Related to Hermaphroditism and Transsexualism." *Transsexualism and Sex Reassignment*. Edited by Richard Green and John Money. Baltimore: Johns Hopkins University Press, 1969.

———, and Anke A. Ehrhardt. *Man and Woman, Boy and Girl: The Differentiation and Dimorphism of Gender Identity from Conception to Maturity*. Baltimore: Johns Hopkins University Press, 1972.

———, and Patricia Tucker. *Sexual Signatures: On Being a Man or a Woman*. Boston: Little Brown and Co., 1975. Baltimore: Johns Hopkins University Press, 1972.

Moss, Howard. "Early Sex Differences in Mother-Infant Interaction." *Sex Differences in Behavior*. Edited by Richard Friedman, R. M. Richart, R. L. Vande Wiele, and L. O. Stern. New York: John Wiley and Sons, 1974.

Moyer, Kenneth E. "Sex Differences in Aggression." *Sex Differences in Behavior*. Edited by Richard Friedman, R. M. Richart, R. L. Vande Wiele, and L. O. Stern. New York: John Wiley and Sons, 1974.

Nuefeld, K. "DES Exposure: What You Should Know." *HERizons* (March 1983), 20–23.

Nyquist, Linda, and Janet Spence. "Effects of Dispositional Dominance and Sex Role Expectation on Leadership and Behavior." *Journal of Personality and Social Psychology* 50 (1986), 87–93.

Oldham, Sue, Doug Farnill, and Ian Ball. "Sex Role Identity of Female Homosexuals." *Journal of Homosexuality* 8 (1982), 41–46.

Orlofsky, Jacob L., and Connie A. O'Heron. "Stereotypic and Nonstereotypic Sex Role Trait and Behavior Orientations: Implications for Personal Adjustment." *Journal of Personality and Social Psychology* 52 (1987), 1034–42.

Panksepp, J. "Hypothalamic Integration of Behavior: Rewards, Punishments, and Related Psychological Processes." *Behavioral Studies of the Hypothalamus*. Edited by P. J. Morgane and J. Panksepp. New York: Marcel Dekker, 1981.

Parke, Ross D., and Barbara R. Tinsley. "The Father's Role in Infancy: Determinants of Involvement in Caregiving and Play." *The Role of the Father in Child Development*. Edited by Michael E. Lamb. New York: John Wiley and Sons, 1981.

Parker, Dennis M. "Determinate and Plastic Principles in Neuropsychological Development." *Brain and Behavioral Development: Interdisciplinary Perspectives on Structure and Function*. Edited by John W. T. Dickerson and Harry McGurk. London: Surrey University Press, 1982.

Payne, Thomas J., Jane M. Conner, and Gep Colletti. "Gender Based Schematic Processing: An Empirical Investigation." *Journal of Personality and Social Psychology* 52 (1987), 937–45.

Person, Ethel Spector. "Sexuality as the Mainstay of Identity: Psychoanalytic Perspectives." *Women: Sex and Sexuality*. Edited by Catherine Stimpson and Ethel Spector Person. Chicago: University of Chicago Press, 1980.

———, and L. Ovesey. "The Psychodynamics of Male Transsexualism." *Sex Differences in Behavior*. Edited by Richard Friedman, R. M. Richart, R. L. Vande Wiele, and L. O. Stern. New York: John Wiley and Sons, 1974.

Petersen, Anne C. "Hormones and Cognitive Functioning." *Sex Related Differences in Cognitive Functioning: Developmental Issues*. Edited by M. A. Wittig and Anne C. Petersen. New York: Academic Press, 1979.

Pfaff, D. "Theoretical Issues Regarding Hypothalamic Control of Reproductive Behavior." *Behavioral Studies of the Hypothalamus.* Edited by P. J. Morgane and J. Panksepp. New York: Marcel Dekker, 1981.

Pleck, Joseph H. *The Myth of Masculinity.* Cambridge, Mass.: M. I. T. Press, 1981.

Radin, Norma. "The Role of the Father in Cognitive, Academic, and Intellectual Development." *The Role of the Father in Child Development.* Edited by Michael E. Lamb. New York: John Wiley and Sons, 1981.

Raymond, Janice G. *The Transsexual Empire: The Making of the She-Male.* Boston: Beacon Press, 1979.

Reinisch, June M. "Fetal Hormones, the Brain, and Human Sex Differences: A Heuristic, Integrative Review of the Recent Literature." *Archives of Sexual Behavior* 3 (1974), 51–90.

———, R. Gandelman, F. S. Spiegel. "Prenatal Influences on Cognitive Ability: Data from Experimental Animals and Human Genetic and Endocrine Syndromes." *Sex Related Differences in Cognitive Functioning: Developmental Issues.* Edited by Michele A. Wittig and Anne C. Petersen. New York: Academic Press, 1979.

———, and W. G. Karow. "Prenatal Exposure to Synthetic Progestins and Estrogens: Effects on Human Development." *Archives of Sexual Behavior* 6 (1977), 257–88.

Rich, Adrienne. "Compulsory Heterosexuality and Lesbian Existence." *Signs* 5 (1980), 631–60.

Rose, R. "Androgens and Behavior." *Hormones and the Brain.* Baltimore: University Park Press, 1980.

———, T. Gordon, and I. Bernstein. "Plasma Testosterone Levels in the Male Rhesus: Influences of Sexual and Social Stimuli." *Science* (November 10, 1972), 643–45.

Rose, Steven. *The Conscious Brain.* New York: Vintage Books, 1978.

Rosko, J. A. "Fetal Hormones and Development of the Central Nervous System in Primates." *Regulatory Mechanisms Affecting Gonadal Hormone Action.* Edited by J. A. Thomas and R. L. Singhal. Baltimore: University Park Press, 1977.

Ross, N. "On the Significance of Infant Sexuality." *On Sexuality: Psychoanalytic Observations.* Edited by Toksoz B. Karasu and Charles W. Socarides. New York: International Universities Press, 1979.

Rossi, Alice. "On *The Reproduction of Mothering:* A Methodological Debate." *Signs* 6 (1981), 482–514.

Ruddick, Sara. "Maternal Thinking." *Feminist Studies* 6 (1980), 342–67.

Sano, Keiji, Yoshiaki Mayanagi, Hiroaki Sekino, Motohide Ogashima, and Buichi Ishijima. "Results of Stimulation and Destruction of the Posterior Hypothalamus in Man." *Journal of Neurosurgery* 33 (1970), 689–707.

Schmidt, Gunter, and Ederhard Schorsch. "Psychosurgery of Sexually Deviant Patients: Review and Analysis of New Empirical Findings." *Archives of Sexual Behavior* 10 (1981), 301–23.

Seavey, Carol, Phyllis Katz, and Sue R. Zalk. "Baby X: The Effects of Gender Labels on Adult Responses to Infants." *Sex Roles* 2 (1975), 103–109.

Seyler, Lloyd E., Ernesto Canalis, Steven Spare, and Seymour Reichlin. "Abnormal Gonadotropin Secretory Responses to Leutinizing Releasing Hormone in Transsexual Women after Diethylstilbestrol Priming." *Journal of Clinical Endocrinology and Metabolism* 47 (1978), 176–83.

Siegel, A., and H. Edinger. "Neural Control of Aggression and Rage Behavior." *Behavioral Studies of the Hypothalamus.* Edited by P. J. Morgane and J. Panksepp. New York: Marcel Dekker, 1981.

Sipova, I., and L. Starka. "Plasma Testosterone Values in Transsexual Women." *Archives of Sexual Behavior* 6 (1977), 477–81.

Spence, Janet, Robert Helmreich, and J. Stapp. "Ratings of Self and Peers on Sex-Role Attributes and Their Relation to Self Esteem and Conceptions of Masculinity and Femininity." *Journal of Personality and Social Psychology* 32 (1975), 29–39.

Stein, Donald G., and Ronald G. Dawson. "The Dynamics and Growth, Organization and Adaptability of the Central Nervous System." *Constancy and Change in Human Development.* Edited by O. G. Brim Jr. and J. Kagan. Cambridge, Mass: Harvard University Press, 1980.

Stoller, Robert. "Etiological Factors in Female Transsexualism: A First Approximation." *Archives of Sexual Behavior* 2 (1972), 47–64.

———. *Sex and Gender: On the Development of Masculinity and Femininity.* New York: Science House, 1968.

Stoneman, Zolinda, Gene H. Brody, and Carol E. MacKinnon. "Same-Sex and Cross-Sex Siblings: Activity Choices, Roles, Behaviour, and Gender Stereotypes." *Sex Roles* 15 (1986), 495–511.

Storms, Michael D. "A Theory of Erotic Orientation Development." *Psychological Review* 88 (1981), 340–53.

Tanner, J. M. *Foetus into Man: Physical Growth from Conception to Maturity.* Cambridge, Mass.: Harvard University Press, 1978.

Thompson, Cherry. "Cortical Activity in Behavioral Development." *Brain and Behavioral Development: Interdisciplinary Perspectives on Structure and Function.* Edited by John T. Dickerson and Harry McGurk. London: Surrey University Press, 1982.

Weisner, Thomas S. "Some Cross-Cultural Perspectives on Becoming Female." *Becoming Female: Perspectives on Development.* Edited by Claire B. Kopp and Martha Kirkpatrick. New York: Plenum Press, 1979.

Wex, Marianne. *"Let's Take Back Our Space": "Female" and "Male" Body Language as a Result of Patriarchal Structures.* Berlin: Frauenliteraturverlag Hermine Fees, 1979.

White, David, Anne Woollett, and Louise Lyon. "Fathers' Involvement with Their Infants: The Relevance of Holding." *Fathers: Psychological Perspectives.* Edited by Nigel Beail and Jacqueline McGuire. London: Junction Books, 1982.

Widiger, Thomas A., and Shirley A. Settle. "Broverman et al. Revisited: An Artifactual Sex Bias." *Journal of Personality and Social Psychology* 53 (1987), 463–69.

Williams, Walter L. *The Spirit and the Flesh: Sexual Diversity in American Indian Culture.* Boston: Beacon, 1986.

Wollett, Anne, David White, and Louise Lyon. "Observations of Fathers at Birth." *Fathers: Psychological Perspectives.* Edited by Nigel Beail and Jacqueline McGuire. London: Junction Books, 1982.

WORKS CONSULTED

Bem, Sandra, L., and Ellen Lenney. "Sex Typing and the Avoidance of Cross-Sex Behavior." *Journal of Personality and Social Psychology* 33 (1976), 48–54.

———, Wendy Martyna, and Carol Watson. "Sex-Typing and Androgyny: Further Explorations of the Expressive Domain." *Journal of Personality and Social Psychology* 34 (1976), 1016–23.

Davenport, C. W., and S. I. Harrison. "Gender Identity Change in a Female Transsexual." *Archives of Sexual Behavior* 6 (1977), 327–40.

Dorner, G., and C. Seidler. "Influence of High-Dosage Perinatal Androgen on the Sexual Behavior, Gonadotropin Secretion, and Sexual Organs of the Rat." *Archives of Sexual Behavior* 2 (1973), 267–72.

Dougherty, C., and R. Spencer. *Female Sex Anomalies.* Hagerstown, Md.: Harper and Row, 1972.

Ehrhardt, Anke A., S. Ince, and H. F. L. Meyer-Bahlberg. "Career Aspirations and Gender Role Development in Young Girls." *Archives of Sexual Behavior* 10 (1981), 281–99.

Fishbain, D., and A. Vilasvo. "Exclusive Adult Lesbianism Associated with Turner's Syndrome Mosaicism." *Archives of Sexual Behavior* 9 (1980), 349–53.

Friedman, Richard, R. M. Richart, R. L. Vande Wiele, and L. O. Stern, eds. *Sex Differences in Behavior*. New York: John Wiley and Sons, 1974.

Green, R., and J. Money. *Transsexualism and Sex Reassignment*. Baltimore: Johns Hopkins University Press, 1969.

Gupta, D., and W. Voelter, eds. *Hypothalamic Hormones: Structure, Synthesis and Biological Activity*. Weinheim, Germany: Verlag Chemie, 1975.

Heim, N. "Sexual Behavior of Castrated Sex Offenders." *Archives of Sexual Behavior* 10 (1981), 11–19.

Hopkins, J. "The Lesbian Personality." *British Journal of Psychiatry* 115 (1969), 1433–36.

Hubbard, Ruth, Mary Sue Henifin, and Barbara Fried, eds. *Women Look at Biology Looking at Women: A Collection of Feminist Critiques*. Cambridge, Mass.: Schenkman, 1979.

———, and Marion Lowe, eds. *Genes and Gender II: Pitfalls in Research on Sex and Gender*. New York: Gordian Press, 1979.

Kando, T. "Males, Females, and Transsexuals: A Comparative Study of Sexual Conservatism." *Journal of Homosexuality* 1 (1974), 45–65.

Karasu, Toksoz B., and Charles W. Socarides, eds. *On Sexuality: Psychoanalytic Observations*. New York: International Universities Press, 1979.

Kelly, J., and J. Worell. "New Formulations of Sex Roles and Androgyny: A Critical Review." *Journal of Consulting and Clinical Psychology* 45 (1977), 1101–15.

Kimball, Meridith. "Women and Science: A Critique of Biological Theories." *International Journal of Women's Studies* 4 (1981), 318–88.

Lev-Ran, A. "Sexuality and Educational Levels of Women with the Late-treated Adrenogenital Syndrome." *Archives of Sexual Behavior* 3 (1974), 27–32.

Luttge, W. G. "The Role of Gonadal Hormones in the Sexual Behavior of the Rhesus Monkey and Human: A Literature Survey." *Archives of Sexual Behavior* 1 (1971), 61–88.

Masica, D., John Money, and Anke A. Ehrhardt. "Fetal Feminization and Female Gender Identity in the Testicular Feminizing Syndrome of Androgen Insensitivity." *Archives of Sexual Behavior* 1 (1971), 131–42.

McCauley, E., and Anke A. Ehrhardt. "Role Expectations and Definitions: A Comparison of Female Transsexuals and Lesbians." *Journal of Homosexuality* 3 (1978), 137–47.

Money, John, and J. Delery. "Iatrogenic Homosexual Gender Identity in Seven 46XX Chromosomal Females with Hyperadrenocortical Hermaphroditism Born with a Penis; Three Reared as Boys, Four Reared as Girls." *Journal of Homosexuality* 1 (1975), 351–71.

———, and M. Swartz. "Fetal Androgen in the Early Treated Adrenogenital Syndrome of 46XX Hermaphroditism: Influence on Assertive and Aggressive Types of Behavior." *Aggressive Behavior* 2 (1976), 19–30.

———, and J. Zubin. *Contemporary Sexual Behaviors: Critical Issues in the 1970's*. Baltimore: Johns Hopkins University Press, 1973.

Morgane, P. J., and J. Panksepp, eds. *Behavioral Studies of the Hypothalamus*. New York: Marcel Dekker, 1981.

Parsons, Jacquelynne. "Psychosexual Neutrality: Is Anatomy Destiny?" *The Psychobiology of Sex Differences and Sex Roles*. Edited by Jacquelynne Parsons. Washington: Hemisphere, 1980.

———, ed. *The Psychobiology of Sex Differences and Sex Roles*. New York: McGraw Hill, 1980.

Pauly, Ira B. "Female Transsexualism: Part 1." *Archives of Sexual Behavior* 3 (1974), 487–507.

————. "Female Transsexualism: Part 2." *Archives of Sexual Behavior* 3 (1974), 509–26.

Stimpson, Catherine R., and Ethel S. Person, eds. *Women: Sex and Sexuality*. Chicago: University of Chicago Press, 1980.

Strauss, Anselm, ed. *The Social Psychology of George Herbert Mead*. Chicago: Phoenix Books, 1962 (1934).

Thoday, J. M., and A. S. Parkes. *Genetic and Environmental Influences on Behavior*. New York: Plenum, 1968.

Thomas, J. A., and R. L. Singhal, eds. *Regulatory Mechanisms Affecting Gonadal Hormone Action*. Baltimore: University Park Press, 1977.

Thompson, N., B. McCandless, and B. Strickland. "Personal Adjustment of Male and Female Homosexuals and Heterosexuals." *Journal of Abnormal Psychology* 78 (1971), 237–40.

Veale, W. L., and K. Leders, eds. *Current Studies of Hypothalamic Function, Metabolism and Behavior*. New York: Karger, 1978.

Walfish, S., and M. Myerson. "Sex Role Identity and Attitudes Toward Sexuality." *Archives of Sexual Behavior* 9 (1980), 199–203.

de Wied, D., and P. van Keep, eds. *Hormones and the Brain*. Baltimore: University Park Press, 1980.

Wittig, M. A., and Anne C. Petersen, eds. *Sex Related Differences in Cognitive Functioning: Developmental Issues*. New York: Academic Press, 1979.

Index

Adrenogenital Syndrome (AGS), 14–15, 21, 156n37
Androgen Insensitivity Syndrome, 8–9
Androgens, 3–5, 8–9, 10–16, 20–21, 52, 156n19; and dominance, 16–17, 52, 158n62; and stress, 16–17, 157n52; in females, 4, 10–11, 14, 16–17
Androgyny, 31, 117, 129
Animal studies, 2–3, 10, 11–12, 14, 16
Arnold, Arthur P., 18

Baker, Susan W., 14–15
Bandura, Albert, 27
Bem, Sandra L., 27, 31–32
Bem Sex Role Inventory, 31, 32
Biller, Henry, 38
Brain development, 30, 36, 160n12, 161n16, 162n46. See also Hypothalamus
Breedlove, Marc, 18
Broverman, Donald M., 32

Chase-Lansdale, Lindsay, 35
Chodorow, Nancy, 40–41, 53–55
Congenital Adrenal Hyperplasia (CAH). See Adrenogenital Syndrome

Diethylstilbestrol (DES), 12–13, 21, 156n29, 156n30, 156n33
Doering, Charles H., 36
Downs, Chris A., 40

Edinger, H., 18
Ehrhardt, Anke A. 8, 14–15
Estrogens, 3–5, 8, 10–14, 17, 21, 156n19, 158n62

Fathers, as role models, 27, 33–35, 39–40, 68–72. See also Gender blending females; fathers of
Femininity: as connection, 41, 50, 54–55, 57; definitions of, vii, 11–12, 14, 32–33, 50–52, 55–57, 89, 127, 128–31; in males, 58–59. See also Gender roles; Gender schema; Stigma
Feminism, 99, 126, 129–32, 138–40, 153
Fetal development, human, 3–6
Follicle Stimulating Hormone (FSH), 4, 21
Freud, Sigmund, 27

Gay men, 92, 117, 119–21, 125, 128
Gay rights, 99, 128
Gender: acquisition theories, 27–30, 39, 59; children's concepts of, 26–30, 43–47, 58, 160n5; definition of, vii, 7; in aboriginal cultures, 43–44. See also Gender attribution; Gender identity; Gender role

Gender attribution: definition of, vii; process of, 26, 48–49, 58, 62, 90, 115, 121–26, 146, 147–49, 148 Fig. 2, 149 Fig. 4, 150–51, 151 Fig. 5, 152–53, 154
Gender blending females: appearance of, ix–x, 68–69, 74–75, 76, 77, 78–82, 84–86, 94, 99, 108–11, 113–14, 116–19, 122, 124, 127–30, 134–35, 139, 152; as surrogate sons, 70–72, 73, 77, 82; brothers of, 69, 70, 72–78, 94–95, 101, 140; definition of, vii, viii; demographic characteristics of, viii–ix, 65–66, 67, 72, 79, 86, 90–91, 95, 122; fathers of, 68–77, 82–83, 92, 94–95, 109, 140; frequency of misattributions, ix, 75, 107–17, 119, 121–24, 146; grandparents of, 66–69, 77, 81, 82, 108, 140; heterosexuality and, ix, 83, 85, 86, 90–99, 103–104, 108, 113–14, 138–39, 141; husbands and children of, 75, 91, 93–99, 113; lesbianism and, ix, 90–91, 94–104, 108, 112–14, 120, 132, 136–37, 138–39, 141, 186; mothers of, 66–70, 75–78, 82, 83, 94, 99, 108, 140; passing as men, 94, 114–16, 119, 121, 122–26, 132–38, 142, 152; peers of, 78–87, 91, 92, 96–97, 100, 102, 108–10, 112, 120, 124, 139; sisters of, 72–78, 82, 110–11, 140; sports and, 77, 78–80, 82, 83, 84, 85, 97; teen years, 71–72, 75, 82–87, 90–91, 92, 95–101, 104, 109–13, 140–41
Gender identity: definition of, vii, 89; development of, 9–10, 13, 16, 20, 27–30, 34–41, 43–45, 62, 65, 77, 79, 82, 89–90, 92, 95, 98, 99, 102, 103, 104–105, 107, 113, 121–26, 126–27, 132, 138–39, 140–41, 145–47, 147–49, 149 Fig. 3, 149 Fig. 4, 150, 151 Fig. 5, 154, 163n1
Gender roles: as indicators of sex and gender, 48–49, 147–49, 150, 151 Fig. 5, 154; definitions of, vii, 15, 31–33, 43, 46, 51–58. See also Femininity; Masculinity
Gender role strain, 60–61, 104
Gender schema, 27, 29–30, 45–7, 166n3; as ideology, 46–53, 55–56, 60–61, 150–54, 151 Fig. 5; dominant, 32–35, 37–40, 43, 46 Fig. 1, 46–49, 51–58, 59, 65–66, 86–87, 95, 98, 102–105, 127, 130, 140, 142, 145–54, 151 Fig. 5, 159n3; male standard of, 25–26, 32, 47–49, 59, 130–31, 152, 153
Gilligan, Carol, 48
Goffman, Erving, 58
Gough Femininity (Fe) Scale, 31
Gupta, D., 18

Harlow, Harry, 12
Hermaphrodites, vii, 12, 16, 155n16, 158n65
Heterosexuality: and femininity, 15, 51, 54–56, 70, 86–87, 89–90, 92, 94–96, 103–104, 130, 141; and masculinity, 56, 89–90, 94–95. *See also* Gender blending females; heterosexuality and
Homosexuality. *See* Gay men; Gay rights; Lesbianism
Hypothalamus, 4, 17–19, 21, 30, 160n15

Impression management, 57–59, 61, 121–26, 127–30, 132–38, 141–42, 146–49, 150–51
Incorrigible beliefs, 1–2, 16, 155n1

Karow, W. G., 13
Kessler, Suzanne, 48–49
Klinefelter's Syndrome, 9
Kohlberg, Lawrence, 27

Lamb, Michael E., 35
Langlois, Judith, 40
Lesbianism, ix, 15, 37, 55, 86, 90, 94–95, 97–104, 108, 112–13, 120, 132, 136, 138–39, 141
Lichtenberg, J. D., 35
Luteinizing hormone (LH), 4, 21

Maccoby, Eleanor, 40
MacKinnon, Catherine, 55
Mahler, Margaret, 36–37, 41
Masculinity: as separateness, 38, 41, 52, 54–55, 57; definitions of, vii, 12, 32–33, 38, 50, 52–53, 55–57, 89, 164n19; in females, 8, 14–15, 38–39, 58–59, 70–72, 74, 78, 80, 83, 85–87, 90, 94–95, 97, 99–104, 115, 128, 132, 139–41, 145, 157n42. *See also* Gender roles; Gender schema; Tomboyism; Transsexualism
Maternity, and femininity, 8, 14, 51, 54–56
McKenna, Wendy, 48–49
Menopause, 5, 6
Methodology, of research, viii, x–xi
Midgeon, C. J., 21
Minnesota Multiphasic Personality Inventory (MMPI), 31
Misogyny, 128, 130, 131, 138, 141–42, 153–54
Money, John, 8, 11, 14
Mothers, as role models, 27, 33–41, 37–40, 53–54, 66–70. *See also* Gender blending females; mothers of

Others, generalized and significant, 45, 59–62, 78, 83–84, 98, 105, 113, 139, 150–51, 151 Fig. 5

Owen, Margaret T., 35

Panksepp, J., 18
Parents: play styles with children, 34–35; preference for sons, 33–34. *See also* Mothers; Fathers
Pituitary gland, 4, 14, 17–18, 21
Pleck, Joseph H., 52
Progestins, 3–5, 10–16, 13–16, 156n19. *See also* Diethylstilbestrol (DES)
Puberty, 4, 6, 8, 9, 20, 71–72

Reinisch, June, 13
Rich, Adrienne, 55
Rose, R., 16

Self (I/Me), 60–62, 104, 121, 150–51, 151 Fig. 5; definition of, 44–45
Separation-Individuation process, 37, 39, 41, 54
Sex: assignment, 7, 9, 10, 12–14, 16, 19–22, 151 Fig. 5, 157n46; definition of, vii, 7. *See also* Sex attribution; Sex identity
Sex attribution, 25–26, 48–49, 146, 147–49, 150–51, 151 Fig. 5, 154
Sex change. *See* Transsexualism
Sex chromosomes, 3–10, 22, 30, 155n14, 155n15, 155n16
Sex hormones, 3–22, 158n61; environmental influences on, 16, 18–19, 22, 30; fetal, 3–4, 12–13, 15–16, 18–19, 21–22; receptor site sensitivity to, 11, 19, 21. *See also* Androgens; Estrogens; Progestins
Sex identity; definition of, vii, 89; development of, 10, 62, 107, 147–49, 150–51, 151 Fig. 5, 154
Sexual assault, 68, 75–77, 82, 93, 94, 98, 111, 113, 132–38, 141, 145, 152, 153
Sexual orientation. *See* Gay men; Gay rights; Heterosexuality; Lesbianism
Seyler, Lloyd E., 20
Siegel, A., 18
Social construction of gender, 89, 147, 150–52, 151 Fig. 5
Stigma: definitions of, 61–62; femininity as, 130, 140–42, 145, 148, 152–53
Symbiotic bonds, 36–38, 40–41, 54

Testicular Feminization. *See* Androgen Insensitivity Syndrome
Testosterone. *See* Androgens
Tomboyism. *See* Masculinity; in females
Transsexualism, vii, 19–21, 43, 46, 75–76, 82, 83, 85, 90, 91, 92, 94, 101–103, 104, 107, 109, 119, 158n63, 158n65, 160n5
Transvestism, vii, 19–20, 119, 128–30
Turner's Syndrome, 7–9

Virilized females, 12–13, 15, 21